The Only Thing I Can Do Is to Fight

Mark T. Dunn

Copyright © 2011 Mark T. Dunn
All rights reserved.

ISBN: 1466312203
ISBN-13: 9781466312203

TABLE OF CONTENTS

Table of Contents	iii
Introduction	ix
Chapter 1 - James ("Jimmy") Barry (1870–1943)	1
Jimmy's Parents	2
The Great Chicago Fire	4
Jimmy's Siblings	7
McGurn's Handball Court and Harry Gilmore	9
1891 – Jimmy's Professional Career Begins	20
1892 – A Year of Politics and Private Knockouts	24
1893 – A Year of National Prominence	26
Barry and Bobby Quade	27
Barry and Pete Shea the "Portland Cyclone"	28
1894 – A Year of Big Fights	32
Barry and "Irish" Joe McGrath	32
Barry and Jimmy Gorman	35
Barry and Casper Leon – First Fight	37
1895 – Becoming the Champion of America	41
Barry and Joe Bertrand	44
Barry and Leon – Second Fight	44
Barry and Jack Madden	50
1896 – Only One Real Match in the Entire Year	53
Barry and Steve Flanagan	56
1897 – Coast to Coast and Across the Atlantic – The Big Time, World Championship and Death	59
Barry and Sammy Kelly	60

Barry and Jack Ward	63
Barry and Jimmy Anthony	66
Barry and Walter Croot	75
Walter Croot Record 1891 – 1896	77
1898 – Life After A Death	82
Barry and Johnny Connors	86
Barry and Johnny Ritchie	87
Barry and Billy Rotchford	88
Barry and Casper Leon – Third Fight	90
Barry and Steve Flanagan – Second Fight	92
Barry and Johnny Ritchie – Second Fight	93
Barry and Casper Leon – Fourth Fight	96
Barry and Casper Leon – Fifth Match	97
1899 – The Beginning of the Rest of His Life	101
Barry and Harry Harris	103
1900 – 1943 – OK Then, Now the Rest of His Life	107
Chapter Appendix	113
Chapter 2 - Captain James H. Dalton (1853-1932)	**123**
The Dalton and Gallagher families	124
1879-1880 - Captain Dalton's Early Career in Chicago	127
1881- Meeting John L. Sullivan	129
A Match with the Champ, Paddy Ryan	134
Hitting the Bridge	135
Local Sports Help Their Friend	139
Trying to Build a Reputation	140
1882–1883 Exhibitions with Sullivan and Ryan After the Big Fight	142
Dalton Loses his Liquor License	144
1883–1884 An Exhibition with and old man	145

Dalton's Marriage Ends With a Bullet	146
Dalton Takes Out a Heavyweight Contender	148
1885–Defies Fly	150
Jack Burke Dismantles Dalton	151
Dalton Nearly Buys the Farm	152
1886–1887 - Boxing is Banned in Chicago	156
Back to St. Louis Where Jack King Breaks his Arm and Loses to Dalton	157
1888–A Career Almost Over	159
Chapter 3 - Patrick J. "Reddy" Gallagher (1864-1937)	**163**
The Gallagher Family	164
Learning his Trade	167
1886 - "One Eyed" Jimmy Connolly	169
George La Blanche – the "Marine"	170
Professor Jimmy Carroll	171
Legal Problems in Cleveland	172
Al Rumsey - Reddy's Instructor is Put Down	173
A Wrestling Career	174
1887 - Pete McCoy and Gallagher	175
Dick Collier – Another Boxing Instructor	179
The Great Jack Dempsey	180
John L. Sullivan Comes to Town	182
An Unsettled Time	183
Mitchell and Reddy Meet	185
Costello and Reddy End up at Odds	187
1888 - The Parson Davies' Specialty Company	189
Personal Loss and a Cancelled Fight	192
Taming St. Louis – Zachritz, McManus and Daly	193
Saving Charlie Mitchell's Bacon	195
1889 - A Time for Changes	197

A Long Layoff	199
1890 - Back to the Ring—Almost	199
1890 - Billy Brennan Killed and Reddy Gallagher Arrested	202
Leaving Cleveland for Good	205
Denver and a New Beginning	206
Fight Possibilities	206
1891 - Young Mitchell Wins	208
A Complicated Subplot and Romance	209
Football over Fights	212
A Mixed Bag	212
1893 - Reddy and "Denver" Ed Smith – the Last Fight	215
1894 - Gallagher and Masterson	216
Reddy Marries Mary McSheehy	217
The Rest of his Life Begins	218
Caught and Squeezed Between Floto and Masterson	219
Gallagher's Success	221
Chapter 4 - Herman Arthur Macziewski, a/k/a Herman Arthur Magesky, a/k/a Arthur Magesty, a/k/a Arthur Majesty, a/k/a A. B. Tracy (1859-1891)	**225**
Majesty's Gackground	226
The Promoter, Charles E. "Parson" Davies	227
1885 - Tommy Warren	228
Majesty-Warren No. 1 – Majesty Hits the Big Time	230
Majesty-Warren No. 2 - a Show for the Bloomington Fans	231

1886 - Majesty-Warren No. 3 – a "Championship" Match at Louisville	233
Travel for Big "Fights"	234
Majesty-Warren No. 4 – a Return to Bloomington	235
Majesty Works with Billy Myer and Streator Fighters	237
1887 – Majesty Returns to Peoria	240
1888 - Majesty-Warren No. 5 – a Fizzle at Peoria	241
1889 - Majesty Returns to Toledo	242
1891 - Majesty Agrees to a Fight	244
Majesty is Killed	247
After the Fight Ended	249
The Legal Proceedings	251
Seville's Dissolute Life	253
Acknowledgements	**255**
Index	**353**

INTRODUCTION

James David Corrothers descended from Scot-Irish, American Indian and African ancestors. He became the poet of black Americans in the early twentieth century. In 1916 he published his autobiography and wrote about his time at McGurn's court on Chicago's near North Side where Harry Gilmore taught him how to fight:

"If I knock a man out, I have *accomplished* something.
If I write a poem, what's *that*?
There's nothing for *me* in writing.
I have no trade, and the only thing I can *do* is to fight."

Corrothers spoke not just for black Americans but for a generation of men looking to *accomplish* something in spite of their handicaps. They were roofers, laborers, teamsters, carpenters and immigrants who found something they could *do* – something that set them apart. They might have said: "If I roof a house what's *that*? If I drive a wagon what's *that*? If I dig a ditch what's *that*? If I fight, that is something I can *do*."

Jimmy Barry trained at McGurn's with Corrothers. Barry grew up in Chicago's "Little Hell" and lived about a block from McGurn's. On December 6, 1897 Barry became the bantamweight champion of the world in London, England knocking out Walter Croot in the last round of their twenty-round match. A few hours later Croot died from a basal fracture of his skull and Jimmy was arrested for manslaughter.

Over the last one hundred years a lot of misinformation has been published about Barry. His real story is told here with the chapter-long biographies of three other Chicago and Midwest fighters: Captain James Dalton, Patrick Joseph ("Reddy") Gallagher and Arthur Majesty. The careers of these men are parts of the history of Chicago and illustrate the efforts of immigrants and first generation Americans to make something of themselves to find social acceptance but more importantly to find self-respect.

These are not just portraits of boxers but snapshots of a post-Civil War generation. Dalton came to Chicago from Cleveland's Irish shanties. He was a tug boat captain on the Chicago River, fought John L. Sullivan and became a small-time part of that city's Democratic machine. Gallagher was a Cleveland boy. He pulled himself from poverty, fought the original Jack Dempsey, Charlie Mitchel and John Herget and ended his life a wealthy real estate owner and sporting editor of the *Denver Post*. Arthur Magesty was a Polish boy from Toledo. Magesty studied at Illinois Wesleyan University, taught shorthand reporting and worked as a newspaper reporter. He fought in Chicago before 8,000 fans and died before about 300 in a small ring in Nelsonville, Ohio where the crowd did not know is real name.

Chapter 1
James ("Jimmy") Barry (1870-1943)

"The biggest little fellow that ever lived"

Jimmy Barry – Undefeated – World Champion Bantamweight fighter – about 1896

> "If I knock a man out, I have *accomplished* something.
> If I write a poem, what's *that*?
> There's nothing for *me* in writing.
> I have no trade, and the only thing I can *do* is to fight."*

> *(*Corrothers, James David*,
> *In spite of the handicap, an autobiography*
> *(1916) – Writing of his days at McGurn's court.)*

On December 6, 1897, Jimmy Barry knocked out Walter Croot in the last round of their twenty-round match in London, England, and became the bantamweight champion of the world. Five feet three-and-a-half inches tall and about 110 pounds, Barry was at the top of his profession. A few hours later Croot died from a basal fracture of his skull and Jimmy was charged with manslaughter and taken to jail.

From 1890 until he retired undefeated in 1899, Barry was the best bantamweight boxer who ever entered the ring and the best fighter Chicago ever produced. Few people remember him, but his life is part of the fabric of Chicago history, and his real story is told below.

Jimmy's Parents

Mary Shields was born in 1826 in County Donegal, the northern-most county of Ireland. Her obituary says that she came to Chicago in 1842, but her death certificate states that she first lived there in 1852. The later date is more likely. In 1842 there were only about 10,000 people living in Chicago, but by 1852 Irish immigrants were leaving Ireland by the tens of thousands, and many of them arrived daily in Chicago. Mary and Garrett Barry were married in 1858. It is likely that she was a daughter of John and Anne Shields who lived on Townsend Street in Chicago's 7th Ward about two blocks from the Barry family.[1]

The Barry family was Roman Catholic, and family religious ceremonies were held at Holy Name Church, which is now Chicago's Cathedral or Immaculate Conception at the corner of Schiller and North Avenue. Immaculate Conception was the church for the Irish Catholics. The Poles, the other prominent ethnic group in the area, attended Saint John Cantius at 825 North Carpenter or Saint Stanislaus at 1300 North Noble, and religious boundaries were honored by ethnic groups even of the same faith.

Garrett Barry was born in County Cork, the southern-most county of Ireland in 1818.[2] He appears in the 1858 Chicago city directory and worked as a laborer, iron moulder, and house carpenter. The Barry family lived at 96 North LaSalle Street about four blocks north of the north side of the Chicago River near the corner of LaSalle and Grand. Their home was north of the grain elevators and the railroad tracks that ran parallel to the river and out to Government Pier on Lake Michigan. The area was a step below a slum. The Barry family was on LaSalle until about 1866, when it moved northwest to 48 Selah Street at the corner of Selah and Division just east of Goose Island.[3] In 1870, they moved to a two flat on the southwest corner of Oak at the intersected with Crosby where the McGurn family also lived.[4]

The Barrys' oldest child, Michael, was born in 1858. Their second son, Thomas J., was born in 1864, Margaret in 1867, and James on March 7, 1870. Michael McGurn, who was a close friend of the Barry family, said that Jimmy was born and raised at the corner of Crosby and Elm. Mary's brother John Shields was only one year older than her son Michael, and he was living with the family when Jimmy was born in 1870.[5]

The Great Chicago Fire

When Jimmy was seventeen months old, the great Chicago fire burned down his home and more than 17,000 other buildings including Immaculate Conception church. The fire started near 137 DeKoven on Chicago's west side near Halsted. Pushed east by strong westerly winds, it jumped over the South Branch of the river, burned the central city, and spread north and south. About 1:00 a.m. whirling cyclonic winds created by the fire carried burning debris hundreds of feet into the air and across the river to the north. Within minutes the grain elevators, factories, and homes on Market, Franklin, Wells, LaSalle, Clark, Dearborn, State, Cass, Bush, Pine, and St. Clair all the way to the water's edge and eventually as far north as Fullerton Avenue were in flames. At the beginning of 1871, there were almost 300,000 people living in Chicago, and over 100,000 people were left homeless. The only home south of where the Barrys lived that survived the fire is now the site of Chicago's Newberry Library and is located at 60 West Walton.

The Barry family escaped the fire. They probably followed others in the neighborhood across the bridge to Goose Island. Stories are told of mothers and fathers running east toward the lakefront seeking refuge by wading out into the frigid water. One account explains that "[r]esidents on the near north side were standing at their doors watching the south side burn when they discovered, to their horror, that the fire was already behind them, driving like a cyclone. The fire moved faster through the north side than in any other part of the city, devouring eleven blocks of houses in less than an hour..."[6] The three flat where the Barrys lived was on the western edge of the fire and burned, but other flats within a block away survived.

The family returned to the north side after the fire and lived in a three flat, this time at 31 Elm Street about a block from their former residence.[7] The lots on Elm were fifty feet wide and one hundred fifty feet long with no alleys. There were eight residential lots on their short block, and about twenty-five people lived on each lot. In the early years, Irish (e.g. Barrys, McGleens, McGreavys, Sullivans, and Shields) and Swedes (e.g. Petersons, Olsons, Johnsons, Larsons, and Ericksons) predominated in the neighborhood. Today the area is made up of modern three flats sold as pricy condominiums and known as Old Town Village.

The family was on Elm for the next sixteen years—from the time Jimmy was four years old until he was twenty. This neighborhood where they lived was sometimes called "Kilgubbin," the "Patch," the "Goose Island" area, or the "gas-house" neighborhood and sometimes "Little Hell." Kilgubbin and the Patch were early names given because Irish immigrants driven out of their homes by English landlords and by abject poverty and starvation squatted there in tar-paper shacks.

The last two (gas-house and Little Hell) were bestowed because in December 1865 the People's Gas Light and Coke Company purchased lots between Division on the north, Crosby on the east, Hobbie on the south, and Kingsberry on the west where it built a gas works to serve the north side. The flames and smoke from the gas works were prominent features in the entire area and reminded people of how hell might appear. The gas works were a block or so from where the Barry family lived and is now occupied by Commonwealth Edison power lines. The area was also part of the home turf of the infamous Market Street gang of pickpockets, strong-armed robbers, and thieves supposedly controlled by "Mad House" John F. O'Malley.

The streets in the neighborhood were dirt but more often just muck and mud. The sidewalks were wooden planks or boards. There was sometimes a foot or two between the three flats lining the streets, but in other places a wall of a newer building completely covered a window of an older flat. The drinking water was drawn from the North Branch of the Chicago River and was polluted with the waste from nearby distilleries, glue factories, and tanneries that dumped their chemical waste directly into the river until its surface looked like an oil slick. Where there were homes the families had gardens, chickens, and sometimes goats in the backyard. There were no playgrounds or public open spaces. The meeting spots were the corners of streets, saloons, and the front steps. Men sleeping off hangovers slept leaning against buildings as fruit and vegetable vendors pulled their hand carts through the neighborhood.

Boys in this part of town would go over to the river to throw rocks at the tugs and ships being towed or to see what they could steal. They usually joined gangs. The Market Street gang's home turf was here, and the head of that gang was supposedly "Mad House" John F. O'Malley who ran a saloon in Smoky Hallow on the west side of the Division Street Bridge.

Unruly young girls were taken from the gutters and saloons and sent to the Industrial School for Girls at 253 Larrabee (now 1316 North Larrabee), two blocks north of Division where they were taught to be domestic servants and to make clothes. When these girls first arrived at the school they were stripped and disinfected before being given a new and clean set of clothing. Their mothers frequently sold their daughters' new wardrobes to buy whiskey. It was not a nice place to grow up.

Jimmy's Siblings

The Barry flat may have been worse than living on the streets. By the time Jimmy was six, his older brother Michael was a hardened criminal and alcoholic. Michael engaged in hand-to-hand fights with the police and committed multiple burglaries and larcenies, but his favorite sport was beating up their mother.

Jimmy was twelve years younger than Mike and a shrimp of a kid. As an adult he was just over five feet three inches tall and weighed about 105 pounds. Mike beat up their mother regularly, and probably Jimmy could do nothing but watch Mike dole out punishment. When Jimmy was six, Michael whipped their mother. When Jimmy was seven, his brother knocked out their mother's front teeth with a chair and threw her down the steps between the second and third floor of their flat. When Jimmy was nine, his brother stabbed their mother in the shoulder with a knife. For these and other offenses Michael Barry spent substantial time in reform school or Chicago's House of Corrections.[8] He was not exactly a good role model for Jimmy, and there were probably many days when Jimmy went to a neighbor asking for help in calling a doctor, the police, or just to assist his battered mother.

Jimmy's sister, Margaret, was also an early alcoholic and violent. When she was eighteen and Jimmy was only thirteen, Margaret married a roofer named James F. Flynn at the Church of the Holy Name in Chicago.[9] She probably wanted out of her parents' house (who wouldn't?) and Flynn was an eligible Irish-Catholic boy of the proper age. He also shared Maggie's appreciation of alcohol.

Margaret and her husband had a stormy marriage. They lived at 66 Larrabee (now 873 North Larrabee) not far from her old home. On January 25, 1903, Margaret threw hot water from a tea-kettle on her husband and then caved in his skull with a hammer. This seemed appropriate at the time as Flynn was beating her with a metal cane. Her husband died on February 6, 1903. Maggie told the police that she was simply defending herself and didn't mean to cause permanent injury. The neighbors had a different story and said that the Flynns were frequently drunk and often engaged in violent quarrels. Margaret was charged with murder and held pending a coroner's investigation but not prosecuted.[10] There seemed to be no witnesses except Maggie's own three small children.

Thomas, Jimmy's other brother, was an upstanding citizen. He married in 1890, and together with his wife, Mamie, had seven children. He worked as an usher at Chicago's Union Depot for at least twenty-five years and was well-liked by other railroad employees.[11]

Jimmy said that before he was a fighter he worked as either a silver plater or a metal polisher. There were many businesses in Chicago that did silver plating in the early 1890s, and a plating business that was reasonably close to Jimmy's home was Chicago Carriage Lamp at 86–88 Market Street. This may be where he worked and learned his trade.[12] At that time many boys started working when they were about twelve or thirteen years old, and they were expected to turn over their earnings to help pay the family bills.

McGurn's Handball Court and Harry Gilmore

Two things probably saved Jimmy from poverty, unemployment, and a life of crime. One is that the McGurns lived at 95 Crosby (the corner of Elm and Crosby) only a few feet from Jimmy's flat. If there was any semblance of a home for Jimmy it was where the McGurn lived.

From about 1873 until 1879, Mike McGurn and his wife Ellen Walsh McGurn operated a grocery store on that corner and also sold liquor. In 1879, the grocery became a saloon, and in 1885, the McGurn family moved to 206 Division where they lived on the first floor of a three flat next to Mike's new saloon. This complex was then about one hundred yards from where Jimmy lived.

Mike McGurn operated his businesses with his son William. Mike was born in July 1843 near Ballina, County Mayo, Ireland, immigrated in 1862, and came to Chicago when he was about twenty-two years old. Ellen had twelve children but only five lived to adulthood. John McGurn was born in Chicago in 1864, Mary Loretta a year later, William in May 1869, Kate in July 1871, and Charlie in August 1883. William would later become a sergeant on the Chicago police force, and his younger brother Charles Garfield McGurn became a well-known and connected captain on the force and a guard for George William Cardinal Mundeline.[13]

In about 1888, Mike McGurn built an indoor handball court behind his saloon. In addition to handball, many Chicago boxers, aspiring boxers, and wrestlers hung out, trained, boxed, and wrestled at McGurn's court. The court was off-limits to women but occasionally the McGurns' young granddaughters and their friends would sneak into the balcony to spy on the boys or watch the athletic events. The wealthy men had their gymnasiums and well-equipped clubs such as the facilities run by the Chicago Athletic Association or the Board of Trade. The average guy did not have similar facilities. Mike McGurn was an important mentor for Jimmy. His court was a place where Jimmy could go to be away from the chaos of his home.

Beginning in 1889, the leading boxing figure at McGurn's was a nationally known lightweight fighter and boxing instructor named Harry Gilmore. In those days anybody who knew anything about the ring knew about Gilmore and particularly his championship fight with Jack McAuliffe who was a near god among Irish immigrants.

Gilmore was a second important figure and role model for Jimmy. The void that existed in Jimmy's family was filled in some small measure by Gilmore. Born in Toronto, Canada, in March 1854, Gilmore was sixteen years older than Jimmy. Gilmore had married in 1878 and started a family. He was a modest and unassuming man. When Gilmore moved to Chicago in 1888, his oldest son, Harry, was already nine years old. Gilmore and his wife, Lizzie, had eight children between 1879 and 1897. Gilmore and Jimmy were men of similar small stature. Gilmore was five feet seven inches tall and weighed about 130 pounds. For several years he held the title of lightweight champion of Canada, and in January 1887, at Lawrence, Massachusetts, he fought the great McAuliffe for the world lightweight championship, losing in twenty-eight rounds.

After the McAuliffe fight, Gilmore moved to Saint Paul. His prominence as a top lightweight contender was ended by the "Streator Cyclone" Billy Myer who administered two successive knockouts to Gilmore. In October 1887, Myer knocked out Gilmore in five rounds at Saint Croix, Wisconsin. Gilmore demanded a rematch claiming that he was the victim of a lucky punch. In January 1888, Myer gave Gilmore his rematch and again knocked him out, but this time in the first round at North Judson, Indiana.[14]

Gilmore became friends with Myer, who was a solid guy, and they traveled together around cities in northern Illinois putting on boxing exhibitions. In February 1888, both Gilmore and Myer were hired by Charles E. "Parson" Davies to appear with two other fighters, Reddy Gallagher and Martin Snee, at Chicago's Casino Theater in a vaudeville-like production called "Gymnasium Scenes." After a short run at the Casino, Gilmore traveled with the Parson Davies Specialty Company putting on boxing exhibitions with Gallagher. While traveling, Gilmore announced that when the tour was over he would close up shop in Saint Paul and move to Chicago. He said that he had been asked by friends to open a boxing school. His status as a top contender was over. Gilmore's long-time backer, after evaluating the results of Gilmore's last five matches, said he had not lost confidence in Gilmore but that he was then very confident that Gilmore would lose.[15]

Despite the downward trend in his own career, Gilmore became popular in Chicago. In October 1888, he was hired as the boxing instructor for the Garden City Athletic Club working at its Clark Street gymnasium.[16] That club was formed in January 1888 with the grand plan that it would rival the best athletic clubs on the East Coast. By the end of 1888, it was in financial trouble and disappeared from the records. The Chicago's sporting community gave Gilmore a benefit to help tide him over until he could find new work. With no job and unable to arrange fights, Gilmore decided to stay in Chicago.

In April 1889, Gilmore was given another benefit. This time the benefit was held at McGurn's court. It seems probable that Gilmore had been running his boxing school there since late 1888. The McGurns had a big family and were active in Chicago Democratic politics.[17] In early 1889, Gilmore began supervising boxing shows presented at McGurn's.

*Harry Gilmore – after his days as a fighter
(Photo courtesy of Tracy Callis)*

Many exhibitions were held at McGurn's throughout 1889 and drew big crowds. The family's facilities were easily accessible from downtown Chicago because a north-south cable car line ran one block east of the court.[18] Gilmore worked at McGurn's until October 1894 when he moved his school to 77–79 Clark Street opposite Chicago's city hall. Although he moved his school, Gilmore continued to offer his boxing shows each week at McGurn's.[19] During 1889, Gilmore was also hired as the boxing instructor at the Chicago Board of Trade's gymnasium where he rubbed shoulders with many prominent Chicago business types.[20]

Mike McGurn said that Jimmy used to fight the boys after school.[21] His friends and family members said that he engaged in regular matches when he was quite young. Jimmy said that he was twelve and weighed about ninety pounds when he started fighting, or "standing off," with boys in the schoolyard. Barry said that necessity made him fight to protect himself from schoolyard bullies. Who first taught him how to fight remains a mystery. McGurn's obituary states that he was interested in boxing and brought out Barry. He may have been Jimmy's first teacher.

Will McGurn said that he was there when Jimmy put on his first glove and beat a fellow twice his size with one hand in three rounds. He used an uppercut that was a new punch for Jimmy. He had seen Tommy White use the punch earlier in the day and he decided to try it out for himself. Someone should have warned his opponent that this kid had a lot of motivation to beat the tar out of someone given the chance. Outside of the ring Jimmy was described as one of the kindest boys in the neighborhood who would do whatever he could to avoid trouble and seldom hung around with other fighters.[22]

In 1887, the McGurns operated both their saloon and their grocery store.[23] At that time handball had become popular in

Chicago. Mike, John and Will McGurn were all championship caliber handball players. In about 1885 Mike bought two lots on the southeast corner of Division and Chatham where two three-story brick buildings were constructed as 206-208 Division. His new saloon was on the first floor of both buildings and the McGurn family lived on the second floor of 206 Division. In about 1888 Mike decided to add a lighted handball court on his property behind his new brick buildings. The court was seventy-five feet long, twenty-five feet wide, and forty feet high with smooth walls made of Portland cement. It was lit by skylights with wire netting covering the glass. At the back of the court was a gallery with seating for spectators. The seating was above a fourteen-foot-high wooden back wall.[24] Over the next twenty years McGurn's court was the home for many local, national and international handball competitions. Cap Anson was a well-known handball competitor at McGurn's and good friend of Jimmy's. In addition, the court was often converted to a prizefight venue and hosted some of the best prize fights held in Chicago.

Shortly after Gilmore began working at McGurn's, Jimmy asked for instruction. The *Chicago Tribune* reported in 1897 that after Gilmore began teaching at McGurn's someone told him that Barry was the most likely person in the neighborhood to become a fighter. Soon after that Gilmore caught a boy peeking in the window at McGurn's and asked, "What do you want?" Jimmy's reply was, "I'se Jimmy Barry." Jimmy said that Gilmore asked, "What makes you think you can become a boxer?" Barry answered, "Because I can whip any boy on the prairie (meaning the vacant land where he and others played prairie ball and which now is littered with aged buildings) and I can't find anyone to give me a decent fight, even among the big kids."

Gilmore gave him a chance, which was Barry's dream come true. Gilmore marveled at Jimmy's natural skill and knowledge of fundamentals. He said that teaching Barry how to fight was like teaching a duck to swim.[25] Gilmore brought out Jimmy as a fighter, and his first appearance was in 1889. Jimmy said that Gilmore taught him proper footwork, how to slip punches, and how to weave.[26]

Within a short time Barry was fighting at the Board of Trade under Gilmore's supervision and picked up the nickname of the "Board of Trade's Pet."[27] There are no records of the fights at the Board of Trade, but articles often refer to fights that happened there and claim that many of them were for prize money. Fighting in Board of Trade arranged matches sometimes involved brutal fights in back rooms, basements, barns and other remote sites.

The first description of Barry as a fighter appeared in late February 1890 in an article about the fighting ability of Tommy Kelly, who was a classy bantamweight known as the "Harlem Spider." The writer had clearly seen Barry fight before February 1890 and wrote: "…there is a little fellow right here that would give him [Tommy Kelly] a great fight, unless Chicago men are greatly mistaken, and that is Jimmy Barry. Jimmy is a two-handed fighter, a hard and quick hitter, and a man that is hard to keep away from.[28] Although there is no byline for this article, whoever wrote those lines knew what he was talking about. This very early description summarized Jimmy throughout his career, i.e. he was two-handed, a quick and hard hitter, and a man hard to keep away from because he believed that his job was to win and the shortest distance to that goal was a straight line to his opponent.

Chapter 1 - James ("Jimmy") Barry (1870–1943)

Typical Chicago handball court, which could also be converted for use as a boxing venue

There were a number of amateur prizefighters in Chicago who hung together and participated in exhibitions and other athletic activities around the city. This group included Tommy White, Frank and Pat Fitzgerald, Dan Kelly, Frank Garrard, Al Schrosbee, Charles Essig, Billy Arthur, Tommy Barrett, and Ben Donnelly.[29] Some of these fighters had been in the ring before Gilmore started teaching at McGurn's. Their matches had taken place at venues such as Chicago's First Regimental Armory.[30] There were also many local men who learned to box or played handball at McGurn's who never made the newspapers but knew the fighters well.

Another of Gilmore's students was James David Corrothers, a welterweight who was only six months younger than Jimmy. Corrothers was of Scots-Irish, American Indian, and African descent. He came to Chicago in 1887 and was considered the poet of his race and later became a minister. In 1916, Corrothers wrote that Gilmore was one of the most modest and gentlemanly men anyone could meet.

Corrothers was asked by his friends to give up boxing. His response spoke for a generation of fighters who gathered at McGurn's to learn to fight: "If I knock a man out, I have *accomplished* something. If I write a poem, what's *that?* There's nothing for *me* in writing. I have no trade, and the only thing I can *do* is to fight." Others who were not poets might have said: "If I roof a house what's *that?*" or "If I drive a wagon what's *that?*" But they all understood what Corrothers meant when he said "the only thing I can *do* is to fight."

Gilmore taught his students how to fight, and after his arrival most of these fighters appeared in Gilmore-promoted exhibitions at McGurn's. Some of them turned professional and began fighting for real money in finish fights. One of Gilmore's matches specifically mentions Corrothers meeting "Texas" Casey.[31] Often Gilmore traveled with his fighters and worked as their manager and second.

Jimmy's reported contests took place during Gilmore's second season in Chicago. He was included in Gilmore's local exhibitions because he was a good fighter.

Chapter 1 - James ("Jimmy") Barry (1870–1943)

Tommy White – one of the fighters trained at McGurn's court by Harry Gilmore. White was a friend of Jimmy Barry. (Photo courtesy of Tracy Callis)

April 1890 was a busy month for Barry. He appeared at McGurn's with Gale on April 5 along with Stift, Garrard (often spelled Girard), and Saint Louis-based fighters. On April 16 he appeared at Chicago's Twelfth Street Turner Hall as part of an evening of exhibitions including a four-round match between Garrard and Billy Young and additional sparring between Barry and Frank Murphy. Gilmore himself appeared that night to spar with White.[32]

A few days later many of the same men appeared at the Madison Street Theater at a Davies-sponsored production where

Barry sparred with Gale, Garrard with Stift, and Australia Billy Murphy with White. Davies customarily had higher quality fighters, and that night the prime attraction was Austin Gibbons and Jack McInerney.[33] Less than a week later Barry was part of a program on Chicago's south side at the Casino Theater and handball court at Twenty-Fourth and State streets where he sparred five rounds with Schrosbee while others on the program included Garrard, McInerney, and Stift. At this point both Barry and Schrosbee were being called celebrated Board of Trade "featherweights." Another later article described a protest to Schrosbee's attempt to participate in a match as an amateur state that the "specific charge against him was that he had sparred with Barry at the Board of Trade Athletic rooms for a purse of $150."[34] All of this taken together suggests that before the spring of 1890 Barry had already been fighting regularly at the Board of Trade.

With no air conditioning, boxing during Chicago summers virtually stopped. In the fall and early winter Barry was back in the ring. On November 15, he sparred four rounds at McGurn's with George Siddons of Peoria, Illinois.[35] Siddons was a high quality fighter and in December was fighting matches in Peoria where Arthur Majesty worked as referee.

1891 – Jimmy's Professional Career Begins

In January 1891, Barry often appeared at McGurn's. These appearances marked the beginning of Jimmy's break-out year as a fighter. Boxing historians list many of Barry's matches and their results without specific identification of the source of their information. Some of the best historians do not agree on his overall record. One source states that his record was 70-0, another

59-0-9, another 68-0, and another 60-0 with 38 KO's. Barry was actually in the ring without a loss for over 150 fights.

It is likely that many of the original sources had some firsthand knowledge of Barry's private fights. These fights were private in the sense that they were not advertised, not open to the general public, and their outcomes were not reported in newspapers. Jimmy's 1891 appearances that were public and are documented in contemporary newspapers are listed in at the end of this chapter.

An excellent record of Jimmy's 1891 fights is found on the Cyberboxingzone. Many of the names of Jimmy's opponents on the list of fights reported in newspapers also appear on the Cyberboxingzone list of fights that were not reported publicly. It is probable that Barry fought many of these same men in both public exhibitions at places such as McGurn's court and in private fights at places such as the Board of Trade's gymnasium that was open only to members and their invited guests or in the back rooms of saloons, in warehouses, or in barns. It is reasonable to think that Barry participated in many such private matches during 1891. Assuming that he did have these matches then who were the men that were his early opponents?

Some of the men on the list of Barry's private fights are fairly well known because they too participated in public exhibitions at McGurn's and other Chicago public venues. These fighters include the Schrosbee brothers, Joe O'Leary, Barney McCall, Joe Gates, and Jack Kelly. Some of these fighters had their own substantial careers in the ring. It would be no surprise that Barry fought these men in private because he frequently fought them in public. However, there are other names on the list of his private fights that are less familiar. These opponents include men such as Fred Larson, Dick Ward, Jack Miller, and Tommy Cassidy. Who were these fighters and did they really exist?

Many sources claim that Barry's first match in 1891 was at McGurn's court with a man named Fred Larson who outweighed Jimmy by ten pounds. Barry knocked out Larson in the first round of that fight. No contemporary newspaper account of this match has been found. Jimmy later said that Larson was known on the north side as the "Swedish Wonder" and had a reputation on the north side as a clever man. There was a Fred Larson who immigrated to the United States from Sweden in 1890 and worked in Chicago as a carpenter. In 1891, this Larson lived only about two blocks from McGurn's court and was about twenty-five years old.[36] This Larson was probably Jimmy's opponent in his first private fight.

During 1891 Barry had two private matches with a person named Tom Cassidy, but there are no newspaper accounts of those matches. In 1891, there was a Tom Cassidy who was born in 1868 and therefore about twenty-three years old. Cassidy's father, John Cassidy, lived on Sedgwick Street in Chicago's 7th Ward only a short walk from McGurn's court.[37] Again, this Cassidy does not seem to have an established record and would probably not have had much ring experience. Later in his career Jimmy had an opponent called Young Cassidy, and this might have been Tom Cassidy, but all of this just amounts to educated guesses.

Barry also is reported to have had an 1891 match with a John Miller. There was a John Miller who lived in the three hundred block of Elm Street about two blocks from McGurn's. This John Miller was about twenty years old and worked as a clerk in downtown Chicago. All of this suggests that the 1891 fights appearing on Barry's record were private fights with his opponents chosen from other men living in the neighborhood around Goose Island, and those men probably trained at McGurn's court under Gilmore's general supervision. Other opponents only came to McGurn's looking to get action. For example, Joe O'Leary, one of Barry's early opponents, was described as a pupil of Jem Mace from London, England.[38]

Jimmy later said he began to fight for money to help support his mother. His sister had married in 1883 and had her own family, his father died in 1885, his mother was already suffering from chronic asthma and was probably not able to support herself. As the last child in the home who was able to provide support, Jimmy probably felt he had a duty to support his mother.

Newspapers provide little insight into what happened during most of the reported matches, but there are a few brief accounts.[39] On Saint Patrick's Day 1891, Jimmy fought three rounds with Al "Shorty" Cleveland before a packed house. The report says that the two men "had it in warm fashion for three rounds."[40] The second time Barry fought Cleveland on June 8, the pre-match article said that the two were scheduled for five rounds "for blood," and Barry fulfilled that prediction by landing on Cleveland's nose in the second round and continuing to pound it until Cleveland was blinded by and choking on blood. Before the end of the fourth round Cleveland's backer threw up the sponge.[41]

Two nights after pounding Cleveland into submission, Jimmy was back in the ring at McGurn's, this time matched with a fighter described as "Young Mellington."[42] This fighter may have been Billy Wellington because the fighters' names are often misspelled in written accounts. There was a William

Wellington that lived on the near north side and who was born in 1869.

In December Barry appeared in a Davies production at Battery "D" in Chicago. The main attraction that night was Davies' new fighter from Australia, Jim Hall, in a match with a local heavyweight named Joe Ferguson. One of the preliminary bouts was between Joe O'Leary and Barry. Jimmy would have been paid for this appearance and was therefore well on his way to a professional career.

1892 – A Year of Politics and Private Knockouts

In April 1891, Republicans by a narrow margin elected Hempstead Washburne mayor of Chicago. Washburne was critical of prizefighting in general, and in early 1892, the Chicago police cracked down. The crack-down was brought on by an evening of entertainment offered by Davies on January 12. The featured fighter was the great Peter Jackson, who undertook the task of knocking out two heavyweights on the same evening. There was a third knockout in another match, and Gilmore cut up a fighter from Saginaw, Michigan.[43] A second big production that an estimated 4,000 patrons attended took place on February 1. That production featured the Australian Hall trying to knock out the fireplug Mike Boden of Philadelphia in four rounds.[44]

On February 15, an evening of entertainment was held at the Second Regimental Armory featuring Andy Bowen of New Orleans and Jimmy Murphy of Chicago. Barry participated in a preliminary match that evening. The police stopped another preliminary match between Joe Doner and Charles Aiken because the fighting had become too aggressive. Then, during the

Bowen-Murphy match, the police informed everyone that there could be no referee and that the fighters could not use seconds. The absence of a referee and seconds would nullify any claim that their match was a professional fight. Finally, during the eighth round of the Bowen-Murphy match, the police ordered the fighters off stage. This led to the cancellation of other entertainment scheduled for February 17.

Two months earlier when a Chicago alderman was supposed to act as the referee in a White-Van Heest match and the police prevented the alderman from acting, he explained his function *vis a vis* the Chicago boxing ordinance to the crowd waiting for the match: "The police says we don't have no referee and make a decision of this little athletic endeavor, which being the case, there will be no referee, and I will withhold my decision until after the fight, that is until some future time, hopin' as everybody is willing." The crowd then cheered, indicating its willingness to await the alderman's decision (and collect on bets) until the police were out of the picture. Chicago was not a place that welcomed prizefighting, and finish fights were forced underground or stopped just before a fighter was counted out.[45]

Despite politics and police interference, Barry's career took off in a big way in 1892. His matches reported in the newspapers are set out in the appendix to this chapter together with the matches reported by the boxing historian for the authoritative Cyberboxingzone.

Finish fights were usually not reported in the newspapers because promoters could not present them in public without possible prosecution. No one was putting up posters saying: "Come to the basement of 309 S. State Street Friday night at about 10:00 p.m. and knock twice. There will be a finish fight between Jimmy Barry and Dan Rowan! Keep it quiet because we don't want the police to know!" The word about such fights was passed by word-of-mouth between bartenders and sports or in the back rooms of the many gyms around town. Because the press was not invited to cover these fights, there are no contemporary newspaper accounts. Many of the private fights where Barry knocked out his opponents undoubtedly took place, and these results demonstrate that Barry packed a powerful punch.[46]

Jimmy Barry in his prime
(Photo courtesy of Tracy Callis)

1893 – A Year of National Prominence

In 1893, Barry grew from a fighter at the top of Chicago's list of bantams to national prominence. Again the year was marked by matches that were reported publicly and others reported only by boxing experts. Most historians report Barry's first fight in 1893 as a first-round knockout of a fighter named Max Eaufeldt (or Saufeldt) on January 8 in Chicago. There appears to be no public account of that match and this fighter has not been found.

There are multiple reports of a private fight between Jimmy and Robert H. "Bobby" Quade that took place on January 14 in Chicago. Quade is the same fighter referred to at the end of 1892 as Bob McQuade, whom Barry was scheduled to fight in Fort Wayne, Indiana. The attempts to carry off that match failed and the fight was moved to Chicago.

Barry and Bobby Quade

Quade was born in 1868 in Kansas City, Missouri. He was a bantamweight fighter who had also appeared in Saint Louis. He had been fighting as an amateur up to and through the spring of 1892. The Barry-Quade fight took place in a cellar described as a cramped apartment on the south side of Chicago. The match was for a purse of $100, all to the winner. Barry weighed 104½ pounds and Quade 102½ pounds. Gilmore took care of Barry during the fight. There was a lot of risk in these fights. The floor was probably dirt but might have been brick. The walls were likely brick. No padding would have been provided.

According to the *Chicago Tribune*, Barry had a very natural style and an easy natural swing, while Quade's style was cramped and his leads poorly aimed. For six rounds it was anyone's fight, but then Quade began to fade and Barry became the aggressor and forced the fighting.[47]

Jimmy was a master of effective combinations. This is what marked him as a two-fisted fighter. He would land a hard left to the chest to bring an opponent's chin down, follow with a right uppercut, and then a straight right to the chin. This approach became a hallmark of his fights over the next nine years. Good fighters could stay with him for a few rounds, but when they showed some hesitation or faded, Barry's foot went down on the pedal. This was his temperament and what separated him from others, ultimately making him a champion. After the Quade fight, Barry was called the bantamweight champion of the Northwest, although there was no organization that laid claim to such a title or definition of what it meant.[48]

Barry's reported fights in 1893 are again listed in the appendix. Some fights that typically appear in the records maintained by boxing historians do not seem to be reported in contemporary accounts. Several of those fights probably did not happen.[49]

Barry and Pete Shea, the "Portland Cyclone"

By June an effort was made to match Jimmy for the "100-pound championship of America" against Jack Levy, who styled himself as the 100-pound champion of England and was often referred to in contemporary accounts as a "Hebrew."[50] Of course this was during a time when Germans were "Krauts," the Irish were "Micks," and "Italians" were "Wopps" and so on.

Before anything was arranged with Levy, a fellow named Pete Shea, the "Portland Cyclone," came east looking for a match with Jimmy, and a ten-round go for a purse of $1,000 was arranged to take place at Roby, Indiana, as a preliminary to a Solly Smith-Johnny Griffin match. Shea had lost in thirty-seven rounds to Fred Bogan at 115 pounds in 1890, but in the future the Barry-Shea match would be called an "engagement of prominence."[51]

Chapter 1 - James ("Jimmy") Barry (1870–1943)

The leading men of Chicago had determined to chase boxing out of Chicago during the Columbian Exposition. The sports moved across the state line into Indiana where they opened a race track and crude hall to stage boxing and wrestling matches. The place where they settled was called Roby and was convenient because trains ran regularly that way and the railroads were willing to add special trains when racing or boxing events were held there.

The night of the Barry-Shea fight became a memorable one in boxing history. The heavyweight champion James Corbett had been ducking a promise to fight the great Peter Jackson, but Corbett was confronted in the ring at Roby by Davies and embarrassed into renewing his promise to fight Jackson—a promise that Corbett later broke.

Both Barry and Shea weighed 105 pounds for this match. Barry's seconds were Gilmore, White, and Griffo and Pat Fitzgerald acted as timekeeper. The first round was devoted to a feeling-out process, but at the start of the second Barry rushed and landed a straight left on Shea's mouth and a heavy right to the head. He hit Shea when and where he wanted. After heavy infighting in the third round, the fighters broke, and Shea then rushed Jimmy to the ropes and landed hard on his stomach and kidneys. Shea continued to be the aggressor to Jimmy's mid-section until Barry landed a hard left to Shea's head.

The fourth round started with another rush by Shea, again pushing Barry to the ropes where they fought hard. Shea looked tired, and when an opponent was tired the green light always went on for Jimmy. He attacked and was stronger, in the end knocking Shea down twice, ending the round with Shea groggy.

One account claimed that Shea was knocked over the ropes twice in the third round and knocked down three times in the fourth. When Shea arose from the last knock down Barry simply pushed him over and Shea was counted out. Another account says that as the fifth round started, Shea staggered up and moved into the ring. His seconds then realized that Shea had not recovered his senses and threw up the sponge. Whatever happened, it was a clear victory for Jimmy.[52]

After the Barry-Shea fight, Levy again wanted a match with Barry, and it was arranged at 100 pounds for a purse of $500 as a preliminary to a Griffo-Lavigne match at Roby.[53] The weight limit was later changed to 102 pounds at ringside and was for the championship at that weight.[54] For reasons that are not clear, the proposed articles of agreement were not signed, and a match between Barry and Johnny Connors of Springfield, Illinois, was arranged at 105 pounds for a purse and stake that together aggregated $1,500.[55] This match did not take place because the governor called out the Indiana National Guard on the day of the match and closed down Roby.[56]

Failing to arrange a match with Barry, Levy agreed to fight Jimmy Gorman of Paterson, New Jersey, at 100 pounds before the Olympic Club in New Orleans.[57] Gorman knocked out Levy in a tough battle. After that match Gorman was described as the 100-pound champion of America. Levy wanted a match with Barry, but Barry was looking for Gorman, and the Olympic Club wanted a Barry-Gorman match for a purse of $1,000.[58]

Chapter 1 - James ("Jimmy") Barry (1870–1943)

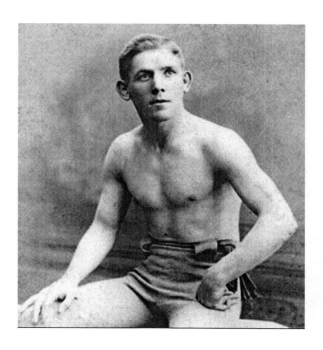

*Jimmy Barry as a young fighter
(Photo courtesy of Tracy Callis)*

After the Barry-Connors match fell through, Jimmy returned to McGurn's for a four-round match with a fighter identified as Jack Fitzgerald. His opponent was probably Frank Fitzgerald and not "Jack" Fitzgerald, but the press used the name "Jack." This was not a title match, and Fitzgerald was a taller, stronger, and heavier man than Jimmy. Nevertheless, Barry took the fight to Fitzgerald and put him down and out in the third round.[59]

Jimmy's final fight in 1893 was six rounds with Johnny Van Heest at McGurn's. Barry was described before this match as "the 105-pound champion," but the champion of what was not explained nor is the outcome reported.[60] After the Van Heest match Barry signed articles to fight the winner of a match between Shea and Steve Flanagan that was supposed to be at the Tivoli Theater on December 22.[61] That match did not happen.

1894 – A Year of Big Fights

The differences between the records of historians and records developed from newspaper accounts nearly stop in 1894. This probably happened because Barry was a nationally known fighter by 1894 and his matches were followed closely and reported extensively. Many of his matches were held in venues outside of Chicago where finish fights were legal and would be reported. Nevertheless, there are some differences that are apparent in the appendix.[62]

In January 1894, Barry was challenged by a New York boxer named Connie Smith. Jimmy agreed to fight, but the match was never arranged.[63] Probably to stay sharp Barry agreed to an exhibition with one of the Fitzgeralds, probably Frank, but it might have been Pat.[64]

After the Fitzgerald exhibition Jimmy agreed to fight Young Cranston (sometimes "Cransden"), described as a pupil of Henry Baker. Cranston needed more time in class. He lasted only three rounds, and Barry's superiority was obvious. He floored Cranston repeatedly in the third round and then used several well-aimed rights to Cranston's jaw to finish the job.[65]

Barry and "Irish" Joe McGrath

On February 6, Barry met an Irish bantam Joe McGrath at the Empire Theater. McGrath was the bantam champion of

Ireland and Billy Plimmer's sparring partner. He was thought to be a capable fighter. Plimmer was the bantam champion of England and was in Chicago with McGrath, appearing at the Empire Theater. Solly Smith had appeared at least once during that week to spar with Plimmer. The local boys such as Gilmore, White, Garrard, Barry, and Fitzgerald would all have been at ringside to see what this English bantam champion had to offer.

With the Englishman inside Chicago's city limits, an issue of national pride arose for Chicago's Irish-Americans. Barry could not just sit and watch Plimmer's show. However, Plimmer was not going to lower himself to meet Barry. On the other hand, McGrath had no excuse.

Accounts of the Barry-McGrath match are muddled because of police interference. The match was touted to be "friendly," but the police were suspicious, and several were at ringside. In the first round the fight became rough. Barry put McGrath on the sod in less than a minute with a straight left and a short right hook to McGrath's jaw, and when McGrath regained his feet, he was put down two more times. There was an obvious message being sent: "How does this compare to the champ, Joe? Tell your boss I'm here and waiting!"

After the first round the police warned the fighters that the bout would be stopped if the rough stuff continued, and the second round was a walk around. At the start of the third Barry went at it again. McGrath clinched to avoid punishment, but at the call of time almost fell down and had to be assisted to his corner. At that point Barry was awarded the match as McGrath was unable to continue.[66] After the match, reports said that Barry would spar with Plimmer, but Plimmer probably had seen enough and wanted no part of Jimmy.[67]

During mid-February, Barry and Frank Fitzgerald appeared for a week as the two star attractions in athletic entertainment offered at Stenger's Hall. Fitzgerald lived at 38 Elm Street just a few yards from Jimmy's home and was the younger brother of Pat Fitzgerald. Like Jimmy, the Fitzgerald brothers had also been employed as metal polishers. Pat Fitzgerald later worked as Barry's trainer, confidant, and manager and was a second in virtually all of Barry's fights. He worked with other fighters too, including White, Con Doyle, and Frank Bartley. Jimmy's appearances with Frank Fitzgerald at Stenger's did not involve serious fighting, but simply gave the public the chance to watch him in person.[68] For its part the press encouraged Gilmore to make a serious effort to push Barry to the front on the national scene.[69]

English lightweight fighter Stanton Abbott was in Chicago in February looking for a match with Gilmore. Abbott's career had started slowly, but he arrived in Chicago on a streak of thirteen matches without a loss, including a knockout of Jack Hopper at Madison Square Garden. Gilmore still had enough of a reputation that Abbott could advance his own career by defeating Gilmore.

Gilmore agreed to meet Abbott at the Second Regimental Armory on February 28. Barry agreed to meet Bob Costello of Buffalo that same night in a preliminary match. George Siler was the referee that evening and was instructed to render a decision if either fighter had the best of the match.

Over 3,000 attended these matches. This was probably ten times as many spectators as typically saw a match at McGurn's. Barry was one of Gilmore's seconds, but Abbott knocked out

Gilmore in five rounds to shorten up that work. Barry then entered the ring and made quick work of Costello. In the first round he forced the fighting and in the second laid out Costello with his customary left hand uppercut followed by a right to the mouth. As Costello was going down, the police entered the ring and ordered the fighters off the platform, but it was evident that Costello was dead game walking. Police stopping a fight before a knockout frequently happened in public matches in Chicago during the 1890s. Efforts were quickly made to match Barry with Casper Leon.[70]

Barry and Jimmy Gorman

In 1894, New Orleans was the place where real fights could take place, and the Olympic Club was the Crescent City's top boxing venue. That club announced a Barry-Gorman match for a purse of $1,000 and a large side stake. Barry signed the articles of agreement for the match to be held on June 2.[71] He was a hot commodity, and the Olympic wanted a Barry-Gorman match before a Barry-Leon match.

Barry, Pat Fitzgerald, and Gilmore left for New Orleans on the Illinois Central and arrived there on May 24 in time to be introduced before 2,000 curious fans at Sportsman's Park for a match between Jack Everhart and "Texas" Jack Burke.[72] Before the Barry-Gorman match the *New Orleans Item* published what it called "Barry's Record." It is not clear how the *Item* developed the reported record. Presumably the *Item* talked to someone familiar with Barry's ring appearances. Even discounting spelling mistakes, there were several fights mentioned by the *Item* that do not appear in other places.

The record reported by the *Item* was: "Defeated Jack Smith [?] in one round, Frank Murphy in six rounds, Shorty Cleveland in three rounds, Billy Millington [sic] in six rounds, Jack [sic] Sloane in three rounds, Joe Gates in seven rounds, Dick Ward in four rounds, Romo [sic] Durvant [sic] in six rounds, Joe O'Leary in three rounds, Joe Gates (again) in four rounds, Bob Quade, 105-pound champion of the Northeast, in ten rounds, Danny Doyle [?] in six rounds, Young Cassidy in four rounds, Young Spitz in eight rounds, Con Sheehan in four rounds, Young Crandsden [sic] in four rounds, Pete Shea in four rounds, Joe McGrath, champion of Ireland, in one round, and Bob Costello in ten rounds." [73]

Another 2,000 fans were at the Olympic on June 2, and Barry did not disappoint. The fighters were in splendid condition, but after the first round it was apparent that Barry would win. Gorman was severely punished, but stood the pummeling until his corner threw up the sponge during the eleventh round. Local papers compared the work that Jimmy did to Fitzsimmons' destruction of Dempsey. This was high praise for anyone familiar with boxing because Fitzsimmons essentially ended a past champion's career, and that fight had been held right there in New Orleans before many of the same fans.

Barry was the aggressor throughout. Gorman had a good seventh round, but when he finally weakened in the eighth round, Jimmy picked up the pace. This sort of thing could kill an opponent's spirit.

There are countless fighters that are willing to rest when an opponent slows the pace and welcome an apparent break and coast to the last two rounds. Barry was not part of that group. When an opponent slowed he saw opportunity. In the tenth round Gorman went down for an eight count and then fell several other times until the gong saved him. The eleventh round started with Gorman being battered to his knees repeatedly, and his corner saved him from a complete knockout.[74] The best fighter on the East Coast at this weight had been dominated and embarrassed by Jimmy.

Jimmy was immediately looking for his next fight. The Olympic Club's plan was to give Levy a match against Connors and then match the winner with Barry. Jimmy was interested in this proposition, but he, Fitzgerald, and Gilmore decided to go back to Chicago and await the outcome of the elimination match.[75]

Once again the summer was slow for boxing in Chicago, and while waiting for matters in New Orleans to be resolved, Gilmore and Barry went on the road to pick up a little spending money. The original plan was for Gilmore to fight Jimmy Gallagher of Pittsburgh on July 3 for eight rounds and Barry to meet a fighter called Eddy Hoven, a 115-pounder, the same night. This fighter Barry was to meet was probably "Kid" Hogan of Pittsburgh, but again many names are often misspelled. Eventually reports said that Harry Brooks was Jimmy's opponent. Whoever the opponent may have been, he was not a well-known fighter and lost to Jimmy.[76]

Barry and Casper Leon – First Fight

In August, Jimmy was matched with Leon, who was another great bantam of the 1890s. Leon was born Gaspare Leoni in Palermo, Italy, on December 2, 1872, and reported that he immigrated to the United States sometime between 1882 and

1885—depending on what census information is accurate. Many Sicilians went to New Orleans, but the Leoni family settled in New York. There were fewer than 4,000 Italians in America in 1850, but their number grew to 44,000 in 1880 and then nearly 500,000 by 1900, with another three-and-a-half million by 1920. Leon became a citizen in 1892. He was almost three years younger than Barry.

Barry and Leon were to fight to a finish at an unspecified place near Chicago at 105 pounds.[77] Disputes over weight became one of the complicated parts of the negotiation. An agreement was finally reached for the men to weigh-in at 3:00 p.m. on the day of the fight. This was a concession to Leon because Barry fought Gorman at 100 pounds, and fighting at 105 pounds posed no difficulty for Jimmy, but Leon needed to lose weight before the fight and wanted a chance to eat after the weigh-in. Years later Barry said he realized that there were few men who could make 100 pounds and he felt that he could whip the bantams. The articles were signed by Barry, Leon, Louis M. Cohn, the fight manager, and witnessed by Gilmore and Charles E. Sherman.[78] Estimates about the purse that would pass to the winner ranged between $1,000 and $4,000.[79]

The first Barry-Leon match took place at Lemont, Illinois, under a circus tent in a picnic grove before about 250 sober, well-behaved Chicago sports that arrived on a special train from the Polk Street Depot in Chicago. Today the town is known because of its Cog Hill golf course, but in the mid-1890s it was the place where many gamblers had gone to avoid the Chicago police. The Barry-Leon fight was billed as for the 105-pound championship of America. Barry had already claimed the 100-pound championship.

Siler was again the referee. Leading lights of the Chicago sporting scene were present, including the dark prince Mike McDonald, Malachi Hogan, Billy Myer and his brother Eddie, White, Sol Van Praag (a future business partner of Al Capone), Big "Sandy" Walters, and many others. Davies rode to the fight on the engine of the train. Eddie Myers worked in Leon's corner, but he was really there scouting for his friend Connors who wanted a chance at the winner.

Casper Leon – the "Sicilian Swordfish" – "Little Italy"
(Photo courtesy of the Cyberboxingzone)

Leon came into the match on a run of ten straight fights without a loss, including four knockouts. He had the advantage—as he always did with Barry—in height and reach. Leon was built like Fitzsimmons and carried the bulk of his weight from the hips up. Some accounts said that he had spindly legs that failed him in long fights. Bert Sugar has described Leon's style based on accounts of the fight. He described Leon as matching Barry in ring science, if not speed. Leon also had the ability to minimize Barry's speed by "subtle sidestepping and occasional right-hand counters."[80]

During the fight Jimmy was again the aggressor. In the fourth round Leon cut Barry's right eyebrow and then made that his target in the following rounds. Leon was saved several times during the fight by the call of time, but after each round he came up smiling and showed no weakness until the fifteenth round when he was knocked off his feet. Barry prepared the way for himself by chopping away at Leon's ribs to bring his guard down. Barry was said to have had the fight in his hands from the eighteenth round forward. He always pressed when an opponent faded, but Leon began clinching to avoid what then seemed inevitable.

Finally, in the twenty-eighth round, Barry made a rush and landed a solid blow on Leon's jaw, knocking him out. Leon had done well for a limited number of rounds, but as time passed he could not keep up. In the future he would always try to have limited round fights with Barry, implicitly acknowledging that his chances were not good in a longer fight.

After the fight Barry was said to be in worse condition than Leon. He had a swollen and heavily inflamed ear, a deep cut across his right eyebrow, and severely battered ribs. Both his eyes were black and blue and his left hand was almost useless. Leon was in a totally exhausted condition.[81] Nine days after the championship match Leon was afforded a benefit at McGurn's and some top fighters appeared to draw a crowd including Gilmore, Barry, Leon, and Young Kelly.[82]

Connors was still looking for a match, and after several failed attempts, the arrangements were made for them to appear in New Orleans as part of a boxing carnival.[83] The match promoter was the Auditorium Club in New Orleans. The bout was scheduled for December 10 for a purse of $1,500, $1,200 to the winner. They agreed to weigh 100 pounds, give or take two pounds, at ringside. The match was supposed to be the first of three successive fight nights and would be followed by Bowen-Kid Lavigne and then Ryan-Dempsey.[84]

Before the match Barry was confident. He had trained down to 103 pounds so that it would be easy to make weight. He announced that if he beat Connors he would issue a challenge to the world for a fight between 102 and 105 pounds for from $2,500 to $5,000 a side.[85]

Less than a week before the match the whole thing was declared off. Connors contracted malaria and was unable to fight. The club tried to induce Madden to substitute, but ultimately an agreement could not be reached and that fell through too. Cancelling the first night of fights was not the worst thing that happened for the carnival. On the second day the Bowen-Lavigne match ended with Bowen's death, and the Ryan-Dempsey fight was then cancelled. For Barry this was a disappointing end to an otherwise very successful year.[86]

1895 – Becoming the Champion of America

By 1895 the differences between newspaper accounts of Barry's record nearly stop. Beginning in 1894 and into 1895, a rematch with Leon was continually discussed, but an agreement could not be reached.[87] Other possible opponents were discussed, including Madden, Connors, Joe Elms, and Plimmer. One account noted that Barry was growing too large for the 100-pound weight class (sometimes called the paperweight class) and would thereafter fight at 105 pounds (usually called the bantamweight class).[88]

Before the end of January, Barry received and accepted an offer from the Olympic Club of Cincinnati to meet Frank Maciewski for a purse of $300 at 110 pounds. At this point, if he wanted a match, Barry needed to give up weight. Maciewski was a New York fighter who had been in Cincinnati since about August 1894. He had one crippled leg, which gave him an odd appearance in the ring, but he had knocked out Kid Thompson of Kansas City during a preliminary match before a fight between Danny Needham and Louis Greeninger of Cincinnati.[89] Then in early January 1895, Maciewski made a good showing during a ten-round match at the Olympic Club with Australian Billy Murphy, but he seemed to be a predominately right-handed fighter. After nine rounds of fighting a signal was given by a Cincinnati police lieutenant to the referee who stopped the fight and called Murphy the winner. This happened to save Maciewski from being knocked out.[90]

Despite their agreement, the proposed Barry-Maciewski fight was prevented by the Cincinnati authorities and did not take place.[91] Jimmy was clearly frustrated. He hadn't fought since mid-September 1894 because of Connors' illness, Madden's reluctance to fight, and police interference with Maciewski. He needed money and said that he was seriously thinking about giving up the game and returning to his trade plating silver.[92]

Charles E. "Parson" Davies was Barry's answer to the need for money. Prior to March, Davies had played no significant role in shaping Jimmy's career. However, Davies was well-known in Chicago as a promoter who made money for his fighters. Davies took a 50/50 split of the net proceeds of his clients' earnings, but he had the ability to find work and arrange fights when others failed. Most fighters understood that fifty percent of $1,000 was better than one hundred percent of nothing.

In early March, Barry began working with Davies as part of his string of fighters. During his career Davies customarily employed a private secretary. Two of his private secretaries were Otto Floto and Harry Glickauf. One of his earlier secretaries, Billy Williams, had died from smallpox in Kansas City leaving a destitute widow. Davies decided to stage a benefit for Williams' widow.[93] Dan O'Leary, the world champion race-walker and a former client of Davies, agreed to act as master of ceremonies for the event to be held at the Waverly Theater on Friday, March 8, 1893.[94] Barry, White, Garrard, Choynski, Leon, Santry, Bertrand, and Gilmore all appeared at the Williams' benefit.[95] Immediately after that benefit, Davies, Choynski, and Ryan left for Kansas City where they would appear at the auditorium there.[96]

Davies' first act on behalf of Barry was to arrange an eight-round bout with Joe Bertrand to be presented at Tattersall's on the same night that Choynski was to fight Dan Creedon, and Frank Childs of Los Angeles was to meet Rufus Sharp of Saint Louis.[97] Within a few days Davies also scheduled a fifteen-round rematch with Leon and was also arranging a fight with Madden in New York.[98]

Barry and Joe Bertrand

In 1894, Bertrand was carrying the title of champion featherweight of the Pacific Slope but also fighting as a bantam. He came to Chicago in the fall of 1894 and had participated in fights with Sig Hart and Joe Thompson. Thompson was a black fighter who weighed 130 pounds. During the Bertrand-Thompson match, Bertrand dislocated his right wrist. After hurting his wrist he had been outpointed by Fred Whitingham in February 1895.

The Bertrand-Barry match took place on March 21. The Fitzgerald brothers and William McGurn were behind Barry for the match. For the first three rounds Bertrand seemed to be in the fight. Beginning in the fourth, Bertrand was simply a target. He was knocked down as often as Barry wanted, and his face was badly battered and bloody. One account said that Bertrand was knocked down a dozen times. Barry finally forced Bertrand to the ropes and pounded him. In the sixth round, Bertrand came up groggy, and a straight right hand sent him to the floor. He remained down for a nine count, stood up, and was knocked down again before the referee declared the match over and gave Barry the fight.[99]

Barry and Leon – Second Fight

Articles for the second Barry-Leon contest were published on March 27 and were signed by Davies for Barry and Louis Cohn for Leon. They agreed to box fifteen rounds under Queensberry rules at the Second Regimental Armory on March 30. The net proceeds were to be divided 80/20.[100] Leon's side thought that he had performed well during the first fifteen rounds of their match at Lamont and believed he had a good chance with Barry in a fight of that length. Choynski worked with Barry as his trainer for the match, and Malachi Hogan was referee. Barry entered the ring at 108 pounds and Leon 112. Before the fight Barry put on as much weight as possible while still staying fit to perform at his top ability.[101]

For years, the accepted story has been that Barry defeated Leon only in their first fight and the rest of their fights were draws. This account serves to enhance Leon's reputation, but it is true only in a technical sense because Barry had Leon knocked out in their second fight just as the Chicago police interfered.

The process at play during the Barry-Leon second fight needs some explanation. To obtain the votes of citizens opposed to boxing, mayors of Chicago often proclaimed during their political campaigns that no finish fights would be allowed within the city limits if they were elected. After being elected, a mayor would sometimes prohibit "slugging," which was designed to perpetuate the idea that boxing exhibitions were simply scientific athletic exercises. Such declarations often amounted to a lie because "slugging" was inherently vague and often in the eye of the beholder. To prevent "slugging," police were sent to fights to monitor the proceedings. The mayor didn't want to see a headline: "In a bloody prize fight X knocked out Y in 15 rounds!" Therefore, just before a knockout the police would stop the fight.

It is likely that in order to achieve a proper balance between the fight promoters and law enforcement the police were paid by the management to lay back and not act too quickly to interrupt the fun. However, if a knockout loomed, then even the management expected the police to spring into the ring and stop the match thereby preserving the illusion that there were no fights to the finish allowed in Chicago. An end to a fight just before a knockout was called a "police finish," and a police finish made it possible for the audience to see a real fight, the police to follow the broad letter of the law as insisted upon by the mayor, and for the promoter to obtain a license for the next fight. This worked just fine if everyone played along with the program.

The day after the second Barry-Leon fight, the *Chicago Tribune's* headline read: "Casper Leon Knocked Out. Police Interfered or Jimmy Barry Would Have Been Given the Decision, Chicago Fight Declared a Draw After Fourteen Rounds of Unusually Lively Work. Italian Counted Out When the Officers Stepped Into the Ring – Honors for Several Rounds Were Nearly Even." Chicago's *Daily Inter Ocean* expressly referred to the fight as a "police finish." Given the way things worked in Chicago, there is no question that Barry had effectively knocked out Leon a second time. Any other analysis is like calling World War II a draw.

Once again Barry was the aggressor, and Leon was knocked down in the second round by a hard right. When he arose, Barry landed three hard blows to Leon's chest, but Leon survived the early crisis. The third, fourth, fifth, and sixth rounds were about even, and the seventh was Leon's by a close shave. Then Jimmy picked up the pace and landed hard on Leon in the remaining rounds. In the tenth, Barry pounded away at Leon's heart like a trip hammer and Leon was fading. It is harder for a fighter to slip punches at this point of a fight. In the eleventh, Jimmy was forced to chase Leon, whose spindly legs were working hard to get away. The *Daily Inter Ocean* wrote that in the eleventh Leon "had long since looked the loser." Barry then caught Leon with a hook and sent him to his knees again. In the twelfth, Barry landed blow after blow while Leon hung on.

*Jimmy Barry in front of a studio backdrop
(Photo courtesy of Tracy Callis)*

The gong saved Leon in the thirteenth round, and in that round he simply clinched to save himself from additional punishment. Finally, a left snapped Leon's head back and a right to the mouth had him wobbling. He was then driven into his corner and sent down. Leon was bleeding from the mouth, nose, and left eye. His ring artistry had not saved him. Barry put him down one final time, and Leon was lying on his back. One account said that the referee had counted time when the Chicago police, on cue, entered the ring and ended the match. Another account said that the referee had counted eight when Leon staggered unsteadily to his feet and a police captain and six officers in civilian clothes entered the ring and ordered Barry and the referee to stop.[102] If it makes fans of Leon feel better to call this fight a "draw" then nothing will change their minds.

Leon relied on the articles of agreement that provided that if he was still "there" at the finish, the fight would be called a draw. He was there only because the police were on their marks, interfered at just the right time, and prevented the referee from calling the knockout. In the 1890s, some writers acknowledged that this fight amounted to Barry's second victory over Leon. For almost a year, accounts said that Barry had beaten Leon in the twenty-eighth round of a finish fight and also in a "police finish." Any fair assessment of this fight should have Barry winning by a fourteenth-round knockout, but as time has passed and dimmed the reality, that is not how others have reported the match, and the illusion is perpetuated that Barry defeated Leon only once.[103] This may have happened because East Coast interests needed Leon to be the top contender and because an army of Italians was flooding into New York and needed an Italian-American hero to worship.

Immediately after the second Leon fight, Davies was prepared to sign articles for a Barry-Madden fight at the Seaside Club on Coney Island.[104] Madden was a good fighter but described as a stiff puncher who was easily rattled in a mix up, which is where Barry excelled.[105] At the beginning of May, Davies took

Choynski, Barry, Ryan, and big Bob Armstrong east where he had lined up matches that would not be stopped by the police.[106] No sooner did they arrive in New York than Madden and his backers backed out of the fight; however, at least one account claimed that Barry was unable to fight because of an injury he sustained in his second match with Leon.[107] After that it was virtually impossible to find anyone willing to fight Jimmy.[108]

Following the second Leon match, Barry's next serious fight was in mid-July, but he was kept busy by Davies. Most of this work involved sparring with Ryan on a daily basis and regularly appearing at benefits that Davies arranged on behalf of John L. Sullivan.

In July, a Cambridge, Massachusetts, fighter named Dave Ross agreed to a fifteen-round match with Barry in Union Garden Hall in Boston. Ross had been fighting for several years and was having a good year. At the end of April he had bested Boyle O'Reilly in a ten-round match and was then taken under Tom O'Rourke's management. O'Rourke and Davies were close friends and probably matched Ross with Barry. This probably happened because Davies was having so much trouble finding a better opponent willing to enter the ring with Jimmy.

The Barry-Ross match was a piece of cake for Jimmy. In the first round, Jimmy landed a straight left followed by another. It worked so well that Jimmy stuck with the punch and continued to tag Ross with his left. After Ross finally landed a blow, Barry followed with a right, left, and another right all to Ross's face. When Ross came out for the second round he was met with a heavy right hand and a left to the jaw. That was it. Ross made two attempts to get up but could not, and the fight was over.[109]

Barry and Jack Madden

More than three months after the Ross fight, Barry was finally able to arrange a match with Madden at the Empire Athletic Club in Maspeth, New York, on October 21.[110] Maspeth is now considered part of the borough of Queens. The club was incorporated in New York in August 1891 by James G. Tighe, William C. Tighe, James C. Kennedy, John Cole, and Michael Falvallo to cultivate rowing, boxing, fencing, wrestling, and trap shooting. James Tighe was a member of the board of the Amateur Athletic Union and a former manager of an amateur boxing club called the Varuna Boat Club.[111] Kennedy was an athletic promoter in New York.[112] Fighters who had appeared in the Empire's ring before Barry included Jimmy Handler, Frank Erne, Jack Skelly, and Griffo.[113]

The Barry-Madden match was supposed to take place a month earlier at the Hudson Athletic Club of Jersey City but the police interfered.[114] Madden claimed to be the eastern bantamweight champion, and somehow Barry had been demoted by the eastern press to the position of western champion.[115]

Jimmy outclassed Madden and put him out in the fourth round of what was supposed to go twenty. After a fairly tame first round, Barry went to work early in the second. He landed one of his well-known combinations: two lefts to the head, a right to the body, and a right to the jaw, sending Madden reeling to the floor. Madden got up and was put back down four more times. The New York backers of Madden must have had their mouths hanging open. Madden clinched to try to stop the damaging attack, but after the breakaway Barry landed another right to the jaw, lifting Madden off his feet. It was during this second round—and probably with the right that lifted Madden off his feet—that Barry broke his right hand.

In the third round, Madden came out looking anxious. Barry was cool and confident. He came to Madden, who clinched again but was straightened up by another left-right combination. Madden tried wrestling and was able to land one good punch before the end of the round.

The fourth started with another right by Barry to the stomach, and Madden clinched again. This time he earned three rights to the jaw, with the last sending Madden through the ropes. Madden crawled back into the ring and rose only to be sent back to the floor again. Finally the referee realized that Madden had no chance and stopped the fight. Barry went to Madden and warmly grasped his hand as the announcer declared him the winner.[116]

The East Coast had been conquered. Gorman was demolished in New Orleans. Leon had been battered twice. Neither Ross nor Madden provided real competition. There was no doubt anymore. Jimmy Barry was the 105-pound champion of America, and no other person could make a credible claim to that title.

After the Barry-Madden match, Davies and his fighters continued to travel from city to city with the Sullivan testimonial aggregation. This device had proved to be an easy way to make money, and Barry was a part of the attraction that packed in crowds.

The big news in prizefighting was the Corbett-Fitzsimmons heavyweight championship match. The fight had been moved from Dallas to Hot Springs to avoid interference by the governor of Texas, and all the contestants were summoned there. Tommy Ryan was part of the Hot Springs production. Davies and his fighters met on the morning of October 30 at the Wabash R.R.

Depot on Polk Street at eleven a.m. to travel to Hot Springs. They planned to stay the night at the Imperial Hotel in Saint Louis before going on to Hot Springs, but they stopped in Saint Louis for only an hour before catching the Iron Mountain Cannon Ball to Hot Springs. The Davies group, including Barry, arrived in Hot Springs at noon on October 31 and stayed at the Arlington Hotel. The next morning they learned that the whole affair had fallen apart. In the end none of the matches went forward and the group went back to Chicago.

The big news for Barry was that he was wearing a plaster cast because he had fractured his right hand on Madden's head during their fight. He had broken the second metacarpal of his right hand, and there was a lump on his hand where the bone was raised.[117] The metacarpals support the hand. The far end of a metacarpal forms the knuckle on the back of the hand and a break at or below there is a common injury for professional fighters. One report said that Jimmy had broken two bones in his right hand.[118] A month later a report said that the injury was so serious that Barry would never again enter the ring because the bone had not healed properly. Davies then hired Dr. Francis McNamara of 277 State Street to take care of Barry's hand.

Dr. McNamara was Davies' personal physician and had saved Davies' life in March 1895. He was the physician for several fighters, including Choynski, and he would later be the physician for the Cook County Jail, which indicates that he was properly connected with Chicago politicians. McNamara did surgery on Barry's hand, and the prognosis was supposedly not good. Surgery may have been necessary because the fracture made it difficult for Barry to make a fist. This may have been a rotational fracture that caused one of his fingers to rest on top of an adjoining finger when he made a fist. Such a fracture would need to be surgically corrected.

When told the story about the condition of Jimmy's hand, McNamara said that there was no truth at all to the stories that Jimmy's hand was seriously damaged. He admitted that there was a small lump at the site of the break, but said that it would gradually disappear and that Barry's hand would be stronger than ever. In fact, Barry was doing so well that he was scheduled to appear with the Sullivan benefit entertainers in Chicago on December 10.[119]

The year of 1895 ended with rumors swirling about future fights. Davies was contacted about a possible fight for Barry with the Australian champion Jimmy Anthony. However, the biggest news involved a possible fight with Pedlar Palmer who had defeated Billy Plimmer to claim the bantam championship of England. The road was open. If Barry could meet and defeat both Anthony and Palmer, he would be the undisputed bantamweight champion of the world.[120] The downside was that Davies was about to depart on a six-month tour with Sullivan and Paddy Ryan and the cast of a play known as "The Wicklow Postman." For Davies' active fighters this was not good news. It appeared that their promoter was out-of-pocket and this would put them on the shelf.

1896 – Only One Real Match in the Entire Year

The year 1896 was a difficult one for Barry. Early in the year he supposedly fought Young Lyons, a man who had been fighting with mixed results in Chicago for many years. It is possible that Lyons was matched with Barry, but virtually all articles about Barry say that he did not participate in a match between his fight with Madden and his fight with Flanagan. Other unreported fights supposedly involved Jim McGuire and Joe O'Donnell. There was a Jim McGuire who often appeared in Chicago newspaper reports and a Joe O'Donnell who was a timekeeper for Barry during his third match with Leon.[121] It remains possible that these fights did take place, but it is also unlikely for reasons explained above relating to the condition of Jimmy's hand.

Davies, Sullivan, Paddy Ryan, and the cast of "The Wicklow Postman" scheduled their tour to reach El Paso, Texas, at the time of a Dan Stuart's famous boxing carnival featuring Fitzsimmons and Peter Maher. Other carnival matches included welterweights Bright Eyes-Walcott, lightweights Everhart-Leeds, and featherweights Dixon-Marshall. Davies had booked a match between Johnny Murphy and Barry as part of the carnival.

Murphy was thirty-two years old and had been fighting since at least 1884. He had been in the ring with some of the best fighters, including Plimmer, Torpedo Billy Murphy, Dixon, and Cal McCarthy. He was larger than Barry and wanted to fight at 114 pounds. Barry wanted the fight at 107 pounds, and this dispute caused a five-week delay in making the match. Ultimately Murphy got his way and planned to enter the ring at 114 pounds. Their match was to be for $2,500 with $500 to the loser.[122] At the same time the Barry-Murphy match was made, Tom O'Rourke was exploring the possibility of a match between Barry and Anthony.[123]

Barry remained in Chicago until late January because he was participating in a handball tournament at McGurn's.[124] He was a quality handball player and continued to play competitively into the mid-1890s. After the tournament ended Barry left for El Paso, arriving there on February 1 and going into training for Murphy.[125] Except for the Fitzsimmons-Maher match that took place in Mexico, the remainder of the carnival fell apart. When it was determined that Barry's match was off and after the Fitzsimmons-Maher fight, Davies continued with the Wicklow Postman tour to California and Barry went back to Chicago where he was tendered a benefit at McGurn's to help cover his expenses associated with the failed Murphy fight. In Chicago Barry resumed playing competitive handball along with Frank Fitzgerald, his frequent ring opponent.[126]

A few weeks later there was more bad news about the right hand that Barry had injured in his match with Madden. Barry was teaching boxing on the north side—probably at McGurn's—when he broke his hand again during a demonstration with a pupil. This was the same hand that was supposed to be stronger than ever after the prior surgical repair.[127] The injury to Jimmy's hand probably had a long-term impact on his ability to fight. After his second break another benefit was given for Jimmy, and Davies wired from Butte, Montana, that he wanted fifty tickets for the show to help support Barry.[128]

A report in 1897 said that after this second break Jimmy gave up fighting, went back to work, and in that process lost weight that he never regained. This layoff probably did not last too long. Five weeks after breaking his hand a second time, Barry was back in the ring for a three-round exhibition with Harry Dalley of Australia. This match was part of a series of matches with fighters from Saint Louis, Cincinnati, Galesburg, Illinois, and Chicago. He also resumed playing handball at McGurn's with some of Chicago's top-ranked players.[129]

A month after testing his right hand with Dalley, his hand appeared to be healed and he was ready to box again.[130] During his lay-off Barry had decided to part with Davies and try making fights on his own. This probably happened for several reasons. White was a close friend of Barry and an arch critic of Davies, whom White did not trust. White had broken off with Davies because he was unwilling to split on a 50/50 basis. In addition, Davies had been away from Chicago for six months, which could not have pleased any of his fighters.[131]

Barry's first effort to arrange a fight without Davies involved a proposed rematch with Leon, who wanted a twenty-five round match at Coney Island.[132] Jimmy met with no success, and the best deal he could make was a match for $200, which would hardly cover training and travel expenses.[133] Barry finally arranged a six-round match with Flanagan to take place at the Caledonia Club in Philadelphia with the fighters weighing 107 pounds. No purse is mentioned in connection with this fight, which probably means the fighters were simply splitting the gate. Such terms are not the type that should have been given to a championship fight or fighter of Barry's caliber. By mid-August there were rumors that Barry would be going back under Davies' management, which probably meant that he thought he could not go it alone.[134]

Barry and Steve Flanagan

Flanagan was called the bantamweight champion of Pennsylvania. He was seven years younger than Barry—part of the next generation of fighters—but a good young fighter who had the reputation of smiling throughout his matches. The terms of the fight favored Flanagan because experience had shown that Barry excelled in longer fights, wearing down his opponents with a relentless attack. He punished his opponents in the early rounds and when the punishment began to show, he became stronger and finished his foe. A six-round fight gave Flanagan a chance to survive long enough that his will would not be broken.

At weigh-in both fighters were 108 pounds. The fight started after 10:00 p.m., and from the beginning Flanagan came up smiling and went on the defensive. This was the same approach that Leon adopted in his fights with Barry. In the first round Barry broke up the initial fiddling around by landing a hard right on Flanagan's heart and Flanagan's smile disappeared. In the second round Barry began to pound Flanagan, landing on his face with his left time after time and following with rights to Flanagan's body. The third round was a repetition of the second with Barry landing hard and with Flanagan backing up. In the fourth round Flanagan landed one flush blow on Barry's face, snapping his head back. The crowd became excited, but Barry's defense was thereafter perfect and he blocked or avoided Flanagan's remaining leads. Barry's solid and relentless work to his body began to show in the fifth round, and in the sixth Flanagan was visibly tired. The decision was given to Jimmy.[135]

Steve Flanagan
(Photo courtesy of the Cyberboxingzone)

By the end of August Barry was again managed by Davies. Jimmy immediately issued a challenge to any man in Great Britain to fight him at 105 pounds and offered to let Plimmer fight at 110 pounds, but there were no takers.[136] A few months later Jimmy modified his offer by saying that he was willing to fight Johnny Murphy at 114 pounds or anyone else at 112 pounds with Palmer, Plimmer, or Sam Kelly preferred.[137] None of these brave men seemed to want any part of Jimmy.

In early October, reports circulated that Barry was suffering from rheumatism. Eight years of fighting had begun to show through a right hand broken three times and rheumatism. Barry was at the top of his skills, but his body was not. Davies had suffered from rheumatism for years and knew what sort of treatment might help. He sent Jimmy to the hot baths at Mount Clemens, Michigan, for two weeks of rehabilitation. Barry stayed there for more than three weeks, returning to Chicago on October 25 in good condition and clear of the pain that had been bothering him. He went to Palos Park, Illinois, to be worked out by Choynski and Schrosbee and was still hoping for a match with either Plimmer or Palmer.[138]

Without anyone accepting his challenges, Barry decided to issue a specific challenge to Sammy Kelly for a match to be held any time before Kelly fought Plimmer in England. Kelly accepted the challenge and promptly returned from England to prepare for a match with Barry. Their match was to be held at the Broadway Athletic Club and billed as the bantamweight championship of America. Kelly was willing to meet Barry at 115 pounds because if he could beat Jimmy and then defeat Plimmer, he would be the undisputed bantam champion of the world. This arrangement was inherently contradictory. Featherweights weighed 115 pounds, not bantams. Barry said that if he defeated Kelly, he would go to England soon after that to look up Palmer.[139] One expert described Barry as "a wicked little cuss with both hands" and thought Barry would have no trouble beating Palmer.[140]

1897 – Coast to Coast and Across the Atlantic – The Big Time, World Championship, and Death

Barry's documented fights in 1897 are provided in the appendix. The important fights were those with Kelly, Ward, Anthony, and Croot. Most of the remaining fights happened because Barry had returned to Davies' management and Davies kept his fighters working between the big matches.

Barry and Sammy Kelly

Jimmy's career in 1897 returned to the frequent fighting that characterized his earlier ring career. In early January, newspapers reported that Barry had been matched with the undefeated Kelly for a twenty-round match at the Broadway Athletic Club for the bantamweight championship of America. There was a dispute about weight with Kelly wanting a higher weight, and Barry again relented.[141]

Kelly was a terrific fighter and arguably the best man Jimmy ever fought. Described as "an exceedingly scientific boxer," Kelly was considered "catlike, cold and persistent" with eyes that never left those of his opponent for a minute. His self-possession was nearly perfect and had been considered a heavy-hitter throughout his career to that point. He did not fight in the style of Flanagan and Leon. He would mix it up with Barry rather than stabbing and retreating. If Barry ever fought a man whose life and approach to fighting mirrored his, that man was Sammy Kelly. However, Barry did not think it would happen that way because he had been told by Casper Leon that Kelly was a "powder-puff puncher."[142]

In mid-January 1897, Barry went east to train at Coney Island. On January 22, 1893, he was working in Dixon's corner at the Broadway AC when Dixon knocked out Australian Billy Murphy before 4,000 fans.[143]

Chapter 1 - James ("Jimmy") Barry (1870–1943)

Barry and Kelly met on January 30, 1897. Jimmy was seconded by Choynski, Armstrong, and Dixon. None of his usual corner men (White, Gilmore, or Fitzgerald) were there that night. Kelly was taller and heavier, weighing 114½ pounds, while Barry weighed only 108. Kelly was fighting as a featherweight and Barry as a bantam. This was one of many fights where Jimmy gave substantial weight at the insistence of his opponent.

In the first four rounds Barry was the aggressor as was his custom. He opened with two lefts to Kelly's face and was then staggered by a right and left to the face and neck from Kelly. What happened to the "powder-puff puncher"? The second, third, and fourth rounds were about even. Barry said that he was stunned and took unnecessary chances, and then in the fifth Kelly backed Barry to the ropes and sent him to the floor for a nine count with what was called a left to Jimmy's jaw. This wasn't supposed to happen. Barry's fights usually were just the reverse.

In the sixth round, Kelly caught Jimmy with a left to his chin, which dazed him for a moment. The seventh round was about even. There are obvious differences between Kelly's strategy and style in fighting Barry and the strategy and style used by Leon and Flanagan.

Two decades later Barry explained what happened in the fifth round of the Kelly match when he went down for a nine count and denied that it happened because of a blow to the jaw:

> He clubbed me one alongside of the head and I thought my brain had been completely uncovered. His wrist landed along my temple and it put me to the bad. I finished the round all right, but when I went back to

the corner I was in a bad way. 'How are you?' my second asked me. 'I'm all right but I can see a couple of Kellys,' I answered, and that was the truth, at the same time winking the bum eye to show him how badly I was hurt.

'There isn't a scratch on you,' he said, eyeing me closely. 'Are you sure he didn't clip you on the chin and make you foolish?' This hurt me and I started to roar. 'Never mind that,' he said. 'If you see a couple of Kellys just smash away at the one with the gloves on,' and he laughed.

My eye was out of commission for five or six rounds and I saw more action in front of me than if they had been coming over the top at me. But I worried along all right and finally there was only one Kelly in front of me. When that came about, I located him and was able to beat him because we were going twenty rounds. But I never want to have that experience again.[144]

In the eighth round, Jimmy seemed to have regained his form. He turned Kelly around with a right to his stomach and two rights to his head. The ninth was even, and in the tenth Kelly landed a strong right-hand uppercut. Barry said that after the twelfth round Choynski was disgusted and doused him with a sponge full of water. In wiping out the water Choynski massaged Jimmy's optic nerve, and this cleared his vision. From this point on the fight was about even until round twenty when Barry sent Kelly to the floor with a right to the jaw. For Kelly this must have been a surprise. "Who is this guy? How could he be pounding away like this after twenty rounds? I had him down and now he's knocked me on my rear!"

Boston papers reported that many spectators thought that Barry had prevailed by a shade, but at the end of twenty rounds it was called a draw, and Barry retained the championship title.[145] Kelly explained (or made the excuse) that he did not "let himself out."[146] Kelly then went to England, where on March 9, 1897, he knocked out Plimmer in the last round of their twenty-round go. Twenty-six years later, Kelly wrote that Barry was the greatest bantam he had ever seen. The opinion of a fighter of Kelly's class is entitled to determinative respect.[147]

Three weeks after the Kelly fight, Davies matched Jimmy to fight Jack Ward of Newark, New Jersey, for $2,000 before the American Sporting Club of New York. For the second time Barry gave up weight. He agreed to fight at 112 pounds. Along with his announcement of the Barry-Ward fight, Davies announced that he would run a special train from Chicago to Carson City, Nevada, for the Fitzsimmons-Corbett heavyweight championship fight and would also take Barry, Choynski, and Armstrong to Carson City and then on to California.[148] Whenever Davies traveled with fighters, a trail of exhibition fights could be expected along the route of their travel. He did not like to pass through a big city without stopping and putting on an exhibition.

Barry and Jack Ward

Ward was a good fighter, but not in the same class as Kelly and Barry. Davies, Choynski, Armstrong, and O'Rourke were in Barry's corner for this fight. Following his usual template Barry forced the fighting in the first five rounds. One account said that Jimmy did all the work throughout the fight, and although Ward was clever, he would not stand up and fight at any stage of the match. In the sixth round, Ward landed several hard shots and the seventh and eighth rounds were about even.

The tenth, eleventh, and twelfth rounds were about even, but by the beginning of the thirteenth round Ward was tired. When his opponents tired, Barry poured it on just as he did in this match. Before coming out for round twenty, Ward was told that he could not win without a knockout. As soon as they shook hands at the beginning of the last round, Ward rushed at Barry and landed a straight left on Jimmy's nose, but Barry countered hard and Ward clinched. Barry then tried to induce Ward to mix it up, but Ward elected to stay away. After the break Barry landed a hard left on Ward's ear and it began bleeding. The match was called "tame" because Ward would not lead at any stage and Barry had the decision safe throughout. The referee awarded the fight to Barry. After the fight his full-steam return from his broken hand was noted, and he was called the cleverest of boxers, with a stiff puncher and a ring general who never lost his head.[149]

On March 6, Armstrong met a fighter called "Muldoon's Thunderbolt" (aka Joe Butler) at the Broadway Club before 2,000 spectators. Armstrong stopped Butler in the sixth round of that fight. As soon as the Butler fight ended, Davies, Barry, Choynski, and Armstrong started on a 2,500-mile trip west. They were in Chicago on the morning of May 8 and in Omaha on the ninth, where Davies told the sports editor of the *Omaha Bee* that a match between Barry and Anthony was quite probable.

Chapter 1 - James ("Jimmy") Barry (1870–1943)

Map of Jimmy Barry's route to California in 1897
(Map by Jill Thomas)

In Denver, Davies modified his earlier remarks about the possibility of a Barry-Anthony match by saying that he was not anxious to schedule Barry for a very hard fight because Jimmy was pretty well worn out.[150] Advertisements about the coming show were in Denver newspapers on March 7, 1897, the morning after the Armstrong-Butler fight in New York.[151] The combination arrived at Denver on the morning of March 11. Davies said that they had expected to be accompanied by Peter Maher, but Maher was too drunk to travel and had to be left behind.[152]

Davies had close friends in Denver, including Masterson, Floto, who had worked for Davies for several years, and Reddy

Gallagher, who had traveled with the Parson Davies' Specialty Company and refereed a fight in Chicago where Billy Brennan was killed. Davies' fighters appeared at Denver's Coliseum on Friday, March 12. The Coliseum was located at 1812 Champa Street. It was the largest venue of its type in Denver and hosted a variety of significant political, business, and sporting events. Barry was scheduled to spar six rounds with the cleverest lightweight fighter that could be found, Armstrong and Choynski were to spar one another, and thirty other people were to take part in the entertainment. If a fighter wanted to make money, this is how it was done. If a fighter signed with Davies he could expect to travel to capitalize on the public's interest in his name.

Davies told the *Salt Lake Herald* that additional exhibitions would be given at Cripple Creek, Victor, and Colorado Springs on their way to Carson City.[153] It isn't clear when or whether these matches happened because the travelers were on a tight timeline. If the fights happened, they were on different dates than originally scheduled. Davies, Barry, Choynski, and Armstrong met Masterson in Salt Lake City, and then all of them went on to Ogden. They were all in Ogden for most of the day on March 14, but Davies and Masterson left on the 2:30 p.m. train for Carson City while the three fighters waited for the Davies' special and then traveled the rest of the way to Carson City with the Chicago sporting crowd and other fans who were going to the fight from as far away as London, England.[154]

Barry and Jimmy Anthony

After attending the Fitzsimmons-Corbett match at Carson City, Davies, Barry, Armstrong, and Masterson continued to San

Francisco where their arrival was welcomed by the local press.[155] Davies described Barry as a natural fighter who was always ready to fight. "In fact, [he's] almost too anxious to put on the gloves. The sight of a bantam causes Jimmy's blood to circulate, and his remark always is, 'I'd like to fight him.'"[156]

Following Barry's arrival, Anthony went to the *San Francisco Call* offices and announced that he would fight only if he was given a month to prepare. On March 28, Davies and Anthony's manager met at the Baldwin Hotel and signed an agreement for a twenty-round fight on April 23 at 115 pounds for the best purse offered by any one of the San Francisco athletic clubs.[157] The timing fit well with what Davies wanted for Barry, but for the third straight match Barry conceded weight.

Davies and Barry took up quarters six miles outside of San Francisco. Davies called it "an ideal spot for work and sleep." Their routine was to get to bed at 8:00 p.m. and be up at 5:00 a.m. They had four eggs every morning for breakfast as Barry tried to get his weight up to 116 or 117 pounds. Davies said that Barry worked like a "fiend" during training.[158] Confident that Barry would take care of Anthony, Davies contacted London's National Sporting Club to try to arrange a match between Barry and Palmer.[159] During this time Palmer was discussing matches with fighters who weighed 120 pounds or more.[160]

San Francisco's National Athletic Club was awarded the Barry-Anthony fight after offering a purse of $2,000 with 75 percent to the winner. The fight took place at Woodward's Pavilion with Hiram Cook as the referee. An estimated 5,000 attended the fight. Among the attendees were three women—a very unusual thing at the time. The women sat in the front and were very conspicuous, causing a degree of scandal.

The fight was Barry's all the way. After eating four eggs and steak for breakfast for six weeks, he entered the ring at 109 pounds and Anthony at the 115-pound limit. Even with added weight Barry was too quick for Anthony, and the *San Francisco Chronicle* reported that Anthony did not get in a single effective blow. Barry rained blow after blow without a return. Although many rounds were uneventful, Barry was clearly outpointing Anthony. Finally, during the last four rounds, Anthony tried to rush Barry but was met with a volley of blows that stopped each of his attempts. At the end Anthony was still standing but was in such bad condition that the referee gave the decision to Barry.[161]

Davies, Barry, and Armstrong quickly left the West Coast heading east. Davies was going all the way to New York for one of Choynski's fights. They were in Denver on April 30, 1897, where Barry and Armstrong gave an exhibition at the Lyceum.[162] On May 3 they were all in Creighton, Nebraska, where Jimmy sparred four rounds with Billy Brown, called the champion of the Rocky Mountains or champion of Montana. Brown had returned to Nebraska from the west and thought he could keep Barry guessing for four rounds.[163]

The following night the aggregation was in Omaha at Boyd's Theater. The press watched Barry perform for four rounds against "Kid" Brown—who was undoubtedly Billy Brown. This time Brown was described as a clever little Denver featherweight. The Omaha press thought Jimmy was a quick and "finished boxer and the hardest hitting little man now before the public." There was also an exhibition that night called a "Battle Royal" in which Armstrong fought Barry and Brown simultaneously."[164]

Davies and Barry returned to Chicago on May 6. Armstrong stopped in Iowa to visit his family and returned later. Upon arrival Barry was asked what he did with his four-round exhibition opponents. He said: "We let 'em off lightly unless they try to rough it." Most of these four-round fights were won in the locker room, but occasionally some fighter would see a chance for stardom and end up seeing stars.

Both Davies and Barry were complimentary of the treatment they received while in San Francisco. Davies said that at one point during the Anthony fight Jimmy landed his right on Anthony's chin and spun Anthony completely around, ending with a clinch by Anthony to prevent himself from falling.[165]

In early summer the authorities stopped boxing in New York, and chances for making real fights in America flickered. Chicago was out for serious fights. New Orleans had been buttoned up after Bowen's death, and possible fights in San Francisco had been exhausted. In June, Davies arranged for his fighters to appear in a Chicago theater along with a sketch entitled "A Bowery Girl." He then sent the sketch, along with Barry and Armstrong, on a tour of Michigan and Wisconsin where the fighters offered to take on all local comers.

In Kalamazoo, Barry was scheduled to spar four rounds with his neighbor Frank Fitzgerald, and Armstrong appeared with Childs. Both Fitzgerald and Childs were probably being paid by Davies. The troupe was scheduled to appear in Grand Rapids on June 16 and later appeared Oshkosh, Watertown, Racine, Kenosha, and Waukegan, Illinois. Their goal was to be in Chicago for a boxing show on July 4.[166] This was the last boxing tour that Davies managed before leaving Chicago and moving to New Orleans.

Several bantamweights made passes at arranging fights with Barry during the summer of 1897. Two of the most prominent were Connors and Dave Sullivan. Davies did not want to make these matches because he felt that Jimmy would be required to give up too much weight and such fights would not be fair. He wrote to Connors telling him that Barry would meet him at 110 pounds at ringside for twenty rounds and a side bet at the club offering the largest purse, but Connors would not agree.

Leon wanted a third match with Jimmy, but Davies told the press that Leon was only willing to fight for an equally split purse, and Barry was not interested in that arrangement. Davies was looking at some bantams in Cincinnati to see whether he could arrange something for Jimmy and also said that he was still thinking about taking Barry and Armstrong to England because the general prospect for a fight was better there than in the States. Barry was disgusted and said that he was thinking about buying a saloon in Chicago and giving up the fighting business.[167] Most fighters did not like road trips where they traveled all day and fought every night.

Barney McCall was a heavier featherweight who had been fighting around Chicago for many years. He had fought Bertrand after the Barry-Bertrand match. Probably to stay sharp, Barry agreed to meet McCall at the Gaiety Theater in Chicago on August 7. Jimmy and McCall boxed five rounds and then McCall gave way to Sig Hart, a young Chicago bantam who sparred like a windmill for three rounds. Hart would be an excellent fighter later in his career but these were not serious matches, only intended to make some money from the gate receipts.

Late in September, Chicago's second Mayor Harrison, Carter Henry Harrison Jr., met with the *Chicago Tribune* to discuss the policies of his new administration. Harrison explained that he saw no reason why boxing exhibitions should not take place in Chicago if conducted with proper restrictions, including a limitation on the number of rounds and "no slugging." He explained that there would be no twenty-round fights and that matches of six to eight rounds were enough under close police supervision.[168] This meant that Chicago could not host a championship fight and boxing exhibitions were doomed. Who wanted to watch a match with no slugging allowed? In addition, Davies had pulled the rug out from under the prospect of going to England and was in the process of leaving Chicago and moving to New Orleans to manage two theaters there. Davies and Barry then split once again.[169]

Jimmy stayed in Chicago. He was planning to act as a second for his pupil Joe Sturch in a September 20 fight with Dave Richards to be held at Cincinnati for the 105-pound championship of the Northwest. Sturch was another fighter who lived near McGurn's. His home was at 36 Gault Place a block east of Larrabee and about two blocks south.

Barry returned home from Cincinnati and on September 27 left Chicago heading for England to meet up with White, who had already arranged a fight in England. In early July, White had learned that a twenty-round match for $1,000 had been arranged for him with Dave ("Nunc") Wallace to take place before London's National Sporting Club in November. When Jimmy left he did not have any fights lined up. He told the *Chicago Tribune* he was going to County Cork in Ireland to see aunts and uncles there if he had to swim to get there. Later articles said that Jimmy was going to Ireland to look up some of his family with the idea that he might be able to arrange a fight in England. Jimmy also said that while he was in England he would fight any man at between 107 and 110 pounds. The speculation was that he would meet an English fighter named Mike Small.

At the time he left Chicago Barry had already engaged in a reported 150 fights. He had beaten Gorman at 100 pounds when Gorman was supposedly the top fighter at that weight. He had defeated Leon and Madden at 105 pounds when they were supposed to be the best at that weight. He had defeated Anthony the Australian champion at 112 pounds and handled Kelly at 115 pounds. There wasn't much left to prove on this side of the Atlantic.[170]

The situation with smaller fighters in the summer of 1897 was complicated. Solly Smith had signed to fight Palmer at 122 pounds (eight stones ten pounds) conditioned upon Smith's winning his scheduled match with Griffin. Once again Palmer was fighting above 120 pounds (eight stones eight pounds). Smith then beat Griffin but opted to accept a fight with Dixon rather than fighting Palmer.

In the meantime in America, Dave Sullivan declared himself bantamweight champion. He said that Barry had not accepted his challenge and therefore he was entitled to be called the champion. In late August, Sullivan and his brother Spike left for England where Sullivan had secured a match with Palmer before London's National Sporting Club. This match was sometimes called a world bantamweight championship match, but others seemed to recognize that this could not be a real championship match and thought that the British had arranged the match only because they thought that Palmer could win easily and this would afford them the opportunity to make back money they had been losing betting on their fighters.

The problems with describing the Sullivan-Palmer fight as the world bantamweight championship was that Sullivan was not the bantamweight champion of America—except by self-acclimation—and both Sullivan and Palmer had agreed to fight at 116 pounds (eight stones four pounds) knowing that the bantamweight limit was generally somewhere between 105 and 112 pounds. It should be remembered that there was no organization that set weights and corresponding titles in America, and the weights customarily used in England did not directly correspond with the weights referred to when American weight classes were discussed.

As a general matter in 1897, fighters in the States weighing 116 pounds were considered to be featherweights and not bantams. To further complicate the situation, Palmer announced that if he beat Sullivan he would retire from the ring. Although the sequence of events is complicated, in 1898, after the Barry-Croot match, Palmer changed his mind and announced that he would not retire. He then agreed to fight Sammy Kelly at 116 pounds, which was again well above the weight usually considered a bantamweight fighter.[171]

Palmer did beat Sullivan but in the process broke a bone in his left arm.[172] This meant that Barry would not be able to fight Palmer within any reasonable time period, but speculation did continue about what might happen if Barry and Palmer did fight.

On October 25, an article appeared in the *Saint Louis Republic* concerning a possible match between Palmer and Barry. Earlier in the year before their split, Davies had turned down matches with Sullivan and Connors because they wanted too much weight. Davies had thrown in the towel on the weight issue with Kelly,

Ward, and Anthony and with the proposed but cancelled fight with Murphy. After the Anthony fight Davies said that he didn't think it was fair to Barry to keep making fights with heavier fighters. Barry probably would have agreed to these fights if Davies had not controlled the situation.

What had changed after the Anthony fight that caused Davies to finally draw a line where weight was concerned? The issue probably was more the condition of Barry's hands than one of weight. The *Saint Louis Republic* article said: "There is only one American lad who might have a chance of beating Palmer and that lad is Jimmy Barry. He has skill beyond that possessed by any of our other little ones, and he is as hard a hitter as [Dave] Sullivan. There is one thing he hasn't got, however, and this is a real good pair of hands. One of them was badly broken in a fight a few years ago, and it is liable to go at any minute in a fight...Barry has cut loose from 'Parson' Davies management and the 'Parson' is understood to be quite influential in boxing circles on the other side of the herring pond, where Barry is at present."[173]

The comments about the condition of Barry's hands probably came from Davies, who was spending a lot of time in Saint Louis in the fall of 1897 arranging a boxing show. Davies' concerns about the weight of Barry's opponents arose after the Anthony fight and were probably directly related to the condition of Jimmy's hands. Jimmy's ring management in the Anthony fight was undisputed. He did what he wanted to do when he wanted to do it. However, accounts of that match said that Jimmy's blows lacked steam. Comments about his earlier fights never questioned his punching power because he had always pounded opponents hard.

Davies had spent more than a year with Barry. They were together every day for six weeks while Barry was training for the Anthony fight. Davies probably decided that he was not going to match Barry with heavier fighters because Jimmy's hands were no longer in top condition. Davies may have felt some indirect responsibility because he had selected the doctor who had failed to properly repair Barry's right hand. Barry also said that he wanted to fight at his own weight. After he left for England, the press reported that Jimmy did not care about meeting Palmer, who weighed 117 pounds but wanted to fight in the range of 107 to 110 pounds, and he did fight in that range when he reached London.[174]

Barry and Walter Croot

Many authors state that Barry went to England to fight Walter Croot. This statement lacks a factual basis. It is similar to saying that Columbus sailed west to find America. Croot was not in the picture as the top English bantam when Barry left Chicago at the end of September 1897. Croot was deemed the English bantamweight representative after London's National Sporting Club decided that the English seven stone ten-pound title was vacant because Palmer had announced his intention to retire and had also gained too much weight to fight at that weight. When Jimmy left for England, the speculation was that he might be matched with Small not Croot.

After Croot's death, Barry wrote to Davies saying that he had hoped to make three or four matches in England and then retire. The fighter Jimmy really wanted at this point was Casper Leon, and throughout September 1897 that was the match he tried to arrange.

When he left for England, Jimmy said that as his own manager and backer he was willing to meet any English bantam with no mention of Walter Croot at between 107 and 110 pounds.[175]

As late as December 6, newspapers wrote that not much was known about Croot. Three or four years before 1897, Croot, Ernie Stanton, and Palmer were "close together as top-notch bantams. Palmer subsequently whipped both Croot and Stanton but both gave him hard arguments. Stanton and Palmer gradually grew to bigger weights, leaving Croot alone in the smaller bantam field, in which place he has not yet found an opponent his equal."[176]

Croot's first big match was in 1891 with Stanton, who knocked him out in the twelfth round. His record from that point forward included being KO'd two more times before he fought Barry. On the other hand, Croot had won six of the last seven matches before his match with Jimmy. Moreover, he had knocked out Mike Small, whom some thought would be Barry's opponent in England.

James Walter Croot
(Photo courtesy of Tracy Callis)

Walter Croot Record 1891–1896

Date	Opponent	City	Place	
1891	Ernie Stanton	East Hampton	LK12	
Jun 4, 1892	Matt Evans	London	W4	Holborn
Sep 19, 1892	Joe Bennett	London	LK11	Kennington Social
Mar 6, 1893	Bill Bolton	London	KO11	Covent Garden
May 1, 1893	Pedlar Palmer	London	LK17	Covent Garden
Mar 5, 1894	Andrew Wood	London	W6	National SC
Mar 1894	Dick Parkes	London	W6	
Apr 16, 1894	Bill Bolton	London	W4	St. Andrews Hall
Jun 28, 1894	Ernie Stanton	Leytonstone	Ex3	
Dec 6, 1894	Ernie Stanton	Leytonstone	Ex3	
Feb 22, 1895	Pedlar Palmer	London	Ex	
Feb 17, 1896	Tom Murray	London	W3	National SC
Feb 17, 1896	Harry Ware	London	W3	National SC
Feb 17, 1896	Con Barrett	London	W4	Covent Garden
Nov 30, 1896	Mike Small	London	KO11	Covent Garden

From early October until the Croot match, Barry had been working with White and trainer Billy Sillick (sometimes "Selleck") in a northwest suburb of London. They were staying at the Two Brewers public house (hotel) at Chipperfield, Herts, which was in a beautiful small village. The hotel remains open to the public today.[177]

Both Barry and White had been in Sullivan's corner when he lost to Palmer with both men fighting at eight stone four pounds. After that, Jimmy wrote to his friend Billy McGurn in Chicago and said that he thought Palmer was "not so much." He wrote that Palmer had a good left but all he did was use it and get away.[178] Two years later Jimmy again said that Palmer had won all his fights using a "choppy" left.[179]

About November 6, when Jimmy had been in England for a month, he was matched with Croot by John Fleming, the former manager of the Pelican Club—which had folded—and at that time the manager of the National Sporting Club. One author claimed that Fleming told Barry that Croot had a standing challenge to meet any man at seven stones and seven pounds for $1,250. Jimmy had only three dollars in his pocket and accepted the match. Their match was to take place on November 15. Fleming was found dead on the morning of November 15, and their match was postponed. Writers noted that the question of weight would be the important factor, with articles saying that they would fight at seven stones and ten pounds (108 pounds). Barry was called the "7st 10 lb champion of America."[180] The fight was delayed twice due to the death of the club's matchmaker but finally set for December 6.[181]

This fight was with four-ounce gloves and for points given during each round with five being the maximum number of points that could be awarded during any round. Points were awarded based on skill and cleverness in attack and defense. Who kept the point total is not explained.

During the first ten rounds, Barry did most of the scoring in what was called a "very scientific struggle." At the start of the eleventh round, Croot began a determined stand and in the eighteenth round had almost equalized the fight. In the nineteenth round, Jimmy forced the fighting and worked at a great pace, finishing stronger than Croot.[182]

After the nineteenth round Jimmy came to his corner and White was nearly crying. White told Barry—whether he believed it or not is another matter—that if he did not knock out Croot in the final round, he would not win the title. A report after the fight said that Barry had "just enough" in hand to win the fight without a knockout.[183] Jimmy did not want just enough. He listened to his friend White, who had enormous ring experience, and when the twentieth round started, Barry went to work as he so often did in the final round of his fights. Any concern about his hands was dismissed. A world title was on the line.

With less than a minute to go in the final round, Barry began to administer a beating like a one-man flash mob. He was moving so fast that Croot probably thought there were two men across from him. With forty seconds to go Jimmy drove a series of lefts to Croot's chest followed by a crushing right to the jaw.[184] One report said that this happened because Croot miscalculated the distance between himself and Barry and came too near Jimmy. Miscalculations happen when a fighter is in distress. Croot's miscalculation led to a sharp right to the jaw that drove him to the ropes and was followed by the final punches. Croot collapsed, lay motionless, and remained unconscious. The referee started to count but, seeing that Croot was out cold, stopped and announced that Barry had won.[185]

When he fell, Croot's head hit the floor. Two days later Davies told the *Chicago Tribune*: "I saw the Slavin-Jackson fight at the National Sporting Club and was surprised that they did not pad either the floor or the posts of the ring." After the Barry-Croot fight the police reported that the ring was about nineteen feet square, covered with felt a half-inch thick, over which was canvas so that the floor was soft and springy to the touch. There was no report about the ring posts.[186] After he did not recover his senses, Croot was moved to an apartment in the National Sporting Club, and when he still did not recover, medical assistance was called. He never regained consciousness and died between about 8:30 and 9:00 a.m. on December 7. The president of the club later said that Croot was a game and scientific fighter but constitutionally weak.[187]

Barry and White learned of Croot's death from a newsboy's calling out the headline on the morning after the fight. The two men went to the National Sporting Club to see what had happened and were met there by Anson, who counseled Jimmy and said that he, Tod Sloane, and Spaulding & Co. in London would raise the necessary funds to provide White and Barry the best legal counsel available.[188]

About 3:00 p.m. on December 7, Barry, White, and several others were arrested. All were taken to the Bow Street Police Court and charged with manslaughter. *The Times* of London in its own direct style wrote: "At Bow-street, yesterday, before Sir James Vaughan, James Barry, 26, of the Two Brewers public house, Chipperfield, Herts; Thomas James White, 27, of the same address; William Watley, 30, of Markham-street,

Walworth, instructor; Arthur Frederlick Bettinson, 35, manager of the National Sporting Club; Bernard John Angle, 44, of Buckingham-street, Strand, stock dealer; and Richard Smith, 36, of Haycroft-road, Brixton-hill, agent were charged with being concerned together between the hours of 10:50 p.m. on the night of the 6th inst. and 12:15 a.m. on the morning of the 7th in causing the manslaughter of one Walter Croot during a boxing contest at the National Sporting Club, Covent-garden-market."

Barry and the police went to view Croot's body, and Jimmy broke down and cried bitterly. *The Times* [of London] quoted a police report stating that Barry said: "Oh, dear; you know I would not do that."[189]

Back in Chicago Jimmy's friends were stunned by the news of Croot's death and Barry's arrest. They noted that Jimmy's friends Anson and Tod Sloane, a professional jockey, were in London but still worried that English law treated deaths in the ring more severely than American law.[190]

Within a few days Dr. George Albert Hammerton, divisional surgeon of police, stated that his post-mortem examination showed no bruises except on the shoulder and the side of Croot's face. He testified that the death was more likely the result of a fall than a blow. A coroner's jury determined that Croot's death was from accidental causes resulting from a basal fracture of his skull due to a fall after the knockout punch.[191] Just as in America, the finding of a coroner's jury was not determinative in a criminal matter. All who had been arrested still faced manslaughter charges. They were again brought to court and released on bail. However, after further review of the facts, the prosecutor refused to prosecute and those charged were finally released about December 21.[192]

Barry told the press he was finished with fighting and wrote to Davies: "I received your cable and I thank you for your kindness towards me. It was tough luck for me. I was going to have three or four contests here and then retire. The Coroner's jury favored me, and we have a hearing on the 14th of December. I think they will let me go. If they do I will start for home as soon as I can, and I will never have another match as long as I live. I will try to make a living at something else. The club has been kind to me."

Jimmy was considered a sensitive soul and was distraught about Croot's death. The idea shared by White and Barry that they would win big money in England did not work out. White lost his fight to Ben Jordan and got the short end of the purse. Then disaster happened at the Croot fight and they ended up reimbursing their friends for legal expenses advanced on their behalf. Neither had a financially successful trip and Barry soon asked Davies to resume his management.[193] White did not like Davies and never again had a manager.

1898 – Life After A Death

On January 6, 1898, Barry and White reached New York on the *Mohawk* after a rough crossing. Their trainer stayed in England, and Spike Sullivan claimed that he had been stranded there by the two fighters. By the time they arrived, Barry had reconsidered his retirement and was prepared to meet anyone in his class. He knew of Leon's challenge and stopped at the *Police Gazette's* office to post a $100 forfeit to fight any man in America at 110 pounds. This was the match that Barry wanted before he had left for England. After Barry left the *Gazette*, Jack Skelly, the manager of the Palace Sporting Club of Trenton, New Jersey, stopped at that office and offered a $1,000 purse for Barry to meet the winner of the Leon-Ward fight scheduled at the Palace on January 12.[194]

Barry and White reached Chicago on the evening of January 8 and were met by a crowd of their north side friends. When Barry learned of Skelly's offer, he said he was willing to accept that proposal and resumed training on the north side. Barry said that he was looking for one more good fight.[195]

Barry's friend Anson also returned to Chicago, and they were both at Kennedy's handball court on January 23 when Anson played a handball game and Barry refereed a boxing exhibition.[196] Tod Sloane went all the way to San Francisco where he was soon riding on California tracks.[197]

A few days after Jimmy's return to Chicago, Davies was notified that Leon had accepted Jimmy's challenge and would meet him at the Palace Sporting Club. This left the situation a little unsettled because Skelly's offer was to have Barry meet the winner of the Leon-Ward fight, and the winner had not yet been determined. White also received offers asking him to arrange fights between Leon and Barry, implying that some thought Barry was willing to arrange fights through White rather than his manager.[198]

In New Orleans, Davies was trying to organize the St. Bernard Athletic Club for some local sportsmen, but whether the authorities would allow any club to stage fights was up in the air. Davies wanted Barry to have a rematch with Kelly on February 23—during Mardi Gras—at his new club. Kelly was fighting at 115 pounds and insisted on fighting at that weight.

He also demanded a 50/50 pot split. Davies was willing to agree to both propositions.

It is not clear whether Davies made concessions because he wanted the new club to have a terrific fight or because Barry wanted to fight Kelly and agreed to the concessions. As Davies was trying to arrange a Barry-Kelly rematch, he learned that in Chicago his heavyweight, Armstrong, had agreed to a fight with Childs without Davies' knowledge and had been knocked out. This effectively ruined all the work that Davies had done in promoting Armstrong and was an embarrassment for him, with other managers laughing up their sleeves.[199]

After Davies, Lou Houseman was Chicago's next leading fight promoter, and he took over the top slot when Davies moved to New Orleans. At the beginning of February, Houseman offered a purse of $1,250 for a Barry-Leon eight-round go in Chicago with the fighters weighing 110 pounds. Barry said he would accept Houseman's proposal provided a side bet could be arranged with Leon's backers. Houseman's direct proposal to Leon and Barry amounted to another shot at Davies. A competitor had made a public offer to one of Davies' fighters without going to Davies, and that fighter was negotiating terms without Davies' assistance.[200]

With Davies trying to arrange fights with Kelly and Leon but no fight firmly arranged, Barry tried to capitalize on his new world champion title or simply get out of Chicago and let his head clear. Encouraged by Cincinnati promoter James Franey Jimmy entered into a contract for two months with a traveling vaudeville troupe known as the Casino Operatic Burlesque Co., and in late January and early February he was in Cincinnati at the People's Theater drawing big houses and offering to take on all comers in four-round matches. Jimmy's friend Tod Sloane returned to Cincinnati from California so Jimmy had the company of one of his closest friends. Fred Bogan had come to Cincinnati in mid-January looking for action and was hired as Barry's sparring partner for three round exhibitions offered along with the rest of the entertainment. At the time Bogan was fighting at 122 pounds. It took Franey several days to secure permits from the mayor for real matches but on February 4, 1898 Jimmy met and defeated Billy Curtis who was twenty pounds heavier and on February 5th he met Danny Rewan, a Cincinnati pugilist who fought at 120 pounds and was described as the best lightweight in Cincinnati. Other suggested opponents included Willie Mack, and Frank Stevenson but those matches apparently were not made. Some reports said that Barry traveled throughout Ohio taking on all comers, but no specific match has been found. He was taking big chances by taking on whatever man showed up in the town he happened to be in that night.[201]

In mid-February, Jimmy was in Detroit again, taking on all comers in four-round bouts, and two days later he was in Louisville, Kentucky, where he met a 138-pound black fighter named "June" Summers. Summers tried to knock out Barry by rushing him in the opening round. Jimmy avoided the rush, found an opening, and landed a hard left on Summers' face. In the second round Barry continued to pepper Summers. When the third opened, Summers rushed again but failed to land a punch. He then clinched and threw Jimmy to the floor where the two rolled over. Then Summers arose and in frustration left the ring. Jimmy was declared the winner.[202] Fights like this could be dangerous and might derail a good fighter's career.

Barry and Johnny Connors

While in Louisville, Barry received and accepted an offer from Houseman for a six-round match with Connors for $1,000. The match was scheduled for Chicago on Saint Patrick's Day. Finally matches were being made. In early March, Jimmy and Davies went to New Haven, Connecticut, to attend a fight between Leon and George Munroe of England. Davies was described as Jimmy's "backer" rather than as his manager. While Barry was in England, Leon had anointed himself the bantamweight champion of America, and Barry attended the Leon-Munroe match to challenge the winner.[203] Leon defeated Monroe in fifteen rounds.

A few days after the Leon-Munroe match, Barry was matched with Johnny Ritchie, a former barber from Saint Louis, to fight at the Chicago Athletic Association at catch-weights. Ritchie was fighting at 115 or 116 pounds and Barry was fighting at between 108 and 110 pounds. This was another instance where Barry gave away substantial weight to arrange a fight. About the same time, Barry also agreed to fight Billy Rotchford of Chicago at 116 pounds.[204]

The Barry-Connors match was one of several held at Tattersall's. Other matches that same night were: (1) George Kerwin-Otto Sieloff for the "light-weight championship of the Northwest and central States," (2) White meeting Griffin (who had recently lost to Solly Smith), (3) Jack Everhardt (called "the champion lightweight of England and the South) "Kid" McGlenn, (4) Link Pope-"Kid" Harris, and (5) Stift-Schrosbee. The Barry-Connors fight was given the honored final fight position.[205] Barry quickly left the vaudeville company and went into training at West Baden, Indiana, a famous hot springs resort and second home for many sporting types. Whether his visit to West Baden indicates that he was suffering from rheumatism again is not discussed in the press.

Barry won his first serious fight after Croot's death by gaining a decision over Connors before a crowd estimated to be upwards of 10,000. This was a rare match where an opponent weighed about the same as Jimmy. Connors entered the ring at 104 pounds. Supposedly there was "bad blood" between the two. Barry was his old self in this fight. He landed blow after blow on Connors' face, nose, mouth, forehead, and neck so that Connors had trouble even throwing a punch. Jimmy was always a combination puncher. In this case he repeatedly threw left jabs to the neck followed by a right to Connors' head. The continued battering weakened Connors, who was only occasionally able to get off a good counter. Jimmy had no trouble and looked better than ever before.[206] Many claim that after the Croot fight Jimmy lost his aggressiveness and willingness to knock out his opponent. This claim does not seem consistent with the Connors match where Jimmy worked over Connors thoroughly.

Barry and Johnny Ritchie

On March 26, Barry met Ritchie for six rounds at the C.A.A. Barry weighed 105 pounds, giving Ritchie a ten-pound advantage. Siler was the referee. Barry had the fight his own way, but Ritchie put up a good battle and cut up Jimmy's face. Siler gave the decision to Barry. Siler said that Ritchie was a clever fighter and had he not gone down three or four times, the decision might have been a draw! It would seem astonishing that a fighter who went down three or four times in a six-round fight might be considered for a draw, but Siler always had his own mind when given the authority to call a fight.[207]

Barry and Billy Rotchford

Rotchford was another north side boxer. He lived at 264 North Franklin not far from where Jimmy grew up. As an amateur, Rotchford boxed at the C.A.A. where he had an unblemished record at 115 pounds. In early 1897, he turned professional and went to the East Coast to arrange matches on his own. His career started well with appearances at the Broadway and Polo athletic clubs, but he later injured his leg and then contracted typhoid fever. When he returned to the ring in the summer of 1897, he began fighting in the range of 118 to 120 pounds.

In late 1897, Rotchford beat Oscar Gardner in twenty rounds in Buffalo. He was scheduled to fight Sammy Kelly at the Polo Athletic, but their match was prevented by the police. In March 1898, Rotchford defeated Maxey Haugh at 120 pounds. Because of his good showings with quality fighters he was matched with Barry.

The Barry-Rotchford fight was a six-round event at Tattersall's at catch weights. This event was arranged by Davies as another of his last Chicago promotions. Choynski was the referee. Before the fight Barry's trainers and friends were concerned about Jimmy giving up so much weight. He gave Rotchford about fifteen pounds.

Barry had a different concern. Palmer had designated four men he was willing to fight for the bantamweight championship: Rotchford, Kelly, Plimmer, and Spike Sullivan. Three of those four had lost previous matches. Barry thought that Rotchford would have trouble getting down to the bantamweight range while Jimmy pointed out that he was willing to fight as low as 105 pounds to obtain a match with Palmer.[208]

The Barry-Rotchford fight was fast and hard-hitting. Where possible, Rotchford took advantage of his weight and longer reach by rushing Barry and then jumping away and firing at longer range. Rotchford also displayed an ability to duck Barry's left, which negated one of Jimmy's best weapons. In the fifth round, Rotchford gave Barry a bloody nose with a stiff jab, but Barry evened matters with a hard right to the head.

The final round was called the "event of the evening." The crowd rose and cheered again and again as both men fought furiously. At the end Choynski called the match a draw, and Davies announced that he would arrange a rematch at Tattersall's for May 9, 1898. Later the rematch fell through over a dispute about the weigh-in. Barry was willing to fight at 118 pounds at ringside, but Rotchford wanted a 3:00 p.m. weigh-in, which would allow him to enter the ring at 120 pounds or more.[209]

Al Schrosbee was shot and killed a week after the Barry-Rotchford fight. He was killed at the Orpheus saloon at 467 North Clark, not far from where Barry lived. In his early career Jimmy and Schrosbee had been in the ring many times. Stories about Schrosbee's death are not written clearly, but it seems that the owner of the Orpheus claimed that Schrosbee and three others were trying to rob his cashier. One story about Schrosbee's death states: "He had the distinction of being the only man who ever gained a decision over 'Jimmy' Barry, but this was many years ago before Barry entered the professional arena." Except for the assertion made in this 1898 story there is no known record of an amateur fight that Barry lost.[210]

Barry and Leon – Third Fight

A third Barry-Leon fight was arranged for Tom O'Rourke's Lenox Athletic Club at the end of May. Davies had nothing to do with this fight. Two days before the fight Barry went to Toronto and gave an exhibition at the Toronto Athletic Club with a fighter identified as Jim Popp's brother. This may have been Willie Popp, but if it was then he was only about sixteen years old at the time of this exhibition.

The Barry-Leon contest was styled as for the bantamweight championship of the world on the theory that Barry was the champion. The match was for twenty rounds. Both men were natural bantams, and O'Rourke arranged an innovation for this fight. He had both fighters weigh in at the center of the ring just before the fight began. Barry had knocked out Leon twice, but the illusion still persisted that their second match was a draw. Leon had his own rationalization. He wrote: "I have to admit that when I was a green boy he got the decision on me in a twenty-eight round bout. When we met again I fought him fifteen rounds to a draw. Since then I know that I have steadily improved. For under Charley White's management and handling I have not lost a fight out of thirty-three in which I have taken part. ... I have always kept in good condition, ready for any ordinary bout, but for my match with Barry I shall make special preparation. I know how good a man he is and to beat him I must be in tip-top condition."

Barry left for New York on May 22 to finish his training for this third fight.[211] He was the favorite before the fight with the odds at two to one. In the ring Barry weighed 109 pounds and Leon 106 pounds—one of the few times that Jimmy outweighed an opponent. Although he was the champion, Barry entered the ring first and Leon followed a few minutes later.

Stories of this fight contain infrequent references to Barry using his right hand. During the first eighteen rounds Barry used his right hand only twice—at least according to the press. He went to that hand only in the final two rounds. This is atypical of Barry's fights and may suggest that Jimmy was having trouble with his right.

A typical article is found in the *Chicago Tribune* and describes the following blows round by round landed by Barry:

First: a light left to the face, a left to the head, a left hard on Leon's face;
Second: no specific punch mentioned;
Third: a right and left to the head, two left jabs on the face;
Four: a hard left on the face;
Five: a good left on the face;
Six: a counter to a left by Leon;
Seven: no specific punch mentioned;
Eight: no specific punch mentioned;
Nine and Ten: described as simple sparring;
Eleven: a cracking good left on Leon's mouth, a left on the face;
Twelve: a good stiff left hand to Leon's chest, another left on the chest;
Thirteen: no specific punch mentioned;
Fourteen: no specific punch mentioned;
Fifteen: a left on Leon's ear, two lefts on the face;
Sixteen: a left and right;

Seventeen: an uppercut (no hand mentioned);
Eighteen: no specific punch mentioned;
Nineteen: a right to the ribs
Twenty: exchanged right and lefts on the head; exchanged hard rights on the head, a right to the head, and a left on the face.

The fight was called a draw by Johnny White, the referee, and the title remained with Barry. Siler had refereed many fights on the East Coast but had been black-balled by the club owners who wanted their own men in the ring. It should be noted that at the end of September that same year, Johnny White called a twenty-five-round Leon-Flanagan match a draw even though most of the audience thought Flanagan had won.

Barry and Flanagan – Second Fight

For some incomprehensible reason Barry agreed to a rematch with Flanagan to take place only three days after a hard twenty-round draw with Leon. It may be that his decision to take this match was driven by money, confidence in his own ability, a need to restore his self-confidence after a draw, or some combination of all of these (or other) motivations. There is no question that his advisors failed him and should have persuaded him not to fight a quality opponent so quickly.

The Barry-Flanagan second fight took place at Philadelphia's Arena. This was a six-round bout that allowed Flanagan to adopt tactics that would have failed in a longer fight. Just as in their first fight Flanagan's approach was to stick and run. In the process he landed more blows than Jimmy, who seemed to be looking for a knockout and could not catch anything but Flanagan's fist.

The first two rounds of the fight were tame, which favored Flanagan's approach. In the third, Flanagan put his left in Barry's face and kept it there because he was scoring and keeping Barry at bay. Flanagan was the aggressor in the fourth round landing with his right and left, but in the process Barry landed a hard right that bloodied Flanagan's nose. After taking that hard right, Flanagan again began running away and in the process slipped and fell through the ropes. The fifth round was Barry's and the last round was fast but described as favoring Flanagan although Barry landed a number of stiff punches. The fight was called a no decision, but there are many comments that Flanagan should have been given the match.[212]

Barry and Ritchie – Second Fight

After nearly two months of inactivity a Barry-Ritchie rematch was arranged. This was another six-round bout at McGurn's with the fighters appearing at catch weights. Jimmy weighed 112 pounds for the fight and Ritchie 115. Sturch fought on the same bill that night. For the first time comments said that Ritchie was in better condition than Jimmy. Barry was a conditioning fanatic, but he was heavier than usual for this fight and never before had an opponent been described as being in better shape.

Barry was the aggressor, but Ritchie was effective in their exchanges. Jimmy worked more quickly than Ritchie, but few of his punches were effective. Those familiar with Barry knew that something was wrong if his punches lacked power. He had been the knockout king. He had always won by punishing his opponents with solid combinations. Neither man was knocked down. No blood was drawn and the disappointing part was that it was over too soon. Ritchie's improvement was noted, but the match was another draw, which was becoming too common in Jimmy's case.[213]

After the Ritchie rematch, Jimmy was matched with Bogan for a fight at Lexington, Kentucky, before the Navarre Athletic Club. As noted above, Barry gave exhibitions with Bogan in Cincinnati at the end of January 1898.

Bogan had been fighting for years. Long before Jimmy started fighting Bogan was the featherweight champion of the Pacific Slope. Bogan often fought at the Seattle Athletic Club with fighters up to 125 pounds. The Barry-Bogan match was scheduled for October 6. The fighters were allowed to be as heavy as 117 pounds for this match.[214] Whether this match actually occurred and its outcome has not been found. Barry was also matched to fight Jimmy Rose at McGurn's on October 6. The Barry-Rose match was cancelled and another fight substituted. This may have happened because Jimmy was fighting Bogan in Kentucky.[215]

On October 17, Barry participated in a four-round exhibition at McGurn's with Sturch. White appeared at McGurn's that same evening. White had started his career at McGurn's, but this was his first appearance there in five years. Between one another Barry and White had amassed a remarkable record never matched by two other Chicago fighters of the same age. A week later Barry was at McGurn's for an exhibition with Cammy Hudson, a 125-pound fighter while White met Jack Daly.[216]

The Waldorf Club was the site of Barry's next appearance on October 29, 1898. This was the opening night of athletic entertainment for that club which had been organized in January 1898 by Max H. Mayer, Jule Marks, and Dan Schuman. The club was located at State and Van Buren streets and was the future headquarters of the Fort Dearborn Athletic Association of Chicago where Barry would frequently appear as a fighter, referee, and second.

Charles Essig, who had been part of the group of fighters trained by Gilmore at McGurn's, was hired as the matchmaker for the Fort Dearborn club. The program at the Waldorf included wrestling, club swinging, and boxing stars including Choynski, Leon, Childs, Essig, Harry Forbes, and Sammy Harris. All the matches that evening were strictly scientific and refereed by Siler.[217] The next night Barry appeared at McGurn's where he sparred four rounds with Frank Bartley before a good-natured and fair-sized crowd.[218]

For several months Barry had been negotiating the terms of a match to be held at the Greater New York Athletic Club with a young bantamweight named Terry McGovern. This effort fell through in early November 1898. Barry said that the club failed to deposit the purse of $1,200 on October 1, 1898, as specified by the terms of the agreement. The club promised that it would make the required deposit, but Jimmy wanted them to show their money. He did not favor a promise over performance. He said that he would be looking to O'Rourke's club to arrange a match with McGovern for $1,500.[219] Jimmy never fought McGovern, and within two years McGovern outgrew the bantam class. If they had fought when they were both in their prime it would have been a terrific fight.

In late 1898, the city of Davenport, Iowa, became the home of athletic clubs where real fights could take place. Jack Leonard organized the Trinity Athletic Club of Davenport and later the Tri-City Athletic Club. On November 18, 1898, Jimmy traveled to Davenport and appeared with Sammy Harris in a four-round preliminary match before a featured 140-pound match between Walter Nolan and Jim O'Leary of Chicago. That same night Leonard announced that his club would offer a substantial purse for either a Barry-Leon or Barry-Harry Forbes match.

Barry and Leon – Fourth Fight

Four days after his exhibition in Davenport, Jimmy was back in Chicago at McGurn's, where he boxed six rounds with Leon. Accounts of this match say that "on points" Barry had the advantage. As with their second match, circumstances intervened to deprive Jimmy of what should have been his third victory over Leon. In this case Barry and Leon had agreed that if both men were on their feet at the end of the six rounds, then the referee would call the set-to a draw.

The six rounds of this match were nothing like the twenty-round draw in New York. In this match Barry returned to his two-hand approach. He was the aggressor from the start and used his "famous one-two style that has won so many of his battles." He swung his right viciously at Leon's head, which left Leon ducking and blocking. At the end of the second round Barry landed a right hard on Leon's wind. Leon landed hard with a jab in the third, but the fourth was Barry's as he landed uppercuts that jarred Leon. Barry also did most of the work in the final two rounds. As stipulated, referee Hogan called the match a draw, but the two men in the ring knew better.[220]

Barry and Leon – Fifth Fight

A week after their six-round show, Barry and Leon were matched for a twenty-round fight at Davenport.[221] Barry confided in a friend—who then confided in a newspaper reporter—that he would retire after this fight. He wanted to retire because of the drudgery of training, uncertainty that matches would actually take place, and the small financial returns earned by bantamweight fighters. He thought another walk-of- life would be more pleasant.[222]

Jimmy left for Davenport on December 28, 1898, and arrived there later the same day.[223] Pat Fitzgerald traveled with him. With the exception of road work Barry had already tuned up for the fight. Leon stayed at Moline, Illinois, across the river and worked out at the Moline Athletic Club. The fight took place at the Claus Groth hall under the auspices of the Tri-City Athletic Club. The hall seated only about 1,300 people. That evening the hall was packed with ticket prices $1.50 to $5 and being scalped for up to $10 a ticket. Hogan had been agreed upon as the referee for this match. A special train to bring sports from Chicago was expected before the fight began, and Kid McCoy sent a telegram that he would be a ringside for the fight.[224]

After the preliminary matches the main attraction was delayed by an hour while everyone waited for the arrival of a train carrying fans from Cedar Rapids. Leon entered the ring first at 11:30 p.m. and Barry was in the ring a minute later. Jimmy's closest friends, White and William McGurn, along with Frank Bartley and Pat Fitzgerald, were in his corner. After five minutes Hogan called the men to the center of the ring and announced that it was for twenty rounds at 110 pounds for the bantamweight championship of the world.

Barry was a two-handed fighter in this match. His first blow was a heavy right hand on Leon's jaw. Both men landed solid blows, clinched frequently, and broke clean as they always had. They were true professionals. Neither man suffered any particular damage.

The pace of the second round was fast. Leon was the first to land with a heavy body blow followed by rights from each to the other's head. Barry then landed a strong hook to Leon's jaw that was followed by a left from Leon. In the process Leon slipped to the floor, but was up quickly and took a left to the head. The third round was again fast with a steady rain of blows from each man and Barry landing a hard right that damaged Leon's eye badly.

Perhaps sensing that Leon was injured, Barry rushed at the beginning of the fourth and took a heavy uppercut as his reward. Leon followed his uppercut with a straight blow to Barry's mouth followed by two hard rights and a powerful left. Leon was apparently not as injured as Jimmy thought. After this exchange the two fought hard at close quarters with neither gaining the advantage.

A hard right to Barry's ribs followed by a stiff left to Leon's head opened the fifth round. Leon again hit Barry's ribs hard and followed with a right to his head. Early in the sixth Leon rushed Jimmy to the ropes fighting aggressively and landing a vicious left on Jimmy's face. After this exchange they backed off and seemed to take stock of the situation deciding how to proceed.

Leon opened the seventh with a light blow to Jimmy's body, and then Barry caught Leon heavily on his head. Leon returned a staggering right over Jimmy's heart, but Barry responded with two stiff blows on Leon's face and a right to his kidneys. Leon returned a blow to Jimmy's kidneys and another to his ribs. The fighting was intense but even.

Jimmy landed three strong blows to open the eighth: a right-left combination to Leon's head and a straight blow to his face. Leon returned hard to Jimmy's body. Both then pounded one another on the kidneys. This round looked like Barry's with the chance that he might be warming and Leon fading, but that was not the case this time.

In the ninth, Barry caught Leon with a right hook to the ribs and then broke a hard blow to his ear. Then Leon rallied with a hard right to Barry's mouth and a left to his body. Barry returned a stinging blow to the stomach at the bell. The tenth was comparatively slow with many clinches before Leon again attacked Barry's ribs with a hard right and a vicious shot to the heart. The match was half over. Neither fighter was showing dominance. Both were working as clean and professional fighters. The title was still in the balance.

The eleventh, twelfth, and thirteenth rounds were more of the same. Leon opened the eleventh by driving his fist into Barry's face and taking three hard bangs on the ribs in return. The customers were getting more than they paid for. If fighters preformed like Leon and Barry, boxing would not have been under constant attack by the authorities. At the start of the fourteenth, Barry decided to take the center of the ring and try to stay there. Leon danced around him throwing rights and lefts to the body. The round closed with Barry delivering two stiff swings on Leon's body and one on his jaw.

The fifteenth round was notable because it echoed early fights in Barry's career. Observers noted for the first time that Barry's blows carried more steam even though both men were landing at a steady pace. At the close of the round Jimmy jarred Leon with a left to the jaw. Seventy-five percent of the way through the fight Barry had a slight edge. White, McGurn, Fitzgerald, and many others among his fans had seen this all before. The final five rounds would be Jimmy's as Leon hung on and dived for the finish line. But it didn't quite happen that way.

The sixteenth round opened with a half-dozen clinches. Both men were tired. Then Leon caught Barry with a hard right to his eye, and Jimmy returned a strong right that jarred Leon badly. A stiff left to Leon's gut stopped another rush at the beginning of the seventeenth round. Jimmy always seemed to know when a round was about to end and gave Leon a hard left hook to the body as the end of that round.

In the eighteenth round, both men exchanged hard right and left hands throughout. Barry was not gaining the clear advantage that he had so often achieved in earlier fights. There was no advantage in the nineteenth round with both fighters scoring and neither man retreating.

As the bell rang for the final round, thoughts of Walter Croot and the final round of that fight must have passed through the minds of many who jammed the hall. Did White tell Jimmy that he needed to knock out Leon to win the fight or did he hold back because he thought such advice had caused the earlier tragedy? Did Jimmy hold back because he was afraid he might kill Leon?

Whatever was said or thought in Jimmy's corner, it was plain that Leon was only interested in holding on. For the first time when they clinched, Leon held on. The crowd could see what was happening and was in turmoil. Hogan tried to separate the fighters, but Leon hung on for life, broke, and then clinched again. At the gong the men were fighting on the ropes, but no decisive blow had been delivered. No one died in this fight, but Jimmy must have felt strong emotions as his undefeated record rested in a referee's hands. Then Hogan called the fight a draw. It was over. He was still the undefeated champion of the world, but Jimmy was disappointed.[225]

Ten days after the fight, the *Chicago Tribune* asked Jimmy about his opinion of the verdict at Davenport. He said:

> I have always been careful to avoid making excuses, but in this instance I have tried hard to figure out why I did not get the verdict. Referee Hogan has admitted that in his opinion I had the best of the first fourteen rounds, and in the remaining six, to the best of my judgment, I at least held my own. During the whole of the fight I did not jump back to avoid a blow more than a dozen times, as I was satisfied Leon could not hurt me. If I had moved out of the way as much as Leon, the public would not have seen much of a contest. Having held the advantage in fourteen rounds, and at least breaking even in the remainder, it looks to me as though I should have won.[226]

Jimmy had a case. Leon was a showy fighter and looked good when he was matched with a workman such as Barry. Leon's style had served him well in his fight with Flanagan in September 1898 when most observers thought Flanagan should have been given the decision. Certainly Leon has been extremely well-treated in boxing history where it comes to his matches with Barry.

1899 – The Beginning of the Rest of his Life

It was customary at the beginning of each year for newspapers to review the year in sports. One review said that Jimmy was entitled to hold the championship for one year after his retirement.[227] Another newspaper wrote: "Jimmy Barry has long been in a class by himself as a bantamweight, but when he allowed Casper Leon to make a draw last week it convinced the followers of the game that the Chicago lad has gone back. Barry is still the champion, however as he knocked Leon out once, and if he retires, as he said he would, Leon must be acknowledged the champion bantam."[228] This analysis undoubtedly irritated Barry and also did not sit well with McGovern, who solved the problem by knocking out Leon in the twelfth round of a scheduled twenty-five round fight held in New York one month after the Barry-Leon draw.

During the first week of 1899, Jimmy was already working as the manager of McGurn's and arranging matches there. He was living in a three-flat at 204 Division Street right next door to McGurn's. He was a boarder with John Euker and his family. Euker and his wife Julia were German immigrants. They had a son, Henry, who was only six months old, and their nephew Carl lived with the family. Jimmy could walk only a few yards to get to work at McGurn's.[229] This was not exactly the glamorous setting associated with some fighters. Jimmy was already living as an ordinary guy doing ordinary things.

Jimmy had started fighting to support his mother. Forty days after he retired, his mother died. She was living in the home of his brother Thomas at 1106 Bonney Avenue on Chicago's west side. She had suffered from chronic asthma for fourteen years. Her death certificate said that she died of "gripe, consumption, chronic bronchitis and asthma." She had lived seventy-three years, lived through the great fire, been beaten nearly to death by one of her sons, seen her only daughter kill her husband with a hammer, and also seen her son Jimmy win a world championship only to be arrested for manslaughter a few hours later. After fourteen years suffering from chronic diseases of her lungs, death may have been welcomed by Mary.[230]

In early May, Jimmy lost a close friend. Pat Fitzgerald had been his neighbor, his trainer, and in his corner just a few months earlier in Davenport. Fitzgerald died in Denver on May 5. Fitzgerald suffered a heart attack. Frank Bartley, another fighter whom Fitzgerald managed, had gone to Denver for a fight there. When Fitzgerald did not appear for Bartley's morning rub-down, Bartley went looking for him and found him fully dressed but lying dead on a bed in the hotel room.[231]

Barry was at loose ends without boxing to occupy his time. He was only twenty-nine years old. In mid-March Jimmy traveled to Saint Louis with Frank Fitzgerald for a Saturday night exhibition.[232] He was reported to have opened a buffet on La Salle Street, but this apparently did not last too long.[233]

Former fighters can find leaving the ring difficult. In April 1899, Barry returned to Davenport where he acted as timekeeper for a fight between Tommy Ryan and Bill Stift and another match between Jack Lewis and Morris Rauch.[234] Jimmy then acted as the referee for matches held at the Adelphi Athletic Club on June 7 and then at the Star Theater on June 23.[235] This work paid him small amounts of money that helped pay his way.

Barry and Harry Harris

In August, Kid McCoy was matched with an obscure Philadelphia fighter named Jack McCormick. The fight was sponsored by the newly formed Fort Dearborn Club. The club held its shows at the Star where Barry refereed. To everyone's surprise, McCormick knocked out McCoy in the first round. The bigger surprise was that the new club's manager introduced Barry after the preliminary matches and told the crowd that Jimmy had been matched to meet Harry Harris for the 112-pound championship of the world in a match promoted by the club. The announcement elicited wild applause. Jimmy went into training at McGurn's. He may have been thinking that he could retain the title for another year if he downed Harris.

Harris was not a mope. He was described as a tall and "reachy" left-handed jabber and was sometimes called "Hairpin Harry." He was the twin brother of Sammy Harris who was another classy little and smart fighter, and together they were the heroes of Chicago's Jewish sporting community.

Harry Harris
(Photo courtesy of Tracy Callis)

Chapter 1 - James ("Jimmy") Barry (1870–1943)

Harry had been fighting professionally since 1896. In November 1898, he defeated Charley Rhoden in the ninth round of a ten-round preliminary fight held before the Corbett-Sharkey heavyweight match. Before his meeting with Barry, Harris had fought a dozen times in 1899 with quality opponents such as Connors, Flanagan, Australian Billy Murphy (who was then well past his prime), and Sig Hart. In the five matches immediately before the Barry fight, Harris had knocked out Dick Sielf in one minute, obtained a TKO against Murphy in four rounds, defeated Hart in fifteen rounds in Davenport, Iowa, knocked out Hart in six rounds in Clinton, Iowa, and then stopped Joe Huguelet in three rounds in Davenport. Harris routinely fought at 112 pounds or less and both men came in below the specified weight. He was better than good.

Barry and Harris fought on September 1, 1899. For Jimmy, nine months had elapsed after his final match with Leon. The Barry-Harris match was the final fight that evening and no other fighter on the entire card had been in the ring when Jimmy had begun fighting. A new generation of fighters predominated, but sometimes it is difficult to take the old horse out of the traces.[236] The *Chicago Tribune* reported the next morning that the consensus was the Barry was far below his previous form and appeared stocky.

Harris opened the fight confident and as the aggressor. This did not happen where Barry was involved. He had always been the aggressor. Jimmy appeared slow, and early in the fight Harris was able to slide inside Barry's right hand. In the second, Barry gave a short glimpse of his past form and landed one good right to Harris' body and two rights to the jaw. This round was clearly Jimmy's.

Round three was Harris'. He jabbed at Jimmy's head at will before Barry landed two ineffective rights to the jaw. Harris seemed to be able to block many of Barry's hardest shots. Jimmy showed well at the beginning of the fourth round, but Harris was still landing on Jimmy's face and his eyes were looking puffy. Just before the bell, Harris staggered Barry with a right hook to the jaw.

Jimmy started the fifth fast, but he soon slowed, and when he did, Harris continued to jab at his face, landed a right uppercut, and finished with a left to the chin. Harris continued to do most of the leading in the sixth and final round. Jimmy fought back, but was not in good enough condition to stand the pace, and Harris had the advantage at the bell. Hogan the referee called the match a draw.

If anything, Barry must have known that his original decision to retire had been correct. He felt that he had lost the match to Harris. The next day he confronted Hogan and said, "That was one decision you muffed. I lost that match last night." Hogan told Barry that he must be punch drunk to make such a claim, and Jimmy responded, "Just to show you what I think about my showing last night, I'm never going to fight again. I know when I'm slipping."

A few weeks later he announced that his day was past. He could not reach his old speed and did not want to risk his reputation. He said, "I have decided to quit. I thought I could fight as well as ever I could, but I find that my muscles have stiffened and that my wind is not as good as it used to be. Besides, it is difficult for me to do any hard training. I have been in the business a long time, and think now is a good time to quit."[237]

Although Barry had quit twice, he was back in the Star Theater's ring with Fitzgerald on December 11, 1899. The two friends provided a three-round exhibition at the beginning of a benefit provided for Frank Garrard.[238]

1900–1943 – OK Then, Now the Rest of his Life

After his pass at returning to the ring, Jimmy laid low. In 1900 he told the press that he was going to become a jockey, but that did not seem to pan out. In the late summer of 1901, Barry and J. O'Neil became the proprietors of the property formerly called McGurn's. They continued to operate the property as a handball court and boxing academy. Not long after taking over McGurn's, Barry's mentor and old friend Gilmore announced that he would begin producing boxing shows there in an effort to revive boxing in Chicago.[239]

In January 1902, Jimmy was approached by Chicago citizens about running for alderman of the 22nd Ward on the Democratic ticket. The article about this possibility noted that Jimmy was the president of the 22nd Ward athletic club, which presented boxing shows at a hall on Market Street and was also a Democratic precinct captain and a "loyal follower of Robert E. Burke in the ward." Jimmy did run using the slogan: "Giving the people what they want." He did not gain much support and lost in the primary election.[240]

Robert Emmett Burke was a power in Chicago's municipal politics. He was known as "OK" Burke because many projects in Chicago did not obtain funding unless Burke had added his "OK" in the margin of the paperwork outlining a proposal.[241] Jimmy's timing in backing OK Burke was bad. In October

1901, Burke was indicted and charged with embezzlement in his capacity as the city's oil inspector. Allegedly Burke had retained about $30,000 of fees to cover bookkeeping problems in the books he was responsible for keeping as oil inspector.[242] Moreover, politicians were concerned about slating an Irishman for the job because the ethnic composition of the north side had shifted to being predominately German. Whatever Jimmy's political aspiration might have been, they were probably ended when in February 1903 his sister, Mary Flynn, killed her husband with a hammer.

By January 1904, the handball court and boxing facilities on Division Street were again being operated by the McGurns. Probably because the Barry & O'Neil business had failed, Barry was given a benefit in June 1904, but that affair raised only $125.[243] McGurn's best days were over. William went to work in law enforcement in 1903, and in 1905, Mike McGurn's wife, Ellen, died. Mike died in early August 1908, and the era of McGurn's court was over.

In February 1910, Jimmy had his second legal experience arising out of the death of a fighter. Barry and Gilmore were arrested when a young man named Albert (Aloise) Wilkowski died after sparring ten two-minute rounds at Gilmore's gymnasium with a fellow named Joseph McCarthy. Gilmore's business was called "Harry Gilmore's School of Boxing and Physical Culture" and was located on the third floor of 35 Adams Street. There were no knockouts in the Wilkowski-McCarthy bout and neither participant reported being injured. Reports said that spectators and pupils of Gilmore cheered the work of both fighters during the match. The press claimed that Wilkowski lacked the appropriate training to be involved in a professional fight even though

Wilkowski had previously traveled to Arkansas to engage in a prizefight with Gilmore's son. Other articles described him as "Kid" Wilkowski and said that he fought under the name of "Jack Coburn of Grand Rapids." After the fight with McCarthy, Wilkowski had gone to a lavatory at the gym and collapsed, striking his head on the floor. He was taken to St. Luke's Hospital where he died later in the day.

The hospital notified the police of Wilkowski's death and they arrested Gilmore, Barry, George Latham, and William Sullivan, all described as employees of Gilmore. No charges were filed pending the results of an inquest to be held the following day. Chicago's police chief claimed that Wilkowski's death was the result of a violation of Chicago's anti-prizefighting ordinance.[244]

Ignatz Wilkowski told a deputy coroner that before the bout took place he understood that his brother was going to Gilmore's academy to participate in a real fight (not a scientific match) and that his brother would be paid $30 if he won, $15 for a draw, and $10 if he lost. All witnesses denied that admission had been charged to attend the fight, but several said that they had attended earlier fights where an admission fee was charged.

The coroner's physician testified that Wilkowski's death was due to a hemorrhage at the base of the brain due to external violence suffered during the match. After the inquest all of the defendants were arraigned in the Harrison Street police court and charged with aiding and abetting a prizefight. The cases were postponed until March 11.[245]

When the criminal cases were called again, they were all non-suited. The grand jury refused to indict Wilkowski's opponent, and the city admitted that it had no evidence of a prizefight other than what the defendants knew, and each of them had refused to testify.[246] While these cases were pending, a newspaper columnist wrote that he had recently seen Barry in Chicago and that Jimmy "looked like a dried-up little old man."[247] Another columnist reported that Barry continued to make friends as he always had and spent his summer months working on Chicago's public playgrounds where he was considered a huge success.[248]

Although some considered him dried up, in 1913, Barry was back in the ring. The Illinois General Assembly was debating a bill that would legalize but regulate ten-round boxing matches. On May 6, members of the state legislature and other notables, including Chicago's mayor, Carter Harrison, were in Springfield, Illinois, to witness exhibitions of scientific boxing. Harry Gilmore's son Fred and Mickey Sheridan, along with Barry and Johnny Coulon, who then held the bantamweight title, put on exhibitions. The Barry-Coulon show went two rounds, and then Coulon went two more rounds with Frankie White. After pleas from Coulon for the legislature to act favorably on the pending legislation, Packey McFarland and Willie Schaefer put on a fast four-round show.[249]

During the First World War, several fighters and former fighters volunteered for military service to help give physical training to American soldiers. Barry volunteered and went to Camp Gordon, Georgia. Other boxing stars who joined the army included Benny Leonard, Coulon, and Johnny Kilbane.

While at Camp Gordon, Barry shadow-boxed with Leonard and was impressed. Jimmy said that Leonard boxed in exactly the same style he had used twenty years earlier, but had the science of punching developed to an extent not found among the old-timers. As to the other fighters, Jimmy said, "Here's the angle: We used to go straight, always in position with left leg and arm advanced, always hitting out straight and as true as possible. Now, these fellows not only do that, but suddenly they start hitting out from angles that we would have considered impossible. Gibbons can hit you no matter in what position his feet and hands are."[250]

Barry and Coulon were at ringside in 1919 when the British flyweight Jimmy Wilde met the American Jack Sharkey. The American defeated Wilde, but that loss was excused in the press because Sharkey weighed 116 pounds and Wilde only 107½.[251] Over the years many have talked about who would win in a Barry-Wilde match.[252] In 1934, one writer called Wilde the best bantam of all time. Coulon immediately protested that Wilde was "just a fair sort of fighter, and nothing more than that." He went on to say that Barry was "the biggest little fellow that ever lived."[253] It should be remembered that Wilde lost to Sharkey, who outweighed him by a little over eight pounds. Barry never lost, although he frequently met quality opponents who outweighed him by similar amounts or higher amounts. For a few examples: Sammy Kelly outweighed him by six-and-a-half pounds, Jimmy Anthony by six, Johnny Ritchie by ten, and Rotchford by almost fifteen.

For twenty-five years, Barry worked in the Cook County clerk's office and as a court bailiff.[254] His former manager Davies died in 1920 in a retirement home in Bedford, Virginia. His frequent adversary Leon worked as a night watchman, developed a protracted illness in 1920, and died in May 1926. His mentor Gilmore led a rich life. In 1912, he entered a burning building to save an elderly woman. He was still boxing at the age of sixty-eight. In 1924, he left Chicago and moved to California because his wife was ill and had been advised to find a home in a better climate. Gilmore died in Santa Monica in September 1942.[255] His close friend Tommy White lived until April 1957.

Jimmy Barry died on April 4, 1943. He had lived in the county tuberculosis sanitarium for four years before his death. The *Chicago Tribune* had covered his career extensively during his life but butchered his obituary. He was survived by his older brother, Thomas J. Barry, and four nieces.

Barry's funeral was held at Immaculate Conception at Schiller and North Park avenues. His pallbearers included Tommy White, Charley White, and Johnny Coulon. Honorary pallbearers included the old fighters Johnny Egan, George Gardner, Riley Bender, Sammy Frager, and Pat Conroy. He was buried at Evanston's Calvary Cemetery.[256]

Jimmy Barry was a man who had every reason to fail. He was a small man in physical stature but a giant in his profession. He had a terrible family life but was a model citizen. There were thousands of newspapers articles written about him and there is not a single word of criticism of him as a person. He became a close friend of many of his ring opponents and had a long friendship with Johnny Connors. He did what he could with what he was given and who could ask for more from anyone.

Appendix
Jimmy Barry's fights reported in newspaper and boxing historian accounts combined in a single table:

1890

Date	Opponent	City		Place
Apr 5	Billy Gale	Chicago	Ex	McGurn's
Apr 15	Frank Murphy	Chicago	Ex	Turner Hall
Apr 22	Billy Gale	Chicago	Ex	Madison St. Theater
Apr 28	Al Schrosbee	Chicago	Ex	Casino Gymnasium
Nov 15	George Siddons	Chicago	Ex	McGurn's
Dec 24	Unknown	Chicago	Ex	Alexandria AC

1891

Date	Opponent	City		Place
Jan	Fred Larson	Chicago	KO1	Not stated
Jan 24	Unknown	Chicago	Ex	McGurn's
Mar 17	Al Cleveland	Chicago	Ex3	McGurn's
Mar 30	Billy Gale	Chicago	Ex	McGurn's
Mar 31	Johnny Van Heest	Chicago	Ex	Turner Hall
Jun 8	Al Cleveland	Chicago	TK4	McGurn's
Jun 10	Young Mellington	Chicago	Sch	Not stated
Jun 24	Joe Gates	Chicago	Sch	McGurn's
Jul 17	Tommy White	Chicago	Ex	McGurn's
Jul 20	Con Doyle	Chicago	Ex	McGurn's
Aug 3	Con Doyle	Chicago	Ex	McGurn's
Aug 6	Al Cleveland	Evanston	Ex	Ducat's Hall
Aug 11	Al Cleveland	Chicago	Ex	McGurn's

Aug 24	Freeman Sloan	Chicago	W3	McGurn's
Aug 31	Billy Boyle	Chicago	Ex	McGurn's
Sep 21	Tim O'Leary	Chicago	Ex	McGurn's
Sep 26	Tommy Foley	Chicago	Ex	McGurn's
Bef Nov 28	Joe Gates	Chicago	KO2	Not stated
Dec 19	Joe O'Leary	Chicago	Ex	Battery "D"[257]
Undated	**reported fights**	**below**		
None	Al Schrosbee	Chicago	W4	Not stated
None	Dick Ward	Chicago	KO3	Not stated
None	Jack Miller	Chicago	W4	Not stated
None	Tom Cassidy	Chicago	W6	Not stated
None	Tom Cassidy	Chicago	KO2	Not stated
None	Joe Cranston	Chicago	KO3	Not stated
None	Joe O'Leary	Chicago	KO3	Not stated
None	Barney McCall	Chicago	W4	Not stated
None	Spud Murphy	Chicago	W4	Not stated
None	Jack Ghetlain	Chicago	KO1	Not stated
None	Jack Kelly	Chicago	KO1	Not stated
None	Young Lyons	Chicago	KO1	Not stated
None	Al Newman	Chicago	KO1	Not stated

1892

Date	Opponent	City		Place
Jan 4	Joe O'Leary	Chicago	Ex	McGurn's
Jan 13	McShane	Chicago	Ex	Turner Hall
Feb 1	Billy Wellington	Chicago	W6	Not stated
Feb 10	Link Pope	Chicago	Sch	Not stated
Feb 12	Link Pope	Chicago	Ex	2nd Reg Armory
Feb 15	Joe O'Leary	Chicago	Ex	2nd Reg Armory
Feb 20	Dan Rowan	Chicago	KO4	Not stated
Mar 2	Billy Joyce	Chicago	KO3	Not stated

Chapter 1 - James ("Jimmy") Barry (1870–1943)

Date	Opponent	City		Place
Mar 12	Paddy Snow	Chicago	KO2	Not stated
Apr 3	Jack Smith	Chicago	W5	Not stated
Apr 4	Frank Fitzgerald	Chicago	Ex	McGurn's
May 10	Kid Corbett	Chicago	W4	Not stated
May 23	Joe O'Leary	Chicago	Ex	McGurn's
Jun 8	Romeo Durand	Chicago	W4	Not stated
Jul 4	Dick Reddy	Chicago	KO4	Not stated
Aug 8	Young Moran	Chicago	KO2	Not stated
Aug 24	N.C. Browand	Ft. Wayne		Not stated
Sep 3	Frank Murphy	Springfield	KO7	Not stated
Oct 11	Joe Gates	Chicago	W6	Not stated
Oct 17	Mike Bradley	Chicago	Ex	McGurn's
Nov 7	Romeo Durant	Chicago	Ex	McGurn's
Nov 14	Romeo Durant	Chicago	Ex	McGurn's
Dec 7	Henry Baker	Chicago	Ex	2nd Reg Armory
Dec 21	Bob McQuade	Ft. Wayne	W10	Masonic Hall
Dec 29	Bob McQuade	Ft. Wayne	Sch[258]	Not stated

1893

Date	Opponent	City		Place
Jan 8	Max Eaufeldt	Chicago	KO1	Not stated
Jan 14	Bob Quade	Chicago	KO10	In a cellar
Jan 16	Frank Murphy	Chicago	Ex	Turner Hall
Jan 20	Billy Murphy	Chicago	KO1[259]	Not stated
Jan 26	Bob Quade	Ft. Wayne	Sch	Not stated
Mar 6	Jack Hopper	Brooklyn, NY	Ex	Not stated
Mar 8	Frank Fitzgerald	Chicago	Ex	2nd Reg Armory
Mar 20	Freeman Stanton	Chicago	KO2	Not stated
Mar 27	Young Kelly	Chicago	Ex	McGurn's
Apr 5	Lou Simmons	Chicago	W6	Not stated

Date	Opponent	City		Place
Apr 7	Con Sheehan	Chicago	W5	Not stated
Apr 8	Young Kelly	Chicago	Ex	2nd Reg Armory
Jul 10	Pete Shea	Roby, IN	TKO4	Roby Arena
Sep 4	Johnny Connors	Roby, IN	Sch	Roby Arena
Sep 6	Tom Cassidy	Chicago	KO6	Not stated
Nov 13	Jack Fitzgerald	Chicago	W4	Tattersall's
Nov 27	Johnny Connors	Roby, IN	Sch	Roby Arena
Dec 4	Johnny Van Heest	Chicago	Ex6	McGurn's[260]
Dec 5	Jack Levy	Roby, IN	KO17	Roby

1894

Date	Opponent	City		Place
Jan 10	Harry Dally[261]	Chicago	TK2	Not stated
Jan 16	? Fitzgerald	Chicago	Ex	Compositors' Club
Jan 22	Joe Cranston	Chicago	KO3	McGurn's
Feb 6	Joe McGrath	Chicago	TK3	Empire Theater
Feb 9	Billy Plimmer	Chicago	Sch	Empire Theater
Feb 18	Young Spitz	Chicago	KO8	Not stated
Feb 19-23	Frank Fitzgerald	Chicago	Ex's	Stenger's Hall
Feb 28	Bob Costello	Chicago	W2	Lake Front Armory
Jun 2	Jimmy Gorman	New Orleans	TKO11	Olympic Club
Jul 3	Eddie Horan	Pittsburgh	Sch	Not stated
Jul 3	Harry Brooks	Bradford Falls	W4	Not stated
Sep 15	Casper Leon	Lemont	KO28	Not stated
Sep 24	Casper Leon	Chicago	Ex	McGurn's
Nov 14	George Church	Chicago	W8	Not stated
Dec 4	Johnny Van Heest	Chicago	Ex6	Not stated

| Dec 10 | Johnny Connors | New Orleans | Sch | | Olympic Club |
| Dec 13 | Jack Madden | New Orleans | Sch | | Olympic Club |

1895

Date	Opponent	City		Place
Feb 11	Unknown	Boston	Sch	Not stated
Feb 19	Frank Maciewski	Cincinnati	Sch	Not stated
Mar 6	Tommy White	Kansas City	Ex	Benefit
Mar 7	Billy Plimmer	Boston	Sch15	Suffolk AC
Mar 21	Joe Bertrand	Chicago	TK6	Tattersall's
Mar 30	Casper Leon	Chicago	D14	Stopped by police
Apr 15	Jack Madden	Brooklyn, NY	Sch	Cancelled
May	Tommy Ryan	Deal Lake, NJ	Ex	Training quarters
Jun 8	Unknown	New York, NY	Ex	Sullivan benefit MSG
Jun 24	Jack Madden	Brooklyn, NY	Sch	Stopped by police
Jun 27	Dan Tynan	New York, NY	Sch Ex	Did not happen
Jun 27	Jimmy Hickey	New York, NY	Ex3	Madison Sq Garden
Jul 15	Dave Ross	Boston, MA	KO2	Union Garden Hall
Aug 19	Dan Tynan	New York, NY	Sch	Did not happen
Aug 19	Casper Leon	New York, NY	Ex	National AC
Sep 16	Jack Madden	Jersey City, NJ	Sch	Hudson County AC
Sep 30	Jack Lynch	Philadelphia	Ex4	Southwark AC
Oct 3	Unknown	Philadelphia	Ex	Sullivan benefit
Oct 5	Unknown local	Cleveland	Ex	Sullivan benefit CAC
Oct 14	Casper Leon	Jersey City, NJ	Sch	Sullivan benefit
Oct 21	Jack Madden	Maspeth, NY	TK4	Empire AC
Dec 21		Chicago	Ex	Academy of Music

1896

Date	Opponent	City		Place
Jan 12	Young Lyons	Chicago	KO1	Not stated

Date	Opponent	City		Place
Feb	Johnny Murphy	El Paso	Sch	Cancelled
Mar 15	Jim McGuire	Chicago	KO2	Not stated
Apr 20	Joe O'Donnell	Chicago	KO3	Not stated
Apr 25	Harry Dalley	Chicago	Ex3	Chicago AC
Jul 24	Casper Leon	Elmira, NY	Sch	Cancelled
Aug 11	Steve Flanagan	Philadelphia	W6	Caledonia Club

1897

Date	Opponent	City		Place
Jan 30	Sammy Kelly	Brooklyn, NY	D20	Broadway AC
Mar 1	Jack Ward	New York, NY	W20	American Sp C
Mar 9	Unknown	Omaha, NB	Ex	Not stated
Mar 12	Unknown	Denver, CO	Ex6	Coliseum
Mar 13	Unknown	Cripple Creek	Sch Ex	Not stated
Mar 14	Unknown	Victor, CO	Sch Ex	Not stated
Mar 15	Unknown	CO Springs	Sch Ex	Not stated
Apr 23	Jimmy Anthony	San Francisco	W20	Nation AC
Apr 30	Unknown	Denver, CO	Ex	Not stated
May 3	Billy Brown	Creighton, NB	Ex4	Lyceum Theater
May 4	"Kid" Brown	Omaha, NB	Ex4	Boyd's Theater
May 4	Bob Armstrong	Omaha, NB	Ex	Boyd's Theater
Jun 15	Frank Fitzgerald	Kalamazoo	Ex	Academy of Music
Jun 16	Unknown	Grand Rapids	Ex	Grand Theater
Jun-Jul	Wisconsin Tour	Several Cities	Ex	Nightly
Aug 7	Barney McCall	Chicago	Ex5	Gaiety Theater
Aug 7	Sig Hart	Chicago	Ex3	Gaiety Theater
Dec 6	Walter Croot	London, Eng	KO20	National SC

1898

Date	Opponent	City		Place
Jan	Unknown	Cincinnati	Ex4	Not stated

Chapter 1 - James ("Jimmy") Barry (1870–1943)

Date	Opponent	City		Place
Jan 31	Fred Bogan	Cincinnati	Ex	Not stated
Feb 4	Billy Curtis	Cincinnati	W4	People's Theater
Feb 5	Danny Rewan	Cincinnati	Ex	People's Theater
Feb	Unknown	Detroit	Ex4	Not stated
Feb 15	June Summers	Louisville	W3	Not stated
Feb 16	Kid Hennessey	Louisville	Ex4	Not stated
Mar 17	Johnny Connors	Chicago	W6	Tattersall's
Mar 26	Johnny Ritchie	Chicago	W6	Chicago Athletic
Apr 18	Billy Rotchford	Chicago	D6	Tattersall's
May 28	Jim Popp's brother	Toronto	Ex	Toronto Athletic
May 30	Casper Leon	New York	D20	Lenox Athletic
Jun 3	Steve Flanagan	Philadelphia	ND6	Arena
Aug 13	Johnny Ritchie	Chicago	D6	McGurn's
Oct 6	Freddy Bogan	Lexington	Sch	Navarre AC
Oct 8	Jimmy Rose	Chicago	Sch	American AC
Oct 17	Joe Sturch	Chicago	Ex4	McGurn's
Oct 4	Campbell Hudson	Chicago	Ex4	McGurn's
Oct 24	Campbell Hudson	Chicago	Ex4	McGurn's
Oct 29	Joe Sturch	Chicago	Ex4	Waldorf Club
Oct 31	Frank Bartley	Chicago	D4	McGurn's
Nov 18	Sammy Harris	Davenport	Ex4	Trinity AC
Nov 21	Casper Leon	Chicago	D6	McGurn's
Dec 29	Casper Leon	Davenport	D20	Tri-City AC

1899

Date	Opponent	City		Place
Mar 18	Frank Fitzgerald	Saint Louis	Ex	
Sep 1	Harry Harris	Chicago	D6	Ft. Dearborn
Dec 11	Frank Fitzgerald	Chicago	Ex3	

119

1900

Date	Opponent	City		Place
Sep 18	Frank Fitzgerald	Chicago	Ex	Tattersall's

Table No. 2: Jimmy Barry's fights typically reported by boxing historians:

1891

Date	Opponent	City		Place
None	Fred Larson	Chicago	KO1	Not stated
None	Al Schrosbee	Chicago	W4	Not stated
None	Dick Ward	Chicago	KO3	Not stated
None	Jack Miller	Chicago	W4	Not stated
None	Tom Cassidy	Chicago	W6	Not stated
None	Tom Cassidy	Chicago	KO2	Not stated
None	Joe Cranston	Chicago	KO3	Not stated
None	Joe O'Leary	Chicago	KO3	Not stated
None	Freeman Sloane	Chicago	KO3	Not stated
None	Barney McCall	Chicago	W4	Not stated
None	Joe Gates	Chicago	KO2	Not stated
None	Spud Murphy	Chicago	W4	Not stated
None	Jack Ghetlain	Chicago	KO1	Not stated
None	Jack Kelly	Chicago	KO1	Not stated
None	Young Lyons	Chicago	KO1	Not stated
None	Al Newman	Chicago	KO1	Not stated
Jun. 8	Shorty Cleveland	Chicago	TK3	Not stated
Jun. 10	Young Mellington	Chicago	Sch	Not stated

1892

Date	Opponent	City		Place
Feb 1	Billy Wellington	Chicago	W6	Not stated

Feb 10	Link Pope	Chicago	Sch	Not stated
Feb 20	Dan Rowan	Chicago	KO4	Not stated
Mar 2	Billy Joyce	Chicago	KO3	Not stated
Mar 12	Paddy Snow	Chicago	KO2	Not stated
Apr 3	Jack Smith	Chicago	W5	Not stated
Apr 4	Frank Fitzgerald	Chicago	Ex	Not stated
May 10	Kid Corbett	Chicago	W4	Not stated
May 23	Joe O'Leary	Chicago	Ex	Not stated
Jun 8	Romeo Durand	Chicago	W4	Not stated
Jul 4	Dick Reddy	Chicago	KO4	Not stated
Aug 8	Young Moran	Chicago	KO2	Not stated
Sep 3	Frank Murphy	Springfield	KO7	Not stated
Oct 11	Joe Gates	Chicago	W6	Not stated

1893

Date	Opponent	City		Place
Jan 8	Max Eaufeldt	Chicago	KO1	Not stated
Jan 20	Billy Murphy	Chicago	KO1[262]	Not stated
Mar 6	Jack Hopper	Brooklyn, NY	Ex	Not stated
Mar 20	Freeman Stanton	Chicago	KO2	Not stated
Apr 5	Lou Simmons	Chicago	W6	Not stated
Apr 7	Con Sheehan	Chicago	W5	Not stated
Sep 6	Tom Cassidy	Chicago	KO6	Not stated
Dec 5	Jack Levy	Roby, IN	KO17	Roby

1894

[Other 1894 fights typically reported by boxing historians]

Date	Opponent	City		Place
Jan 10	Harry Dally[263]	Chicago	TK2	Not stated

Feb 18	Young Spitz	Chicago	KO8	Not stated
Nov 14	George Church	Chicago	W8	Not stated
Dec 4	Johnny Van Heest	Chicago	Ex6	Not stated

1895
[Other 1895 fights typically reported by boxing historians]

Date	Opponent	City		Place
Feb 11	Unknown	Boston	Sch	Not stated

1896
[Other 1896 fights typically reported by boxing historians]

Date	Opponent	City		Place
Jan 12	Young Lyons	Chicago	KO1	Not stated
Mar 15	Jim McGuire	Chicago	KO2	Not stated
Apr 20	Joe O'Donnell	Chicago	KO3	Not stated

1898
[Other 1898 fights typically reported by boxing historians]

Date	Opponent	City		Place
Jan 31	Fred Bogan	Cincinnati	Ex	Not stated
Feb 16	Kid Hennessey	Louisville	Ex4	Not stated

Chapter 2
Captain James H. Dalton (1853-1932)

Captain James Dalton
(Photo courtesy of Tracy Callis)

From 1881 until the mid-1890s, Chicago's working men knew about Captain James H. Dalton and his brothers. While men called "captain," "major," or "colonel" were usually aging veterans of the Civil War, Dalton held his title as commander of the tug *J.C. Ingram*. He was a leading sporting man, a protégé of the infamous Mike McDonald, and a fixture in Chicago's Democratic politics. A hundred years later the only thing known of Captain Dalton is that he once fought John L. Sullivan. His life and times deserve more, and his story is retold below.

The Dalton and Gallagher Families

James H. Dalton was born May 26, 1853, the oldest child of William and Katherine Gallagher Dalton. His father was born about 1829 in Ireland, and his mother was born about 1834 in Canada.[264] The Daltons were poor. In 1860, the total value of the property was $40. They lived at 156 Root Street in Cleveland's 11th Ward where William was employed as a machinist.

Cleveland's 11th Ward was one of roughest places a family could live. It was shantytown, pinned in on the east by the Cuyahoga ship channel and the south by the New York Central tracks. The street, railroads, and river all led to Lake Erie, where the Irish worked twelve hours a day on the docks unloading the Great Lakes schooners and ships that connected the city with the rest of the world. For twenty-six days of this work each month men brought home about $8.[265]

Bill and Kate Dalton married in the early 1850s. After James, his parents had nine more children between 1857 and 1876: Katherine (1857), William (1859), John C. (1861), Charles A. (1864), Andrew (1867), Robert (1869), George (1872), Lawrence Vincent (1874), and Mary E. (1876).[266]

Andrew Gallagher was a laborer whose family lived at 150 Root Street. Only three residences separated the Gallagher and Dalton families. Kate Dalton was the Andrew Gallaghers' oldest child. Her parents lived under the same conditions as the Daltons. They too had emigrated from Ireland. Their six children had been born in Canada, where they had stopped on the way to Cleveland. Kate's youngest brother, Mike Gallagher, was the same age as her own first child, Jim. Jim Dalton and Mike Gallagher grew up idolizing Charley Gallagher. He was Jim's uncle and Mike's big brother.[267]

Charley Gallagher fought his way out of poverty. He fought Jimmy Elliott in 1868 when Elliott was the heavyweight champion of America. In 1869, he twice fought Tom Allen, who was then the heavyweight champion.[268] Growing up in a family with a champion prizefighter, the younger Gallagher and Dalton boys must have boxed for years before the Dalton family moved to Chicago.

In 1860, Bill Dalton was a teamster. He drove a horse-drawn wagon taking freight from the docks to the railroads. In the mid-1870s, he was a pile driver probably working on the lake and in the river driving wooden piles for docks and levees. By 1880 he was captain of a dredge in Chicago and worked in and around the mouth of the Chicago River, keeping it navigable for Great Lakes ships. Dredges worked full time on the river pulling muck up off the bottom and dumping it by conveyor belts along the river banks where possible so that there was a constant smell of sewage for a block on each side.[269] In 1880, all of the Dalton boys above the age of eleven were working on dredges or tug boats in and around Chicago. That was a huge economic and social move upward for the entire family, and their success was obtained through back-breaking hard work.

Captain Jim Dalton came to Chicago around 1874, three years after the great Chicago fire.[270] He was among the tens of thousands of men and women who rushed to Chicago in the mid-1870s to participate in the employment opportunities incidental to rebuilding the core of the city. In 1870, there were about 300,000 living in Chicago. By 1890, there were about 1,150,000 living there. Dalton was probably familiar with sporting men in Chicago because his uncle Charley had fought in Chicago in the late 1860s, and Charley's exploits with Elliott and Allen would have been legend.

The first record of Dalton in Chicago is in Chicago's 1877 city directory. He was living at the Williams Hotel, 61 Kinzie Street, one block north of the north branch of the Chicago River and close to Government Pier where the river joined Lake Michigan.[271] Jim's younger brother John C. came to Chicago around 1877, but the entire Dalton family was living on Peoria Street in Chicago by 1880.

On April 6, 1878, Dalton was commissioned as captain of the tug *Protection* operated by the Vessel Owners' Towing Co. (V.O.T.)[272] V.O.T. was incorporated in Chicago in 1871 by John L. Higgie. The Higgies were Scotsmen whose family had immigrated in the late 1840s. Higgie's brother Captain Francis Balfour Higgie had located in Racine, Wisconsin, where he sold fuel to lake vessels and served as captain of several Great Lakes vessels. Captain Higgie, although strongly opposed to slavery, had assisted in turning over Dred Scott to a sheriff seeking to recover him for his southern slave owner.[273]

V.O.T.'s office was at 244 S. Water Street. John Higgie was president and John Oliver secretary.[274] The company also operated in Cleveland.[275] It was one of the largest towing companies in Chicago, and its primary competition was the Union Towing Association.[276] It seems probable that some of the Daltons had worked for V.O.T. in Cleveland before coming to Chicago.

Boys in the Dalton family began working on tugs and dredges when they were about fifteen. This was a rough business where tug owners competed for work and reputation. Every man's job was important, and if anyone failed to perform everyone could suffer. In 1880, young William was a fireman on a tug, John C. was a deck hand, and sixteen-year-old Charlie was a tug fireman. James Dalton had probably been working on tugs for seven years before settling in Chicago. By 1882, John C. and William were promoted. John was the engineer on V.O.T.'s tug *Van Schnick* and William was the engineer on V.O.T.'s tug *Hood*.[277]

1879–1880 Captain Dalton's Early Career in Chicago

Dalton was a good-sized heavyweight for his time, but in the early part of his career he was often called a middleweight and sometimes a light heavyweight. He stood between five feet nine and a half and five feet ten and a half inches and during his career weighed between 154 and 190 pounds. As with most men he put on weight as he got older.

Some claim that Dalton boxed John J. Dwyer in early 1879. The Dalton-Dwyer match apparently happened on April 5, 1889, as part of a testimonial for the English champion Joe Goss given at Chicago's Metropolitan Theater. Dalton sparred with Dwyer as part of the entertainment. Something happened during their match that angered Dalton, and he punished Dwyer severely.[278]

Dalton apparently made a good impression during his exhibition with Dwyer and was scheduled for another similar exhibition. On Saturday, June 5, 1879 at Chicago's Metropolitan Theater, Dalton sparred with a fighter named James Taylor as part of a benefit given for the middleweight champion Mike Donovan. James Taylor described himself as lightweight champion of the

Northwest.[279] Chicago's prince of darkness Mike McDonald was the master of ceremonies for this benefit. Dalton's participation suggests a relationship with McDonald. It seems likely that between his arrival in Chicago and 1881 Dalton engaged in several other unreported matches with Chicago area fighters.[280]

Dalton was favorably mentioned in the local press about a month after sparring with Taylor. It seems that M.A. Stewart had filed a criminal complaint of adultery against his wife and a man identified by the *Inter Ocean* as "James Holland, or Hailoran, or Hollaran," a pugilist. Some newspapers had identified the male respondent as Dalton. The *Inter Ocean* pointed out that those references did an injustice to the real Dalton who was a pugilist and "well known about town" in the fistic area "but who is as well a hard-working engineer, and has never been guilty of such a crime as is charged against Holland."

At the end of 1879, Dalton was a real defendant in a legal action. He was one of two people named in a civil action to recover 150,000 board feet of lumber that was being held aboard the schooner *S. Bates*.[281] Such legal actions were common between towing companies and their customers and usually involved the company refusing to move a tow as a practical way to force payment of a fee.

In February 1880, the second annual athletic prize exhibition was held at the Athenaeum Gymnasium at 50 Dearborn Street near Randolph. The Athenaeum was then at the core of Chicago's sporting world. Professor Charles Duplessis was the boxing instructor at the gym. Tommy Chandler, another popular boxing personality, trained at the Athenaeum. An audience of about 400 attended this competition. The program included a half-mile run on an indoor track, an exhibition of club swinging, tumbling, trapeze acts, work on horizontal bars, dumb-bell lifting, and several boxing shows. One of the sparring matches was between men identified as Benedict and Dalton. This was undoubtedly Captain Dalton.[282] His opponent was surely George Benedict, who had participated in another sparring exhibition at the same gym a few months earlier.[283] Dalton's participation indicates that he frequently used the gym and knew the people there.

At the end of 1880, Dalton was instrumental in saving the life of a man whose skiff had overturned near the exit from Chicago's harbor. Dalton was made captain of the *Ingram* in July 1880, and in November of that year he spotted the man floating on the surface of the lake supported by two oars. Although the accident had happened near the lifesaving station, it had not been observed. Dalton directed his tug to where the man was floating and pulled him freezing from the water.[284]

1881 – Meeting John L. Sullivan

Captain Dalton is known for his four-round exhibition with John L. Sullivan on August 13, 1881. This was Sullivan's first appearance in Chicago, and the event drew 3,000 customers. Dalton would not have been scheduled as Sullivan's opponent that evening without first establishing a local reputation as a capable fighter during the matches discussed above.

Sullivan had been fighting professionally for about seven years when he battered Steve Taylor at Harry Hill's saloon in the Bowery on March 31, 1881. His fight with Taylor was important because prominent members of the New York press were present for the mugging, and their stories after the fight quickly spread the word about John L.'s brutal approach to boxing.[285] He was on the trail to a heavyweight championship fight after mauling Taylor.

Sullivan's next fight was on May 16, 1881, against John Flood, the "Bullshead Terror," for a purse of $750 on a moonlight barge that was taken north on the Hudson River. Flood had worked as an enforcer in Harry Hill's saloon and had also been a New York gang leader. Their fight was arranged in Hill's establishment and was held on the barge to avoid police interference. The brutal way that Sullivan beat up Flood focused the attention of sporting men interested in such contests in the same way an artillery barrage catches the attention of lowly infantryman in a foxhole.[286]

On July 11, 1881, Sullivan's trainer, Billy Madden, took him to Philadelphia where he knocked out Fred Crossley, a rank amateur. Sullivan then gave the crowd a three-round exhibition with Madden to make up for the brevity of the Crossley fight. Eight days later Sullivan knocked out a hapless fellow named Dan McCarthy (sometime reported as "McCarty") in another one-round pound. After passing through Trenton, New Jersey, where he gave an exhibition with Madden, Sullivan headed for Chicago.

Years later an article in the *Winnipeg Free Press* provided some insight into Sullivan's appearance in Chicago. Charles E. "Parson" Davies had written to Billy Madden and told Madden that he had two heavyweights who could stop Sullivan. Madden then went to Chicago to meet with Davies and arrange a match. While Madden was in Chicago, Sullivan was visiting with his parents in Roxbury. Madden then wrote to Sullivan from Chicago and told him that the likely opponents were James Dalton and Jack Byrnes (sometimes "Burns") of Michigan.[287]

On August 7, the *Chicago Tribune* reported that Sullivan had rented McCormick Hall to put on a sparring exhibition on August 13. Madden offered any boxer in Chicago $50 to stay in the ring with Sullivan for four rounds. Sullivan was asked why he made such a liberal offer. He replied that he had already disposed of the best fighters on the East Coast, and no man had yet been able to stand for four rounds. Should anyone in Chicago win the $50, Sullivan said he would be happy to pay the money.

The Chicago event included an exhibition by Madden against local talent. Ed Dorney, a Chicago fighter turned promoter, had lined up an unknown whom he intended to match against Sullivan. Davies was arranging the details of all the entertainment.[288]

When he arrived in Chicago, Sullivan went to meet McDonald at his saloon and gambling resort on South Clark Street. McDonald's place was the heart of Chicago's underworld. He controlled other saloon owners by having local police on his payroll. Gambling joints and taverns paid protection to McDonald to avoid being raided by the authorities.

McDonald took a look at Sullivan and exclaimed, "Holy smoke! Is this bank clerk the famous Boston Strong Boy?" McDonald thought that Sullivan had lost a lot of weight since he had defeated Professor John Donaldson in Cincinnati. Sullivan responded with a smile, "I strip big." McDonald then said that Sullivan would not have a chance against either Dalton or Byrnes. Mike was prepared to gamble on Sullivan, but he didn't like the idea of paying $500 of overhead to see Sullivan put down. Sullivan then offered to demonstrate his skills against any of the "husky birds" that McDonald could find working in Chicago's stockyards. He said he would lay them out inside of ten minutes.[289] McDonald agreed, and the next day Sullivan, Madden, Tom Chandler, Davies, and McDonald met in a gym that Chandler operated above Chicago's Board of Trade.

McDonald had gathered the elite of Chicago's nightlife to watch Sullivan perform. The Boston boy was fitted out with skin-tight gloves. The first of three longshoremen was put into the ring and lunged at Sullivan, who side-stepped, took one pace forward, and whipped out his right hand so that it landed with terrific impact on the man's chin. He crumpled to the floor spurting blood. The next man climbed into the ring and Sullivan was on him in a flash. He banged the man under the left ear and stretched him out like a dead beef cow. Sullivan began pulling off his gloves and McDonald cried, "Hey, wait a minute! There's three minutes left and one more of 'em you've got to whip." Laughing, Sullivan replied that there wasn't anyone left to fight. "Number three is halfway home now."[290]

On August 13, John Brucks was named to spar with Madden in his preliminary match. Brucks was a competitive race-walker who had participated in several local walking matches promoted by Davies. Many race-walkers had no special athletic training and were just reasonably fit men. It is likely that Davies had drafted Brucks to try out boxing with Madden for the evening. It may be that Brucks had received some instruction from Chandler. In the introductions that night, Brucks was described as the champion of California. If he walked fast enough he might be able to stay away from Madden. The unknown scheduled to take on Sullivan was James Dalton.[291]

Dalton was a rough customer, a friend of McDonald and also the nephew of the former heavyweight champion of America. Reports at the time said he was under the supervision of Ed

Dorney, but this probably wasn't a formal relationship.[292] It is likely that Sullivan knew about Dalton's background and also knew that the captain came from a family in the fight game. McDonald himself acted as master of ceremonies at the August 13, 1881, exhibition at McCormick Hall. This gave McDonald an up-close look at Sullivan against a good local opponent.

The day after the exhibition, the *Chicago Tribune* reported that Dalton proved that he was "no mean opponent." For the first two rounds he held his own, but in the third round Sullivan made one of his patented rushes, smashing Dalton viciously until he had "considerably disfigured the ambitious tugman's countenance." Dalton was somewhat groggy by the time the fourth round was supposed to begin. He did come to time, but Sullivan then knocked Dalton stiff, and the tugman was not able to recover within the allowed time. Dalton was credited with a good showing, and Sullivan gave him $25 for the effort.[293] Sullivan was very complimentary of Dalton after the fight, describing the captain as the best man that he had yet met.[294]

Sullivan returned to Chicago for a scientific exhibition on September 3, 1881. This show was more spectacular than predicted. Abe Williams, a black fighter from Bloomington, Illinois, won a cup for defeating Charles Saunders in a three-round lightweight match. There was a middleweight bout between Harry Clifford and Pete Gibbons. William Bradburn from Pittsburgh, who later became a class heavyweight contender, and Tom Doherty of Chicago fought three very fierce rounds with Bradburn prevailing. There was an abbreviated heavyweight fight between William Owens and John Anderson that was cut short by an injury to Owens. Duncan Ross, a Cleveland-based multi-sport athlete, wrestled a Greco-Roman match against Johnson, followed by a catch-as-catch-can match, blending several wrestling methods so that throws were used, but a variety of submissions holds were also permitted in an effort to pin an opponent to the mat or require him to submit.[295]

A Match with the Champ, Paddy Ryan

Two days after the Chicago exhibition, word came from New York that "friends of Paddy Ryan," the reigning heavyweight champion, had covered McDonald's $1,000 deposit for a fight with Sullivan.[296] As it turned out, Ryan's backer was Fox of the *Police Gazette*. He had given authority to the *Gazette's* sporting editor, William Harding, to back Ryan for up to $5,000. This was the big time in 1881, and Dalton had played a role in the build up for a heavyweight championship fight. Little did he know that history would make this exhibition the high water mark in his life and that he would be remembered as the man who met Sullivan when the big boy first came to Chicago.

Davies invited Ryan, the champion heavy, to come to Chicago for a scientific match with Dalton. This gave the public a chance to compare Ryan's performance against Dalton with Sullivan's earlier showing. Davies went to New York to arrange the details of a proposed bare-knuckle Ryan-Sullivan match that promised to be the biggest thing ever in boxing.[297] The Ryan-Dalton exhibition was held on October 1, 1881, and went well with about 2,000 customers attending.[298] Again, Captain Dalton—a poor Irish kid from Cleveland's shantytown—was a part of the story.

Hitting the Bridge

While Dalton was making a name for himself inside the ropes, things weren't going so well outside the ropes. The captain hit the Chicago newspapers prominently on October 4, 1881.

In 1881, more ships arrived at Chicago every day than the combined new arrivals at New York, San Francisco, Philadelphia, Baltimore, Charleston, and Mobile combined.[299] Arrivals included a nearly equal mix of schooners and propeller-driven vessels from Buffalo, Toledo, Detroit, Milwaukee, Ashland, Superior, and Toronto. Row boats moved between piers and vessels. Black smoke, gray smoke, and soot filled the area along the entire length of the river. Small children lined picked spots open to the public to throw rocks at the tugs and their tows. On the loop side of the river, six- and seven-story buildings walled in the water. The other side of the river was lined was railroad tracks, piers, boat slips, docks, and lots filled with goods waiting to be moved. The river was deluged with tug and ship traffic, making it difficult for ground traffic to conduct commerce between the east and west sides of the river.

To facilitate traffic movement, there were twenty-seven bridges crossing the river, and virtually all of them were so-called pivot bridges. These bridges turned on a central pivot point that was built into a pier sunk in the middle of the river. Building piers in the middle of the river further narrowed the passageways on the river and made it more difficult to bring ships and boats up and down the already narrow river.

When river traffic approached a bridge, the captain of the vessel traveling under its own power or tug captain towing a vessel was supposed to look for a big red ball that was raised and lowered on a rope by the bridge tender controlling traffic at each bridge. Each bridge tender had his own house on the bridge and was the czar of his bridge. If the red ball had been hoisted up, this indicated that the bridge was closed and river traffic and tugs and their tows should hold away from the bridge. If the red ball was down, the bridge was open for river traffic. When the ball was up, this also alerted pedestrians and ground-based traffic that entry onto the deck of the bridge could continue. When the red ball was put down, then ground traffic knew the bridge was about to pivot open and to stay off the bridge's deck. In these situations, huge traffic jams would build up on either side of the bridge as businessmen, teamsters, vendors, and mothers were left standing in positions one upon the other watching river traffic move on the water.

The visual red ball signal was accompanied by a ringing bell to alert people that the bridge was about to pivot. The bridge tender would ring the bell and close gates at either end of the bridge's deck before turning the bridge so that it would be parallel to the banks of the river, which would allow the water traffic to move up or down the river. The bridge would sometimes pivot with traffic on its deck. Vehicles and people on the bridge deck when it pivoted would be stuck there until the river traffic passed and the bridge could be repositioned. The only progress such traffic could make was to move from one end to the other of the bridge itself while waiting for the river traffic to pass by.

Captain Dalton had been doing his work with the tug *Ingram*. At about 5:00 p.m. the *Ingram* was slowly towing the schooner *William L. Preston* down the river. The *Preston* was light, meaning that it was not carrying cargo, and was therefore riding high on the water. The ball was up and the Adams Street bridge was loaded with traffic. Captain Dalton signaled with his tug's whistle asking the bridge tender to lower the ball and pivot the bridge so that he could pass down the river with his tow.

The bridge tender saw the *Ingram* when it was at the Van Buren Street bridge and knew that it was coming up the river toward the Adams Street bridge towing the *Preston*. He also heard Dalton's tug whistle. When he saw the *Ingram* approaching, he immediately concluded that even at its slow rate the *Ingram* would reach his bridge before traffic on the deck could clear off. If Dalton tried to pass under the bridge, then the mast of the schooner would hit the bridge because the schooner was riding high on the water.

Fearing a collision when the bridge was full of traffic, the bridge tender began ringing his bell to alert ground traffic to clear off the bridge immediately. The bridge tender also disengaged the bridge so that it would be ready to pivot. He said that he also took this action to reduce the anticipated damage to the bridge if it was hit by the schooner's mast.

Most of the ground traffic got off the bridge safely. D.T. Beloiz was in a horse-drawn buggy that was still on the bridge's deck when it disengaged. Because the schooner was riding high on the water, its mast did hit the side of the bridge. When the schooner's mast hit the bridge the impact made it pivot, and this frightened the horse. The driver was able to jump out of the buggy, but the horse lurched forward and went off the deck of the bridge, pulling its buggy into the river where the horse then drowned. Some accounts claimed that the horse went off the bridge because Beloiz tried too late to drive the buggy off the bridge.

The bridge tender faulted Dalton for not controlling the schooner's movement. He thought that Dalton could see that that mast would hit the bridge but did not move his tug alongside the schooner to slow or stop it soon enough to prevent the collision with the bridge.[300]

Dalton was charged with violating a city ordinance by allowing the schooner to hit the bridge.[301] The bridge tender, William McAuliffe, told his story in court, and Dalton said that he was moving at only one mile an hour as he approached Adams Street.

Bridge tenders such as McAuliffe were junior grade dictators of the territory around their bridges. This tender and V.O.T. had long-running differences about the way he operated his bridge, and the company later tried to have him arrested in connection with a second incident at his bridge.[302] For his part, Dalton admitted that the red ball was up, but said that he heard the bell ringing and took this as a signal that he should come ahead. He didn't see any danger that the schooner's mast would hit the deck of the bridge.[303]

The judge held that Dalton had violated the city ordinance and fined him $100. This ordinance violation case was only the beginning of the litigation. An arbitration followed by an appeal of the arbitrator's award and a federal law suit all followed. The central legal questions related to the application of a federal law designed to limit the liability of ships involved in accidents at sea. Did this law apply when a ship was on a river and not moving under its own power? Did it apply when the damage from a collision was to a bridge over the river rather than another ship? The resulting federal decisions are found in dozens of modern legal treatises.[304] Few know that the captain of the tug involved was a heavyweight prizefighter who was well known in Chicago.

About one month after the accident, the V.O.T. published its list of captains and engineers for the coming season. Dalton was not included on that list, and he probably lost his job because of the accident at the Adams Street bridge.[305]

Local Sports Help Their Friend

The Chicago sporting community pulled together behind Dalton when he faced financial difficulty because of the big fine imposed. Within three days, a benefit was announced for Dalton to be held at McCormick Hall on Saturday, October 15, 1881. The *Police Gazette* donated a gold medal valued at $100. In addition, a silver goblet would be awarded for the best middleweight sparring. The contestants that evening included Williams, the Bloomington fighter, Paddy Golden, Eugene McCarthy, John Scully, James McLaughlin, Ed Duplessia, Joseph Schooll, Dorney, and Jack Bowen. Ross and Thomas Eck participated in a high jump contest, and there were also wrestling and club swinging events.

An Irish heavyweight named Con Morris challenged Dalton a few days before the benefit, and Tom Chandler offered to spar four rounds with Dalton at the benefit for $50.[306] Dalton offered $25 to any man who would spar with him four rounds under Queensberry rules. The press noted that Sullivan had given Dalton lessons designed to improve the captain's punching power.[307]

It turned out that Dalton did not spar with Morris at the benefit. Instead, a separate Dalton-Morris match was arranged for November 15, 1881, to be held within fifty miles of Kansas City and for $500 a side. With Morris out of the picture for the benefit, Chandler was substituted as Dalton's adversary. Dalton trained for this exhibition with "Soap" McAlpin.[308] Then, about a week later, Morris backed out of the Kansas City match and gave up the forfeit money he had posted.[309]

Trying to Build a Reputation

In early December 1881, the *Daily Inter Ocean* carried an article reporting that Dalton had booked the Industrial Art Building in Philadelphia for December 19, 1881, for a first-class pugilistic show.[310] It is highly unlikely that Dalton could make such arrangements by himself. It is probable that the arrangements for this show were made by Davies. Dalton's opponent that evening was Mike Cleary, an Irish-born fighter who had immigrated to Philadelphia and who would later be matched for real fights with fighters such as George Rooke, Jack Burke, and Charley Mitchell. Dalton's 1881 match with Cleary was for a purse of $200.[311]

In January 1882, Dalton was a hot commodity. Rooke, the champion American middleweight, and Mike Donovan, past middleweight champion, were touring together trying to capitalize on the interest in boxing that had been stirred up by the impending heavyweight championship match. When Rooke and Donovan showed up in Chicago on January 21, 1882, they both wanted part of Dalton. Rooke and Dalton had scheduled an exhibition in McCormick Hall for January 23. Dalton had a benefit scheduled with old Tom Allen at Chicago's Central Hall that same day.

Rooke and Donovan both challenged Dalton. Rooke offered Dalton $50 to show up on Monday evening and spar with him.

Donovan offered to bet $100 that he could defeat Dalton on Tuesday night at Dalton's own benefit.[312] Dalton responded to these challenges in a long letter that was published in the *Daily Inter Ocean*. He contended that his reputation in Chicago was well known and people there knew that he would not run away from a fight. He thought both Rooke and Donovan were a couple of hippodromers trying to enhance their own attendance at his expense. Dalton said that he considered Donovan to be a "poor, old, broken-down pugilist," and it could earn him no credit by beating Donovan. However, he offered to post $200 with Mike McDonald as a forfeit to secure a fight for a purse of $1,000 with Rooke at New Orleans on the same day, under London prize rules, as the Sullivan-Ryan fight. He wanted to beat Rooke with his bare hands.[313]

During their show in Chicago, both Rooke and Donovan replied to Dalton's letter. Rooke, who had been specifically challenged by Dalton, did not accept the captain's terms. Rooke offered to fight Dalton eight weeks from January 23, 1882, at catch weights for a $1,000 a side. A catch-weight fight would not qualify as the championship fight that Dalton wanted, and a fight for $1,000 a side was a big difference from fighting for a purse of $1,000. Most fighters needed a backer for a fight like the one Rooke proposed.

Donovan offered to fight Dalton on the same night that he met Rooke as middleweights and for $1,000 a side. Of course, this proposition would mean that Dalton would have to weigh in as a middleweight for his fight with Donovan, but Rooke could be much heavier. Their response was nonsense to anyone who was paying attention. However, all of the give-and-take further indicates the depth of Dalton's involvement in prizefighting.

1882 – Chicago Exhibitions with Sullivan and Ryan After the Big Fight

On February 7, Sullivan beat the tar out of Paddy Ryan and began his long run at the top of the boxing world. Paddy explained that he had a hernia and his truss slipped.

Sullivan quickly returned to Chicago, where he arrived at about 7:30 a.m. on Saturday, February 11. After checking in at the Commercial Hotel, he went to McDonald's place to bask in the glory. That evening Sullivan appeared at an exhibition given in his honor at McCormick Hall. Three Daltons were involved that night: James Dalton and his younger brothers John C. and William.[314] McDonald was the master of ceremonies, while Sullivan and Madden pranced around the ring with Sullivan mimicking moves that he had made during his bashing of Ryan a few days earlier. There were no films at the time, so it was nice to give the locals an idea of how the execution had been administered in Mississippi with Madden playing the part of Ryan.[315]

Near the end of February, Ryan also headed for Chicago, where he was given a benefit at McCormick Hall. Benefits were a staple of fighting at the time. The general idea was that the defeated fighter had lost the prize money and the costs involved in training and therefore must be down on his luck. Promoters put on benefits where the vanquished could appear and receive part of the gate to help tide him over until he could pull himself together. Ryan's event in Chicago took place on February 25, 1882. It was poorly attended. Ryan never was a particularly popular champion. Again, the same three Daltons appeared. John C. and Bill sparred together and Captain Dalton sparred with

Ryan. McDonald acted as referee.[316] The three Dalton boys were an important part of Chicago's sporting community.

After the Adams Street bridge accident, Dalton left the tug business and opened a saloon at 59 South Desplaines Ave. His place was about three blocks west of the Chicago River and south of Randolph Street. It was a rough neighborhood, and it is probably fair to say that Dalton's place was a dive. He provided live entertainment in the form of friendly women who sat inside booths and were visited by patrons of the pub. Exactly what happened inside the booths is not explained, but one can use his imagination.

Although Dalton was in the saloon business, he kept busy prizefighting. In the eleven months between June 1882 and May 1883, the captain had three matches with John Donaldson, who much later acted as sparring partner for James J. Corbett when Corbett was preparing for his championship match with Sullivan. Donaldson was another fighter from Cleveland's 11th Ward and had lived only about five blocks from the Dalton and Gallagher families.[317] He was a year younger than Dalton and roughly the same size. It seems probable that the Daltons and Donaldson had known each other for many years. Moreover, by 1882, both the captain and Donaldson had met Sullivan in the ring with similar results.

In the early 1880s, Donaldson moved from Cleveland to Milwaukee, where he was operating a gym. As a new face in Milwaukee, it was important for him to draw talent to that city in order to develop a reputation. On June 14, 1882, Donaldson and Dalton put on the first exhibition in Milwaukee. The following month, Donaldson issued a challenge to fight any man in the world except Sullivan.[318] Then on August 12, 1882, Donaldson came down to Chicago for another four-round exhibition with Dalton.

Dalton Loses his Liquor License

In late 1882, the big news was a heavyweight fight that was being promoted by Davies between Jimmy Elliott, the washed up former champion, and Sullivan. The idea that McDonald and Davies would bring Sullivan to Chicago for a fight with a convicted felon angered Chicago's mayor, Carter Harrison. The mayor elevated Austin Doyle to superintendent of the Chicago Police Department, and Doyle quickly reorganized the department to put Harrison's political supporters in key roles.

On November 23, newly promoted lieutenants led raids on the gambling dens. The mayor revoked the liquor licenses of many of McDonald's supporters. These actions by the mayor and the police were intended to make the going difficult for Davies. Despite these actions, preparations for the Sullivan-Elliott fight continued to move forward.

On November 25, 1882, Elliott sparred with Dalton. This was intended only as a show to sharpen up Elliott and so that the public could see Elliott in action with Dalton, who had given Sullivan a rough time in 1881. Again, Dalton was playing a role in a planned heavyweight championship fight.

No one wanted something to happen that would endanger the proposed heavyweight fight. Nevertheless, during the Elliott-Dalton contest, Elliott sprained a ligament in his right hand, endangering the match with Sullivan. Moreover, the Elliott-Dalton fight was an insult to Harrison and his plan to crack down on vice—which, by definition, included boxing.

The next day Harrison retaliated by revoking Dalton's liquor license. The alleged offense related to the private boxes that Dalton operated where men could meet the female performers face to face. Because of his sprained hand, Elliott had to ask Sullivan to postpone their fight.[319] Ultimately, this delay in the Sullivan-Elliott fight led to the murder of Elliott by Jere Dunne.

After his liquor license was pulled and while boxing was closed down in Chicago, Dalton took an athletic show on the road. A Rockford, Illinois, newspaper reported in mid-May 1883 that Dalton was making arrangements to give an exhibition in its local opera house (including club swinging, fire-eating, mesmerizing, and ventriloquism). This show would be offered in Beloit, Janesville, Racine, and Madison.[320] On May 29, 1883, Dalton appeared at the Stadt Theater in Milwaukee with Paddy Ryan in a friendly show with soft gloves.[321]

1883–1884 – An Exhibition With an Old Man

Davies continued to look for a fighter who could be matched with Sullivan. William Sheriff, the "Prussian," was one of the oldest of the older heavyweight fighters and came to Chicago to try to get into fighting shape to see whether he could make the grade. In October 1883, Sheriff had fought a seven-round draw with Charley Mitchell. On May 19, 1884, he was knocked out by Cleary in Philadelphia. But in early 1884, he was training in Chicago under the dual direction of James Connolly of Boston and Davies.[322]

Sheriff expected to train for sixty days before issuing a challenge to some of the leading artists of the profession. He made Chicago his headquarters and opened a sparring academy in the city enlisting eight pupils. He also trained in the basement of Vere Davies' saloon at 219 Randolph Street, which had been fitted up for ball exercise.

As part of his training Sheriff sparred with Dalton on January 22. The Prussian was a short, square-built fighter who was quick and agile. Dalton looked good in this fight, and the press remarked favorably about the captain's long reach. However, in the third round of the fight, Dalton moved in close to Sheriff and was dropped to his knees. The two men were told to back off in the fourth round and finished the fight with only light sparring. Coverage of this match noted that on the following night Sheriff would spar with a 200-pound Chicago saloon keeper named Mike Driscoll.[323]

On February 23, Dalton defeated Driscoll in five rounds. Their meeting took place as part of a benefit for Driscoll organized by Davies. In the first round Driscoll drove Dalton against the ropes and bloodied his mouth. Dalton seemed stunned by the attack—after all, this was supposed to be a benefit—but he pounded Driscoll hard in return. In the second round Dalton drew blood from Driscoll's left eye, and the crowd grew so excited that Davies had to make a little speech to quiet things down. During the final three rounds Dalton had complete control of the fight, and Driscoll's face looked as if he had been on the losing end of a bare knuckle fight.[324]

Dalton's Marriage Ends With a Bullet

On January 13, 1883, Dalton married Mary Jane Kerwin in Chicago.[325] Apparently this was not a happy marriage. Within fifteen months Mary Jane, described in the press as a "large, fleshy woman with red hair," tried to shoot her husband.[326]

About midnight on March 7, 1884, Dalton was in the barroom attached to the Park Theater at 333 South State Street enjoying a few brews with his friends. Mary Jane and some of her friends entered the bar from the area of the theater's auditorium. She had previously lived in a women's boarding house at 316 South State and probably had a lot of friends in that area. When she spotted her husband she drew a .22 caliber, self-cocking revolver and shot across the room, shouting, "Take that!"

The bullet struck him in the right side about three inches below his armpit, penetrated the pea-jacket he was wearing, broke his skin, and then fell to the floor. Mary Jane was trying to get off a second shot when one of Dalton's friends wrestled the gun away from her, and she ran out of the bar and into an establishment at 331 State Street. She was quickly found and taken by the police to the Harrison Street station house.

Later that night Mary Jane was brought from her cell to be interviewed by the press. When she learned that her husband was not hurt, she said that she was glad to hear the news. She went on to explain that Dalton had been promising to kill her and when she saw him in the bar, she decided that she had better take the opportunity to shoot him before he killed her. The press said that Mary Jane had a "bad reputation" and had been living on Van Buren Street near Clark—an area frequented by ladies of the night.[327]

A few days later Mary Jane appeared in criminal court. At this point she was described as the "divorced wife" of Captain Dalton. He did not appear because he and Mary Jane had reached a compromise and he was not pressing charges. The judge was not satisfied with their private resolution of a criminal matter and ordered her held on $1,000 bail pending her indictment by the grand jury.[328]

Although he had been shot, Dalton was also scheduled to meet a man named Tom Anderson on March 10, 1884, just three days later. He was prepared for that fight, but it was stopped by an injunction obtained by the owner of the hall where the fight was to take place.[329]

The Dalton-Anderson match took place on March 22. It was scheduled for four rounds at the Buckingham Theatre on State Street. Supposedly Anderson and Dalton didn't like each other and their fight was for blood.

After some preliminary sparring, Dalton landed several heavy blows on Anderson's face and cut him badly around his eye. At this point Lieutenant Shea intervened, seized Dalton's gloves, and revealed that the gloves were fastened with iron buckles used to mutilate Anderson's face. Dalton said the buckles were only to fasten his wrist protectors, but Anderson said it was a dirty trick. The match was stopped, but no arrests were made.[330] On April 28, Dalton and Driscoll had a rematch. Their second fight was with small gloves under Queensberry rules. This time Dalton was prepared and knocked out Driscoll in the first round.[331]

Dalton Takes Out a Heavyweight Contender

In early 1884, Davies was trying to promote an English heavyweight named Jem Goode as a viable opponent for Sullivan. In the process Davies matched Goode with Dalton at Battery D on the evening of May 19. The political situation in Chicago had eased for Davies and made it possible for him to promote important sporting events.[332]

Four thousand people showed up for the Dalton-Goode fight. The sports of Chicago knew what Dalton could do in the ring, and Goode was the big draw. The fight was with small, soft gloves for five rounds under Queensberry rules. This was a serious fight and not something like the Sullivan or Ryan exhibitions. Tom Chandler acted as referee and McDonald assumed the role of time keeper, giving him more control over the outcome than the master of ceremonies.[333]

Goode did not show well, and Dalton did not play the flunkey role. It may be that Dalton saw an opportunity for himself if he could defeat Goode. Perhaps he thought he could move into the ranks of heavyweight contenders by putting Goode down. In the second round Dalton made a rush and fought Goode all over the platform. The *Daily Inter Ocean* wrote that his performance in this round would be memorable in the annals of Chicago sparring. In the third round he made another rush and put Goode down and off the stage between the ropes, giving Goode a slight push for extra measure as he went over the edge. Goode had to circle the entire stage before he was able to try and reenter the ring.

As Goode climbed back in the ring, Dalton rushed at him again, this time with the two banging away at close quarters until Goode went down in his corner. While Goode was on the floor, Dalton swung at him again. When the fight was renewed, Dalton rushed for a fourth time, forcing Goode out of the ring and then grabbing his ankles to help knock him off the platform a second time and kicking out in Goode's direction. A foul was claimed by Goode's handlers.

While Goode was trying to get back into the ring, the referee gave the match to Dalton because Goode had not returned to the stage within ten seconds. McDonald overruled Chandler, making the outcome of the event uncertain. The papers remarked that Goode was in better condition after the fight and that Dalton had a fearful cut on his left eye. The result of this fight was that Goode's reputation needed rehabilitation if he was ever expected to have a show against Sullivan or any other serious heavyweight contender.[334] Dalton said that except for Sullivan, his fight with Goode was the hardest fight he ever had.

After beating Goode, Dalton did not fight again until a rematch with Anderson on December 5. Their fight took place in a theater at 333 State Street. The police were again present, fearing trouble because rumors circulated that Dalton had used brass knuckles during his first fight with Anderson. This was an apparent exaggeration of the iron buckles that Dalton had on his wrists during that match. In their second fight, Dalton was the better man from the start. The police watched closely but did not interfere as Dalton gave Anderson a black eye and made him bleed profusely from the mouth and nose. Because the fight was a "scientific" affair, it was called a draw, but the real outcome was apparent.[335]

1885 – Defies Fly

The world of prizefighting in the early 1880s had its own lexicon. One of the words in that lexicon was "defy." A defy could be directed to a particular fighter or to several fighters at the same time. Sometimes defies appeared to be drafted by a promoter rather than the fighter himself. For example, in January

1885, Dalton issued a defy to Dominick McCaffrey to fight him in a fair stand-up fight with bare knuckles for from $1,000 to $2,000 a side at any place within one hundred miles of New Orleans.[336]

Bradburn issued a defy to Dalton. Bradburn said that he had learned that Dalton had criticized him, saying that he could "only stand a punch or two" before folding up. To spice up his defy, Bradburn insulted Dalton, and his insults provided insights about some previous fights. Bradburn wrote that when Sullivan fought Dalton, he allowed him to stand four rounds so that Dalton could "hold his reputation and open a saloon."[337] This may have been exactly what happened because Dalton did use his take from his fight with Sullivan to open a saloon. Bradburn also wrote that Tom Chandler, a man twenty pounds lighter than Dalton, made him think he did not know how to fight, and he claimed that Elliott had knocked out Dalton with a single blow and then "took him aside and gave him fatherly advice and told him to quit the business, for as a fighter he would be a failure."

Bradburn proposed a fight with Dalton using kid gloves for $500 a side and the winner to take 75 percent of the gate. The things that Bradburn wrote were not what a promoter would likely include in his defy, but they did provide tabloid-like information about the fight game at the time.

Jack Burke Dismantles Dalton

Davies continued to look for a heavyweight to match against Sullivan. In early 1885, he went to New York to try to match Jack Burke, Alf Greenfield, or Mitchell with Dalton.[338] On January 23, 1885, Davies announced that he was planning an athletic entertainment at Battery D that would be one of the best Chicago had ever seen. The promised show was a Burke-Dalton fight on February 2.

Paddy Ryan acted as the referee for their match. Burke was no Jem Goode. The *Chicago Tribune* reported that Dalton was noticeably out of shape and was entirely at the mercy of Burke.[339] In contrast, the *Herald* reported that both men were in good shape. Although Dalton was the local man, the crowd was with Burke from the beginning, and he was noted to be a "clean, quick hitter, with plenty of science."[340]

In the first round Burke delivered seven successive left-handers full on Dalton's nose and mouth and then drove him to the ropes, where a right-hand put him down for an eight count. Burke stood at a distance and waited, smiling at Dalton, who faced the music like a man. During the remainder of the fight, Burke did not use his right hand and controlled Dalton with his left alone. Even using one hand he was too much for Dalton, and the crowd cheered for the victorious Irishman. Dalton had reached the pinnacle of his career when he beat up Goode. Although he fought for many years after February 1885, his career was effectively over after Burke took him apart.

Dalton Nearly Buys the Farm

Soon after the Burke fight, the world of boxing nearly ended for Dalton. After being schooled by Burke on February 2, Dalton traveled to Louisville for a fight with Cleary, a really tough customer. In making this move, Dalton left his home territory and stepped out of his league.

The Cleary-Dalton fight was held at Liederkranz Hall in front of 2,000 paid fans. Dalton was not in good shape. This time his physical stamina was not the issue. He was badly bruised and had a puffed-up eye and a severely cut lip from his match with Burke. After only two minutes and forty-eight seconds, Cleary caught Dalton with a straight right. Cleary had one of the best rights in the business and he knocked Dalton cold.

It was more than four minutes before Dalton recovered consciousness. The *Cincinnati Enquirer* reported that when Dalton was hit, he "fell full length, his head striking on the bare stage with such weight that the sound produced was heard all over the large hall." Dalton's first words when he came to were: "I ain't knocked out, am I?"[341]

He would not be the first or the last fighter to ask that question, and 100 percent of the time this is a question a fighter's backers don't want to hear or answer. To add insult to injury, Dalton and his brother John were stranded first on a New Albany and Chicago Railroad train and then in a private home near Lafayette, Indiana, for four days between February 9 and February 13 when a surprise snowstorm blockaded the railroad.[342]

Dalton limped back to Chicago with the news that he had been scheduled for a rematch with Cleary during the second week of March in New Orleans. This was to be a fight to the finish—as if he hadn't been finished in Louisville. The New Orleans contest would be Dalton's third serious fight in about five weeks against high-quality opponents.[343] After packing his bags, Dalton headed for New Orleans to go into training for his rematch with Cleary.

Ten days later, Dalton was returning to Chicago from New Orleans on the Illinois Central's New Orleans express train. A

Saint Louis express train had stopped on the track about nine miles south of Kankakee, Illinois, because of a broken wheel. Flares were set out behind the train to warn any following trains, but the New Orleans express was traveling too fast to stop and plowed into the sleeping car on the Saint Louis train, telescoping it into the baggage car. One passenger was killed and many passengers, including Dalton, were injured.

Little attention was paid to Dalton's injury in original accounts because it was learned that he was traveling on a pass that the railroad had issued to Alderman Gaynor of Chicago. Gaynor was one of the aldermen considered to be a "sport" and thought to be in McDonald's back pocket. The railroads regularly gave free passes to politicians for their personal use as a way of influencing them toward railroad corporations and railroad legislation. Every alderman in Chicago had a free pass from the Illinois Central. Politicians were not supposed to give up their passes to other people.

When asked what Dalton was doing with his pass, Gaynor said that Dalton had asked him whether he could help get him a pass. Gaynor had sent a friend to procure a pass, if possible, from the IC. According to Gaynor, the friend had misunderstood and procured the pass in the alderman's own name. He said that he was unaware of his friend's mistake, and he would never have abused a railroad pass. Chicago aldermen were and remain proficient at making such lying answers: "I have made mistakes in my life. None of us are perfect. I have apologized and consider this matter in my past." In Chicago this means: "I made the mistake of being caught in the act. Everybody gets caught sometime. I am sorry I got caught, but I still have enough clout that you had better just forget about it because you can't do anything about it anyway." The scheduled Dalton-Cleary fight in New Orleans was cancelled because of Dalton's injuries.

Dalton would not fight again until May 1885, when he was matched to fight the heavyweight champion of Colorado, John P. Clow, another quality fighter.[344] In the meantime, his younger brothers John C. Dalton and William "Billy" Dalton appeared in lesser roles during the summer of 1885.[345]

Dalton fought Clow at the Park Theater on May 15. At least this time when he went to the Park no one was shooting at him. Their match was panned. It seemed that Dalton was not on form and continually led short. Clow was afraid of being hit and spent his time running away. After five rounds, referee Billy Lakeman called the match a draw. The general impression seemed to be that under ordinary circumstances Dalton could have handled Clow, but either he could not or did not perform well.[346]

About one month later Dalton was in Saint Paul, Minnesota, to act as a second for Cardiff in his fight with Billy Wilson.[347] At this point in his career Cardiff had become a dirty fighter. He knocked Wilson down in the second round and then stood over him threatening to hit him again if he attempted to rise. Despite this behavior, Cardiff was given the fight. Dalton was acting as a second for Cardiff, and while all this was happening he jumped into the ring and got into a fight with Wilson's second. The whole affair was an embarrassment to legitimate boxing.[348] There are several matches in 1885 that are sometimes attributed to Captain Dalton that actually involved his brother John Dalton.

1886–1887 – Boxing is Banned in Chicago

The year 1886 was difficult for prizefighters in Chicago. Early in the year there was another crackdown on prizefighting and wrestling. Several factors led to the change of attitude about the sports, and some of the problems were created by people who participated in the events.

In early 1886, there were a series of national high-profile wrestling and boxing matches that were particularly brutal. In March 1886, Dempsey defeated La Blanche. The last round of their fight was described in words such as: "The Marine was bleeding like a stuck pig, and Jack was puffing and blowing. The gloves of both were in tatters and covered with blood."

On the wrestling side there were two significant matches in early 1886 in Chicago. During the first match Evan "the Strangler" Lewis choked out his opponent. In the second match Lewis appeared to intentionally break his opponent's ankle. These and many other similar events played into the hands of that part of society (the "Law and Order League" types) that was opposed to prizefighting and wrestling.

Chicago's prizefighting squeeze also happened because of some major sociological issues. The anarchists, socialists, and bomb throwers who threatened a reign of lawlessness were confronted by the Chicago police in what became known as the Haymarket riot. Among the leading citizens of Chicago was a prevailing opinion that the wage classes brought on their own poor living conditions by improvidence and misdirected efforts. This view was coupled with a low opinion of the "foreigners" that largely made up the wage classes and their trade unions and that gave rise to such entities as the American Protective Association.

In May a ban on boxing and wrestling went into effect in Chicago, and its athletes looked for a place where they could fight without interference. Saint Louis had an excellent fighting community that included the formidable Daly brothers, Tom Allen, and Tom Kelly who had once been the middleweight champion of America.

Chased out of Chicago, boxers looked for another place to fight. On April 2, Dalton went to Saint Louis to meet a boxer named Fitzwilliams. Dalton was twice the size of his opponent. He was to knock out Fitzwilliams in five rounds using two-ounce gloves or forfeit $100. In the first round Dalton pounded Fitzwilliams and put him down three times. In the second he caught him with a hard right hand to the jaw. Fitzwilliams went down but pulled himself to his feet. As he began to resume fighting Fitzwilliams gave his best impression of a soccer player by falling to the ground and rolling around screaming that his ankle had been broken. A doctor was called and Fitzwilliams was carried off on a stretcher, ending the match.[349]

Back to Saint Louis Where Jack King Breaks his Arm and Loses to Dalton

Before the boxing ban, Chicago had hosted important Burke-Mitchell and then Burke-Sullivan fights. After the ban, a Dalton-Mitchell match was scheduled to take place in Saint Louis on July 3.[350] In mid-June, Dalton returned to Saint Louis for a fight with Jack King of Pittsburgh. This match was supposed to help Dalton prepare for his match with Mitchell.

Dalton and King fought six rounds at the packed People's Theater for the gate receipts. Tom Kelly was Dalton's second and Bob Farrell worked with King. Old Tom Allen was the referee. King was the aggressor in the fight, and he appeared to be out on his feet when time was called at the end of the third round. However, in the process of beating up the captain, King had broken a bone in his right wrist. Years later, Al Spink wrote that he had attended this match and it had scarcely commenced when King accidentally hit a stage tree and broke his right arm at the wrist. Dalton recovered and from that point forward beat King at will. Tom Allen awarded the decision to Dalton.[351]

In the end, Dalton did not fight Mitchell. Charley was having a bad time of it. In May 1886, he too had lost a good fight to Burke in Chicago, and then on June 11, 1886, he was beaten up by Cardiff in Minneapolis. Mitchell stopped fighting after the Cardiff match and began promoting fighters. He did not fight again for almost eight months. Dalton also left the ring for months after his fight with King in Saint Louis.

Dalton may have stepped out of the boxing ring because he had opened a new saloon at 109 South Halsted Street. This saloon was on the west side of the Chicago River and just south of Monroe Street, but it was a step up from his first saloon. It was important for a sporting personality to be seen at his business place as often as possible, and this put a crimp on traveling out of town.

Unfortunately for Dalton, the general crackdown by Chicago authorities continued into 1887. Organizations such as the Citizens' League pressed the mayor and police department to strictly enforce the liquor laws. On the evening of May 3, 1887, the police raided a large number of saloons.

On the west side, 109 South Halsted was among eight places closed.³⁵² Dalton's liquor license was revoked for a second time a few days later.³⁵³ A month later Dalton's bartender, John Smith, was arrested for selling liquor without a license.³⁵⁴ With his saloon blacklisted and no license, Dalton left the liquor business. From 1888 through 1900 he gave his employment as "engineer."

In late 1887, a Dalton-Cardiff match was scheduled to take place in Milwaukee. Apparently Cardiff thought that this would be a step down for him. He was trying to arrange a fight with Jake Kilrain. Sullivan had broken his arm hitting Cardiff on his hard head, and Kilrain was claiming that the heavyweight championship belonged to him because Sullivan was not defending his title. Cardiff saw himself poised to be a champion, and a fight with Dalton would not help him reach that objective. The Cardiff-Dalton fight did not take place.

1888 – A Career Almost Over

Dalton turned thirty-five in 1888. He was getting old for a fighter, and there was no real prospect that he could regain the position he held after he had defeated Goode. Nevertheless, he did not stop fighting. On February 1, he fought a hard-drinking brawler named Tom Kinnard, the "Michigan Cyclone," at Milwaukee. The fight was stopped by the police before the end of the second round. The general opinion was that this action saved Dalton from being knocked out.³⁵⁵ Only four years later, Kinnard died from delirium tremens.³⁵⁶

Down and out of the saloon business and the ring, some of Chicago's sports came together to put on a benefit for the captain at Chicago's Academy of Music. Those helping out included

Bradburn, Paddy Carroll, and John McDonongh. Dalton and Bradburn once again sparred for the paying customers.[357]

Dalton faded from history after the Kinnard fight. Shipping traffic in Chicago began to evaporate in the mid-1890s, and there was little use for the tugs and dredges that had played such a prominent role in the 1870s and '80s.

In 1892, Dalton was living on Chicago's west side at 518 West Austin Avenue. His brother Charles moved to Racine, Wisconsin, in about 1900. His brothers Bill and Lawrence Vincent Dalton became stationary engineers and stayed in Chicago. John C. Dalton, who also fought professionally, ran a saloon on Rush Street for many years before returning to work on sailing ships. It seems likely that the captain worked in his brother's place because he had been blacklisted and could not obtain a liquor license. John's son and namesake died during the great Spanish flu epidemic of 1918 and John died in Cleveland in 1931. Jim's brother Andrew also worked as a bartender but died in 1893. Robert became a marine engineer. George Dalton died in an Illinois asylum and Jim's sister Mary seems to have disappeared from the records.

In 1905, Sullivan came to Chicago on a "lecture" tour decrying the use of cigarettes and liquor. He appeared at the Waverly Rink. Among the old-timers appearing were Captain Dalton, Tommy White, and the great world champion bantam Jimmy Barry.[358] They must have had a good laugh hearing Sullivan talk about the evils of a good stiff drink.

In 1921, the famous sports writer Alfred ("Al") Spink met with Dalton and then wrote a syndicated story about their get-together.[359] It seems that the captain had called Al and asked to meet with him. He wanted to introduce Al to a friend identified as "Professor Bonjour" from France. Dalton was working with Professor Bonjour to plan a trip to France where the captain would give boxing exhibitions.

Spink recalled the good old days when Dalton met Sullivan in the summer of 1881. He remembered that Sullivan never trained when he was on tour, and on the night he met Dalton, Sullivan was as "full as a drunken sailor after a ten-day shore leave." Dalton, on the other hand, was in shape and caught Sullivan off guard.

During their meeting in 1921, Dalton told Spink that he was sixty-two years old. He was actually nearly seventy. Spink wrote that he had expected to meet an old man when Dalton phoned for an interview. Instead Dalton entered the room "a fine-looking, upstanding fellow, as fashionably dressed as a real champion, which is going some, with a fine black moustache and dark, curly hair to top it all." During their meeting Dalton assumed a boxing stance and aimed blows at an imaginary opponent, shooting out his left and countering his imaginary opponent with his right. Spink said he was "speedier than some of the young crackerjacks of today."[360]

Captain James H. Dalton died on January 4, 1932. He was seventy-eight years old. He was hit by a "Ford auto" while crossing the street. The cause of death was described on his death certificate as accidental. It was an inglorious way for an important old-time boxer and tug boat captain to die. This man from Cleveland's shanty town entered the ring against some of the best fighters of his time, including Sullivan, Paddy Ryan, Goode, Burke, and Cleary. He survived and prospered at a time when many others failed and then he faded away from the public's memory. He is worth remembering.

The captain's brother Lawrence was the informant for his death certificate. He reported that the captain's occupation was stationary engineer and he had last worked in June 1930. James H. Dalton was buried at Calvary Cemetery at the southeast corner of Evanston, Illinois, January 7, 1932.

Chapter 3
Patrick J. "Reddy" Gallagher (1864-1937)
"An ideal middleweight"

Patrick Joseph "Reddy" Gallagher
(Photo courtesy of Tracy Callis)

Patrick Joseph "Reddy" Gallagher was born February 7, 1864 in Clarksville, Tennessee. His father, John, and mother, Julia, were born in Ireland but lived in Tennessee for five years before his birth. The third of the Gallagher's seven boys, Reddy also had a younger sister, Ellen.

Reddy learned to fight in Cleveland and earned a national reputation as a tough middleweight willing to take on the world's best, including Jack Dempsey, Charlie Mitchell, and the undefeated John Herget. Samuel J. Kelly, a famous Cleveland sports writer and historian, wrote that Gallagher was "an ideal middleweight, strongly built, of medium height, with close matted red hair" and a model boxer. Reddy could "absorb a heavy punch, step about, and deliver a staggering blow when an opening came."[361] He was also a professional wrestler, and after 1902 he played right guard and was the captain of a professional football team.

On October 28, 1894, Reddy married Mary McSheehy in Denver. They were together until his death from pneumonia on November 13, 1937. While he lived in Denver, Reddy was in partnerships with the infamous Bat Masterson and then the slightly less infamous Otto Floto. He was the beloved boxing instructor at the Denver Athletic Club (D.A.C.), owned the Lewiston Hotel, operated a real estate company, and was the sports editor of the *Denver Post* from 1929 until his death in 1937. His remarkable life story has been largely ignored but is retold briefly below.

The Gallagher Family

Reddy's father and mother were Irish immigrants, and his father supervised railroad construction crews. This was not a desk job. A crew supervisor reported to the chief engineer and the general superintendent of the railroad. He was expected to keep grueling schedules and suppress labor trouble. The faster railroad tracks were laid, the less money a fledgling company had to spend and the sooner it could start making money. To do these things a supervisor had to be meaner, stronger, and smarter than the uneducated but wily and poverty-stricken refugees of the Irish potato famine that he supervised.

Reddy's father probably worked for the Memphis, Clarksville, and Louisville Railroad. The M.C.L. was constructed between 1854 and 1861 to create a more direct connection between Louisville and Memphis. Its rail was laid through Clarksville, where Reddy was born, and then across the Cumberland River and southwest to Memphis.[362]

Clarksville was pro-slavery. Soon after the attack on Fort Sumter, it voted 561 to 1 in favor of Tennessee's joining the Confederate States of America.[363] Union forces moving south along the Cumberland captured Clarksville in 1862 and held the city until the end of the war.

Census information indicates that the Gallagher family was in Tennessee from 1859 until at least 1864.[364] His father probably worked for the railroad throughout the war. When the Confederate states lost the war, many southern railroads failed and were sold for a song to northern interests. In July 1866, the M.C.L. defaulted on its bonded indebtedness and by mid-1867 was in receivership. The railroad stopped paying its employees in February 1868. A brief strike followed before the railroad folded.[365]

About the time that the M.C.L. folded, the Gallagher family left Tennessee and moved to Whiskey Island on the northwest side of Cleveland, Ohio. It is likely that the family lived at 143 West River Street in an area west and north of the Cuyahoga River and south of the shipping yards where the cargo from lake steamers was transferred to railroad cars. It appears that Reddy's father first operated a grocery store at 143 West River Street and later opened a saloon and lived at 164 West River Street.[366]

The Gallagher family became part of Cleveland's west side Irish. Reddy's younger siblings, Ellen, Frank, Robert, and John, were all born in Ohio between 1867 and 1874 and the family lived there until at least 1877. Reddy's youngest brother, Charley, was born in Minnesota in 1879. Information published at the time of Reddy's death states that the family lived on a farm in Minnesota, but in 1880 the entire family was living at 2410 South Seventh Street in Minneapolis, which is now north of Interstate 94 and near the University of Minnesota's Medical Center. By 1880 Reddy was already working as a laborer. The family lived in Minnesota for several years before returning to Cleveland in the early 1880s.

Reddy's father was a rough customer. A family friend named Patrick McKenny explained that "one evening a short time ago, the old man told me why he always thought 'Reddy' would be the flower of the flock. When they were born, one by one he held them up by the ear. 'Reddy' was the only kid that didn't squeal."[367]

Reddy's mother also had a tough side. In Cleveland in 1874, when Reddy was ten years old, his parents were both sued because his mother had thrown a piece of coal at a man named James Mullen and broken Mullen's arm. Mullen was awarded $425 in damages.[368]

Not all of the Gallagher boys lifted themselves out of poverty and the dead-end character of Cleveland's west side. Frank was about five years younger than Reddy. For many years he operated a saloon at 30 Main Street in the 8th Ward. He produced a criminal record that was nearly as impressive as Reddy's ring record.[369] Robert Gallagher, who was born in 1871, lived with his brother Frank in the back of Frank's saloon and assisted in some of Frank's criminal activity.[370]

Terry Gallagher operated a saloon at 30 Elm Street—on the corner of Elm and Winslow—in the 8th Ward. His saloon was a dive situated in the middle of a block of other saloons and boarding houses. In 1891, the remaining members of the family that were not living at Frank's were living above Terry's saloon.[371] Charles, the youngest Gallagher brother, also developed a nice little criminal record that began when he was only twelve.[372]

Jack Gallagher was born in 1874 and tried to follow in Reddy's footsteps. He participated in some prizefights without too much success and in the 1890s worked for Reddy at the D.A.C.[373]

Learning his Trade

As a young man Reddy worked for Albert H. Rumsey, a leading Cleveland sporting man.[374] Politically connected with the Democratic Party, Rumsey held an appointment from Ohio's governor as a railroad policeman. He was also the chief shipping master for Cleveland's Lake Carriers Association. He was responsible for preventing theft from the docks, determining which ships landed where, and keeping the Seamen's Union from organizing workers. Rumsey was good at his job.[375] Reddy's father's experience as a railroad crew supervisor would have been valuable to a man like Rumsey, and he probably worked for Rumsey during the shipping season on Lake Erie.

Reddy was a hard-nosed west side kid. He said that he began fighting when he was four years old.[376] Rumsey took him under his wing when Reddy was about eighteen years old and for five years trained him on the docks and at his South Euclid Avenue gymnasium.[377] In the mid-1880s, other sports venues opened where Reddy appeared to box or wrestle.

The Cleveland Athletic Club opened its gym on Frankfort Street in the mid-1880s. Before 1884 that gym had been operated by Duncan Ross. The club had a running track, baths, and other athletic paraphernalia and ran track and field events, wrestling and boxing matches. Reddy would frequently stop at the Frankfort Street gym to punch the bag and spar with other fighters who gathered there.[378]

Another sporting venue known as the White Elephant opened on the fourth of July 1884 east of Cleveland's Central Market. The White Elephant provided billiard rooms, bowling alleys, and a shooting gallery and was another place where prizefights were held. Reddy sometimes appeared at the White Elephant for boxing and wrestling shows.[379] He was one of four advertised contestants during wrestling matches held at the White Elephant in February 1885. The other participants were Lewis Rabshaw, Mervine Thompson, and Dick Pooler.[380] Reddy also appeared at Curry's Hall on Ontario Street not far from Cleveland's Central Police Station.

Reddy was taking on all comers at the Frankfort Street gym almost every night during the latter months of 1884.[381] He began to make the local newspapers during the fall season of 1885 when he challenged Rabshaw, who had several fights under his belt, when he was called out by Reddy.[382] They agreed to a finish fight with bare hands under Queensberry rules for $50 or $100, but no record of their match has been found.[383] Reddy also worked as second during a wrestling match held at Cleveland's Armory in June 1886.[384]

Chapter 3 - Patrick J. "Reddy" Gallagher (1864–1937) "An ideal middleweight"

1886 – "One-Eyed" Jimmy Connolly

Reddy arranged a small glove finish fight with Professor James Connolly of Boston at the end of July 1886. Connolly was known as "One-Eyed" Jimmy and was well-known in boxing circles as freeloader and troublemaker. Connolly claimed to have fought draws with Billy Bradburn and Frank Glover who were both promising Chicago heavyweights. The date for the Gallagher-Connolly match was postponed because of threatened police interference.

Connolly stayed in Cleveland until August 19, when he and Reddy finally met at Yingling's Hall on Clark Avenue. In the fifth round, Connolly caught Reddy with an uppercut that staggered him, but Gallagher came back strong and drove Connolly across the ring punching him at will. At the opening of the sixth round, Gallagher continued to pound Connolly until the police showed up at the door. At that point the professor announced that his hands were shot and Gallagher was too strong for him. He withdrew from the ring and Reddy was awarded the fight.[385]

The police arrested Gallagher and Connolly and charged them with misdemeanors. They were summarily convicted, filed motions for a new trial, and posted $200 appearance bonds; however, when their motions were called, both the pugilists failed to appear. Their bonds were forfeited and that seems to have been the end of the matter.[386]

Rumsey liked what he saw in Gallagher during the Connolly fight. He offered to pay $50 to any man who would arrange a match between Reddy and a fighter from Toronto, Sam Bittle, for $1,000 a side. Both sides were willing to make the match, but the threat of additional criminal prosecution dissuaded the parties from going forward.[387]

George La Blance – the "Marine"

While prize fighting violated Ohio law, sparring exhibitions did not. The line between the two forms of entertainment was indistinct. Local sports decided to put out a feeler to see how far they could go without additional criminal prosecution.

In September, the "Marine" George La Blanche came to Cleveland to spar at the Academy of Music. He was more than seven years older than Reddy and had been fighting professionally for nearly four years. Six months earlier, La Blanche had been in a middleweight title fight with the "Nonpareil" Jack Dempsey at Larchmont, New York. La Blanche lost that contest, but showed well and was regarded the top contender. A few weeks before coming to Cleveland, La Blanche had knocked out Bittle in Denver and sent Bittle into early retirement.

Reddy was about the same size as La Blanche. Advertising for their exhibition said that the contestants would be using big eight-ounce gloves. Some of Reddy's friends tried to dissuade him from appearing. They were afraid that La Blanche would murder Reddy even when sporting the big gloves. Rumors circulated that some real fighting would be permitted by the police and this could be bad news for Reddy. Nevertheless, he wanted the opportunity to be in the ring with an international star like La Blanche. Climbing over the ropes and doing well while facing an opponent of La Blanche's quality could skyrocket a young fighter's career. Every promoter in the country would see the result and think about using the new man to attract a crowd.

The Gallagher-La Blanche show started slow, but then La Blanche began to force the fight. Gallagher retaliated with a hard uppercut that excited the crowd. During their three rounds of sparring, La Blanche landed some heavy body blows, but Reddy too landed some hard shots on La Blanche's nose and neck. The police were present but took no action to stop the affair, which suggests that they had probably been taken care of before the match. It was noted that Reddy had a bad habit of sticking out his tongue while he fought and would likely lose it if the practice was not corrected quickly.[388]

Professor Jimmy Carroll

In mid-August a young baseball player from Cleveland named William Smith was the third baseman for an international league team playing in Toronto. Smith and some friends went swimming near Hanlon's Island, a popular summer resort. Smith stood on the shoulders of a teammate and dived into the water head first. He fractured his second cervical vertebra and died the next day.

Smith had been the sole support for his widowed mother, who was prostrate because of his death. Local sports decided that they would put on a benefit to help support Will's mother. La Blanche agreed to participate. Others who offered their support included Jimmy Carroll, James Brady, and Gallagher.[389]

Smith's benefit was held on September 18 at Cleveland's Academy of Music in an upscale area east of the river. Reddy was matched with Carroll, a lightweight fighter who had been a professional for fourteen years. Carroll was a well-known international fighter, and in years to come he and Reddy would become friends.

Carroll was in Cleveland for two reasons. First, he was on the run after participating in a twenty-two-round private fight with Dick Collier. Their fight had been staged on Coney Island, New York. Collier had emigrated from England in early 1886 and was considered the past middleweight champion of England. He came to the States to make money. During his first year here, Collier was not very successful, but he then found work as the boxing instructor at the Cleveland Athletic Club. Carroll and Collier had taken the express train from New York back to Cleveland to avoid New York legal authorities.[390] In addition, Carroll and La Blanche were beginning to promote a fight that they would have in Saint Paul, Minnesota, at the end of October 1886. With Carroll in town, Gallagher had the unique opportunity to battle a second top-rated middleweight within one week.

There was a good crowd at the Smith benefit. As might have been expected, Carroll demonstrated more ring generalship than Reddy. He was a clever fighter who could glide in the ring. Carroll would later be the manager of Bob Fitzsimmons, a future world middleweight and heavyweight champion. Without regard to the outcome of their match, the exhibition with Carroll was another terrific opportunity for Gallagher.

Legal Problems in Cleveland

There was strong anti-prizefighting prejudice among wealthy and religious elements of Cleveland's society. Part of the problem was that Irishmen dominated the profession, and the Irish were considered threats to good order. The Irish were predominately Roman Catholic, and many thought that the Irish owed their allegiance to the pope rather than to the government of

Chapter 3 - Patrick J. "Reddy" Gallagher (1864–1937) "An ideal middleweight"

the United States. When push came to shove, the white Anglo-Saxon Protestants were sure that the Irish would side with the pope. The Irish were also fond of alcohol, which was considered a corrupting influence, and they were also dirty, poverty stricken, and participants in such gross entertainment as prizefighting. This all needed to be stopped, and the upper class made many attempts to kill fighting.

Ohio's statutes were amended in April 1884 to suppress prizefighting. Under Ohio law any two persons who agreed to willfully fight, box at fisticuffs, or engage in a public sparring or boxing exhibition with or without gloves of any kind, or who aided, assisted, or attended such an exhibition, and any owner or lessee of the property where such a match took place could be fined $250 and imprisoned for from one to three years. An exception in the statute permitted exhibitions like those Reddy engaged in with La Blanche and Carroll. The exception provided that the statute did not apply to sparring in public gymnasiums or athletic clubs. This exception left a lot of room for interpretation and presented great risks for local fighters like Reddy.[391]

Al Rumsey – Reddy's Instructor is Put Down

Reddy had learned to fight from Rumsey, his mentor and first boxing instructor. Rumsey operated his public gymnasium on South Euclid, and it fell under the exception to Ohio's anti-prizefighting law. Rumsey was known as "Professor" because of his work as a boxing instructor. On November 2, Rumsey decided to put on the gloves with his pupil for a four-round, medium-glove fight before a crowd assembled at his own gym.

Gallagher's solid left hand proved too much for his old professor. It took only two and half minutes for Rumsey to decide that he had taken enough punishment. He wasn't the type of person who quit a fight easily, and his early retirement from the fight indicates that Reddy was for real and not a mere exhibition fighter.[392]

A Wrestling Career

Many Cleveland fighters were proficient in both boxing and wrestling. The antecedent for this may have been Duncan Ross, a Cleveland athletic instructor. Ross boxed and wrestled professionally. He styled himself as the "world's greatest athlete." It was a humble appellation, but consistent with his view of himself.

Ross was also a self-appointed talent scout. In 1884, he brought out Mervine Thompson and named him the "Cleveland Thunderbolt." The Thunderbolt was a raw commodity. Ross had watched Thompson performing in a wrestling tournament and promoted him in other tournaments. Later Ross saw greater potential in promoting Thompson as a prizefighter and arranged boxing matches for him in Cleveland areas. By April 1884, the *Police Gazette* reported that Thompson had made $20,000 from his fights in and around Cleveland.[393] Gallagher was another Cleveland man of the same era who boxed and wrestled at the professional level.

Lucien Marc Christol was a long-time professional wrestler who had immigrated to the United States in the early 1870s. He came from France, although other sources claim that he came from Cuba. He was a very good Greco-Roman wrestler who made his home in Cincinnati. The prohibitions against prizefighting did not apply to wrestling. Reddy wanted to make money—a primary preoccupation during his adult life—and in mid-November he put out word that he wanted to wrestle Christol best two out of three falls using collar-and-elbow in jackets, side hold, and Greco-Roman styles.[394]

Christol agreed to the match with the provision that one match would be collar and elbow, a second Greco-Roman, and the final format selected by the contestant who won the toss of a coin.[395] It seems probable that this match did take place, but its outcome does not seem to be reported.

1887 – Pete McCoy and Gallagher

After the matches with Connolly, La Blanche, and Carroll, there were many potential opponents mentioned for Reddy. Ross wanted to back him for a fight with William Evans, a Cleveland fighter. Ross offered a purse of $200 for the match. George Forbes, a local gambler and trotting horse owner, wanted to arrange a fight between Gallagher and Mart Hanley, a pug from Omaha. Pete McCoy, a higher class middleweight who was fighting out of Bridgeport, Connecticut, was another possible opponent.[396]

Reddy fought McCoy on January 25, 1887, at about 6:00 p.m. before an estimated 300 people at Curry's Hall in Cleveland. There were several sports from Pittsburgh who attended the match, and betting was in McCoy's favor at $100 to $40. McCoy weighed in at 177 pounds, much bigger than Gallagher's 153 pounds. Tom Costello, a leading Cleveland sporting promoter, acted as referee for the match. The men fought in a twenty-foot ring, a small ring that gave an advantage to the bigger, more experienced McCoy. After this fight McCoy said that Reddy was the best man he had ever fought.[397]

In the first round McCoy feinted rapidly and forced Reddy to miss several good shots. Then Reddy nearly stopped McCoy, who then regained his composure between rounds. The fighters displayed good footwork and an ability to slip blows until McCoy nearly put Gallagher out in the fourth. In the fifth it became evident that Reddy was younger, stronger, and in better condition than McCoy. He landed a powerful blow to McCoy's jaw and several vicious blows to his ribs. He seemed to have McCoy nearly gone.

In the sixth McCoy rallied, but in the middle of the round the police broke down the back door and arrested the principals, seconds, referee, and every member of the audience they could round up.[398] Among those present at ringside was Judge J.C. Hutchins, who usually presided over Cleveland's police court but was on temporary leave from his assignment, and also a Cleveland police detective named Jack Reeves. Judge Hutchins was the judge who would usually hear cases involving prizefighting misdemeanors.

When the police entered, Detective Reeves suggested to the judge that he should consider himself Reeves' prisoner. As the uniformed officers milled about, Detective Reeves took the judge by the arm and in an official manner escorted him out of the hall. The two men then disappeared around the corner avoiding the paddy wagon being used to transport other patrons to the jail.[399]

The criminal cases of those who were not as fortunate as Reeves and Hutchings were called into Police Court on the morning of January 26. McCoy and his trainer, John Files, pled guilty with the idea that they could pay fines and leave town. To their surprise they were fined and sentenced to thirty days in the workhouse. Both men filed motions for a new trial and posted $500 appearance bonds. Their cases were set to be reheard the following morning. After being released on bond, McCoy and Files left town on the 11:40 p.m. train headed for Philadelphia. Seeing what happened to McCoy and Files, Gallagher pled not guilty, and his case was continued until the following morning.[400]

The next morning when the criminal cases of McCoy and Files were called on their motions for a new trial, neither appeared. Their lawyer, Jay Athey, appeared and submitted his clients' written consents to a trial before a judge alone. He then presented affidavits and witnesses on behalf of his clients. The affidavits provided an idea of what went on during the McCoy-Gallagher match.

F.H. Brunell, sporting editor of the *Plain Dealer*, swore that he had been at the McCoy-Gallagher match and that the two men were simply boxing in a very scientific way. Brunell said that he had witnessed sixty to a hundred sparring exhibitions, and it was plain to him that the McCoy-Gallagher match was not a prizefight. He pointed out that many respectable men of Cleveland had attended the match. He swore that both McCoy and Gallagher acted in a very orderly and gentlemanly fashion. He noted that the contestants were wearing three-and-a-half-ounce gloves, and in prizefights the contestants wore one or one-and-a-half-ounce gloves.

George Forbes, who had offered to be Reddy's backer in an earlier fight, swore that what happened at Curry's Hall was nothing more than a sparring exhibition and certainly not a prizefight. In addition, a prominent Cleveland contractor testified that he was familiar with prizefighting and the McCoy-Gallagher match was not a prizefight.

When the McCoy and Files cases recalled, again they were not present. The judge ordered their bonds forfeited and the original sentences executed. As they had made no headway with the judge on behalf of McCoy or Files and then reiterated Gallagher's demanded for a jury trial. Other pending cases were continued.[401]

Reddy's case was heard by a jury on February 2. He knew that he had a better chance with a jury than with the judge. The prosecution called Sergeant Bradley of Cleveland's police force. Bradley testified that he was inside Curry's for two or three minutes before the match began. He saw chairs arranged around a ring. There were enough chairs for about two hundred men. He watched Gallagher and McCoy enter the ring with their seconds. Gloves were on the floor in the respective corners and he watched the men put on the gloves. He watched the first round of the match and thought the two men were hitting each other in earnest. On cross examination he said that he thought that Curry Hall was not a public gymnasium. He was shown the gloves used during the fight and agreed that they were three-and-a-half-ounce gloves, but thought that they had only slight padding on the hitting surface than lighter gloves.

An Officer Flannigan was also called. He said that he had watched the fight for five full rounds and part of the sixth. Flannigan thought the two men were hitting hard and said that he knew that damage could be done even with big gloves.

Brunell appeared for the defense and said that he could see no one managing the fight. He said the crowd had picked Costello as referee. Other witnesses for the defense included Rumsey, a Mr. Curry, who owned the hall, and Reddy. Curry testified that his hall was used as a public gymnasium. Reddy said that he had been hired by Costello to spar eight rounds with McCoy in a scientific fashion. He said he did not know McCoy and did not have a fight with him. After three hours of deliberation the jury returned a verdict of not guilty. Reddy was acquitted and avoided time in jail.[402] After this trial, the template for avoiding prosecution in Ohio seemed to have been established.

None of the prosecutions seemed to slow down the efforts to book fights for Reddy or to promote him as an important part of Cleveland's sporting community. Two days before the trial, friends of Reddy and Jack Fogarty tried to match the two men for $500 a side for a match to take place somewhere near Pittsburgh.[403] In addition, at the end of February, Reddy was appointed referee for an important wrestling match between Ross and James Faulker.[404]

Dick Collier – Another Boxing Instructor

That Collier and Reddy had both boxed Carroll within a two-day period in September 1886 gave Cleveland sports an opportunity to discuss and evaluate the merits of the two fighters against a common opponent. Soon a dispute arose over whether Collier or Reddy was the superior fighter. Collier was an English-style fighter. During this period it was generally accepted that English fighters used a style that was not generally followed in America.

An English fighter was said to stand stiff-legged in the ring and was expert at throwing crisp punches. He did not generally bend at the knees nor weave from side to side. American fighters stood with one foot advanced in front of the other and slightly bent at the knees.

Local press reported that backers had posted money for a finish fight between Collier and Gallagher for $250 to $500 a side at 155 pounds. The fight was planned to take place in a small, central

Ohio town. It is possible that the two men did fight during the fall of 1886. One of the problems with establishing records for fighters of Gallagher's era is that to avoid criminal prosecution good fights were often held in secluded places, using assumed names and not reported in the popular press.[405] Many fights can be found only in record books that do not rely on source material.

Collier and Gallagher met on March 18 at the Cleveland Athletic Club for a purse of $300.[406] After some cautious sparring in the first round, Reddy rushed Collier and pounded his short ribs with his left hand and followed with a right to Collier's jaw. Collier went down like a log and could not regain his feet. Reddy was declared the winner in just one minute and seven seconds.[407] Any question about Reddy's right-hand power seemed to have been addressed by this result.

The Great Jack Dempsey

After the KO of Collier, interest in Reddy grew exponentially. All sorts of possible fights were quickly mentioned. Arthur Chambers wanted to match his fighter Fred Woods with Reddy. Jack Fogarty was a prospective opponent, but he had injured his hand. He said he had moved Reddy to the top of his list of fighters he wanted to meet. However, Jack Dempsey became Reddy's next opponent.

Before his match with Dempsey, Reddy and Harry Pank purchased the Frankfort Street gymnasium that had been operated by the Cleveland Athletic Club. Pank was a well-known horseman, billiard player, and all-around member of the Cleveland sporting community. He had been Reddy's second during his match with McCoy, which infers a close relationship between the two. Reports said that Pank also acted as Gallagher's trainer.

Chapter 3 - Patrick J. "Reddy" Gallagher (1864–1937) "An ideal middleweight"

There are implications to the purchase of the gymnasium that seem to be reinforced by later events in Reddy's life. Unlike many fighters, Gallagher liked to save and invest the money he made. There are no reports about Reddy leading a dissipated life, giving away money, buying expensive gifts, or wasting his earnings. By purchasing a gymnasium, Reddy and Pank obtained a venue for future fights in Cleveland. This facility allowed Reddy to fight at a place that would fall within the exception to prosecution under Ohio law. In addition, in fights staged at his own gymnasium, Gallagher would not pay rent and thereby increase the net profits divided by the fighters, including himself.

Jack Dempsey in fighting pose
(Photo courtesy of Tracy Callis)

Dempsey and Gallagher met at the Frankfort Street gym for a six-round fight with four-ounce gloves on May 2. Gallagher weighed 155½ pounds. Pank and Thompson were his seconds. Dempsey weighed 151 pounds and was seconded by Denny Costigan and Charles Perkins.

The first round of the Dempsey-Gallagher fight favored Reddy, but Dempsey was smiling at the end. To some it appeared that Dempsey was sizing up his opponent to evaluate his ability. In the second round Dempsey rushed Gallagher and stabbed him repeatedly with his left, driving Reddy back to his own corner. Dempsey started a left toward Gallagher's head just as Reddy was throwing his right, and their arms collided. The radius in Dempsey's left arm was broken about halfway between his elbow and wrist, but he fought on. Gallagher didn't know what had happened, but he forced Dempsey back until the round ended. At the call of time Gallagher was bleeding from his mouth and Dempsey from his nose. The spectators were getting their money's worth.

Dempsey used his right exclusively in the third, fourth, and fifth rounds. The sparring was good and Gallagher took some hard rights to the head. In the sixth, Gallagher landed a hard blow on Dempsey's chin as the fight ended. It was soon disclosed that Dempsey's arm was broken. The match was called a draw, but the injury to Dempsey's arm somewhat diminished the acclaim that Reddy should have earned for his good work against a fighter of Dempsey's caliber.[408]

John L. Sullivan Comes to Town

The big fight news in Cleveland in May was that John L. Sullivan and his combination of prizefighters was coming to town to put on their traveling dog-and-pony show. The other fighters with Sullivan included La Blanche and Carroll, who had both already been in the ring with Reddy. Patsy Kerrigan, Joe Lannon, and Steve Taylor made up the rest of the show that appeared at the Academy of Music. The press speculated that Reddy would spar with both Lannon and La Blanche. However, the only exhibition involving Reddy was with La Blanche.[409] After the show Reddy was invited to travel with Sullivan's combination but declined because he was hoping to arrange a fight with Jack Burke, an English heavyweight who was under the management of Parson Davies.[410] Although he was fighting as a heavyweight, Burke was closer to Reddy's dimensions. It was unlikely that Burke would stoop to fight Reddy without a substantial up-front financial guarantee.

An Unsettled Time

The summer of 1887 was unsettled for Reddy. After only a month as co-owners of the Frankfort Street gym, Pank and Reddy began talking about selling. They may have purchased the place to provide a venue for the Dempsey match or may have decided that neither of them had the time to manage the gym. It was then sold to another local sport named Mike Ryan.[411]

Reddy wanted to fight, and the prospects during the summer weren't good, so he proposed touring in towns surrounding Cleveland.[412] In addition, Costello said that he was trying to arrange a match between Reddy and Peter Nolan of Cincinnati. By early June, Reddy had gone to Pittsburgh where he joined a boxing combination including Jake Kilrain, Charles Mitchell, Patsey Cardiff, O.H. Smith of Iowa, Joe Page of Pittsburgh, and

Will Clarke of Philadelphia. This combination had been on the road for a month visiting such cities as Albany and Baltimore before turning west.[413]

The Kilrain-Mitchell combination was planning a week of appearances in and around Pittsburgh.[414] They had been organized by Richard K. Fox, the publisher of the *Police Gazette,* who was a confirmed hater of Sullivan willing to finance anyone who could bring Sullivan down. Fox was in the process of anointing Kilrain as the world heavyweight champion because Sullivan had broken his arm and was drinking like a fish and not defending his title. Reddy joined their combination in the hope that he could arrange matches with Kilrain, Mitchell, or both and to make money.

During his time with the Kilrain-Mitchell combination, Gallagher developed a friendship with Mitchell that may have prevented Mitchell from being killed about eighteen months later. Their friendship developed from a particular incident.

Gallagher was in Mitchell's dressing room one night in June when the diamond heavyweight championship belt sent by Fox to Kilrain arrived by messenger. Mitchell opened the package, showed it to Reddy, and urged him to try it on. Reddy put on the belt, and just then Kilrain arrived. He was angry when he saw Reddy wearing his belt. Kilrain said that he or Mitchell would fight Reddy any day of the week and put him in his presumptuous place.

Mitchell knew that he had caused this incident but also realized that a unique opportunity existed for him. Gallagher had fought a draw with Dempsey. Mitchell was the subject of constant criticism because he had avoided fighting Dempsey. Mitchell concluded that if he fought and stopped Gallagher that would put an end to the claims that he was afraid or Dempsey. Mitchell proposed a six-round match with two-ounce gloves in Cleveland where a good crowd would be present to watch their local favorite.[415]

There was a substantial shift in the ranks of the heavyweight contenders coincidental with the Mitchell-Gallagher match. At the time that Mitchell had agreed to fight Reddy, Kilrain agreed to fight Jem Smith, the heavyweight champion of England. Kilrain had been anointed by Fox as the heavyweight champion of the United States. If he defeated Smith he could claim to be heavyweight champion of the world. On the other hand, Mitchell, in defeating Gallagher, could only claim that he could handle the fighter who had fought a draw with Dempsey. In this way Kilrain was pushed forward as a heavyweight while Mitchell dropped back and was left to hope that Smith could whip Kilrain and thereby recast all the contenders. Reddy was only a pawn in this chess match—unless he beat Mitchell.

Mitchell and Reddy Meet

Word came from Pittsburgh that Mitchell and Gallagher would fight.[416] There were estimates that as many as 20,000 people would attend the match if it was held on Long Island.[417] In the end the match was held at the Cleveland Athletic Club's gymnasium before about one hundred high-paying customers.

Mitchell outweighed Reddy by twenty pounds at the time of the fight. Kilrain was in Mitchell's corner as his second. The men fought for a purse that was divided 75/25. Accounts of the match are not consistent, but agree on the outcome. The spectators were on their feet throughout the fight. When after six rounds the referee awarded the fight to Mitchell, his decision was met with "indignant and vociferous opposition."[418] Six months after this fight Mitchell fought a thirty-nine-round draw with Sullivan in France.

All but one account of the match agree that there were no knockdowns and that both fighters took hard blows from his opponent.[419] Gallagher was the aggressor in the first round and hit Mitchell hard several times. Mitchell's cleverness was apparent. He kept his left at play—not heavily, but frequently—in Reddy's face and on his ribs. Reddy opened the second with a left to Mitchell's chin, got a heavy left to the eye in return, and then caught Mitchell hard on the mouth with a left. After that exchange Reddy was on the defensive, but in the fourth he decidedly had the best of the fight. In the last two rounds Reddy was not only on the defensive, but tried to keep away from Mitchell so that he could not be hit. At the end Reddy's left eye was closed and his right was clotted with blood.[420] Mitchell was not marked but later claimed that he had broken his little finger and his right hand had swollen so much that he was unable to put on a boxing glove.[421]

This last claim helped give the appearance that while Dempsey managed only a draw with Gallagher after he broke his arm, Mitchell had defeated Gallagher with a broken hand. Reddy described Mitchell as a dirty fighter who would resort to every trick in the book. He said that before their fight Mitchell had rubbed his skin with a preparation to make him slick, put resin on his gloves, and soaked his gloves in water just before the fight began.[422]

After the fight there were many articles about who Reddy would fight next. He wanted to fight Burke, but Burke was leaving the states for Australia.[423] Nolan was again mentioned as a possible opponent, and Johnny Regan, who was being backed by East Coast money, was another possibility.[424] If Reddy could not line up Burke, then he favored a match with an English middleweight named Ben Davis.

While waiting for his next match, Reddy, Thompson, Mark Lamb, and Al Woods left Cleveland on September 4 for a tour of "All Stars" under E. Humphrey that took them to Akron, Kansas City, and then other cities in Ohio, Kentucky, and Indiana.[425] They appeared in Newark, Ohio, on September 12 and 13 at the Opera House.[426] After their tour Gallagher returned to Cleveland and, in early November 1887, gave a four-round exhibition with Collier at the Academy of Music.[427]

Costello and Reddy End Up at Odds

After his Dempsey and Mitchell matches, it became more difficult for Reddy to arrange matches with good fighters. Men ranked near the top of their weight classes saw Reddy as a risk, and less experienced fighters knew that their ring records would probably suffer if they fought Reddy.

In late 1887, Costello began trying to arrange fights for Reddy. There is no evidence that Reddy asked Costello to act on his behalf. Costello proposed fights with Bittle, La Blanche, McCoy, Danny Kelleher, Dominick McCaffrey, and Con Riley, a lesser-known middleweight from Middletown, Ohio.[428]

Short on prizefights, Gallagher turned to wrestling to make money. On November 12 he wrestled a famous Japanese wrestler, Matsada Sorakicki, and won $50 by lasting fifteen minutes without being pinned.[429] Then on November 17 he lost to a professional wrestler from Detroit, Michigan, William B. Johnson, who was touring under William Muldoon's management. The Gallagher-Johnson match was for the best two-out-of-three falls using different styles popular at the time: collar-and-elbow in jackets, catch-as-catch-can, and Greco-Roman. Reddy pinned Johnson in catch-as-catch-can but lost the two other matches and said he was giving up on wrestling.[430]

The press reported that Costello had arranged a Gallagher-Riley match to be staged in Dayton, Ohio, on December 16. Other fights Costello proposed were with Jim Fell of Grand Rapids on December 29 and Jack Fogarty of Philadelphia on January 8, 1888. The Riley fight was to be a six-round match with big gloves.[431]

Riley was a 170-plus-pound fighter. Reddy, however, did not appear for the match and Thompson was substituted. The upshot of all of this was that Reddy declared that Costello had never been authorized to arrange any fights on his behalf. Costello said that he was dropping Gallagher and cancelling the Fell and Fogarty fights.

Costello's practice was to claim 50 percent of his fighters' winnings as compensation for his managerial services. Reddy and Costello probably argued about money. Reddy had a high regard for the money he made fighting and was not inclined to share it with a promoter. Whatever happened, the other fights Costello arranged were called off.[432]

Finally Reddy arranged a fight with Bittle. Probably because Reddy's conflict with Costello had put him on the outs with Cleveland sports, Gus Wilson, a horseman, took Reddy under his wing and Reddy trained for the Bittle fight at Wilson's gymnasium in Canton.[433]

Back in the ring and boxing again, Reddy was on familiar territory. His match with Bittle took place at the new Cleveland Athletic Club gym before about fifty spectators who paid $5s each to watch. Gallagher weight 153 pounds for the match. Bittle was heavier, weighing in at 167 pounds, and looked fat. Three-ounce gloves were used and it went the full six rounds. Police surrounded the crowd and everyone thought arrests were imminent, but the fight was allowed to go forward.

Gallagher knocked Bittle down several times in each round and Bittle went down another dozen times to avoid punishment. He seemed to pretend to slip, which irritated the crowd. Reddy drew first blood in the second round and had Bittle collapsing on the ropes at the end of that round. Bittle's only hard blow during the match was a hard right to Reddy's jaw at the close of the fifth round. The referee gave the fight to Reddy as the clear winner.[434]

1888 – The Parson Davies' Specialty Company

In early 1888, Charles E. "Parson" Davies of Chicago was the leading boxing and wrestling promoter in the United States. Chicago authorities had cracked down on boxing and chased fighters out of town. On January 18, Davies and many other sports had traveled to North Judson, Indiana, to see a short match between Billy Myer and Harry Gilmore with Myer knocking out Gilmore in the first round. Three nights later Davies had refereed a match between Tommy Warren and Arthur Majesty in Peoria, Illinois, but about the only thing he could promote in Chicago was wrestling.

Davies decided to create the Parson Davies' Specialty Company to take Evan "the Strangler" Lewis and Bill Muldoon on the road as the stars of his new company. He planned to take the company to Milwaukee, return to Chicago for a week at the Casino Theater, and then work east through Chicago, Detroit, Pittsburgh, Buffalo, and other large cities. Davies offered $50 to any man who could stand before Lewis for fifteen minutes in catch-as-catch-can style and $100 to any man who could throw Lewis within the allotted time. Davies made the same offer for Muldoon in the Greco-Roman style. Davies also forwarded a challenge to Jack Wannop, an English catch-as-catch-can wrestling champion, on behalf of Lewis.[435]

After the specialty company's opening in Milwaukee, Davies added fighters to the company. On February 11, Gallagher arrived in Chicago. He was described as being every inch a fighter but a man of gentlemanly manners on his way to the top of the middleweight ranks. Then Davies added Martin Snee, a lightweight fighter born in New York in 1865 and fighting out of Boston. Snee had come west looking for a match with Billy Myer.

After their fight in North Judson, Myer and Gilmore had been traveling around northern Illinois putting on boxing shows in places like Streator and LaSalle. Davies hired both of them to appear along with Gallagher and Snee as part of a variety show called "Gymnasium Scenes," which was scheduled for a one-week run in Chicago. On the evening of February 13, the specialty company appeared at the Casino Theater in Chicago. Each of the fighters signed for twenty weeks under Davies' management. Reddy appeared with Gilmore in Chicago the day after he signed with Davies.[436] Some of the places the combination appeared included Detroit on February 17, where Reddy sparred three rounds with John Collins.[437] On March 21, the combination was in Buffalo and in Williamsburg, Virginia, on March 28.[438]

Davies never left his athletes idle, and they probably appeared in many cities in between. In mid-March Reddy spent a week in Cleveland. The Specialty Company was in Rochester, New York, and that city did not allow boxing, so Reddy was out of work for a week. When visited by the Cleveland press, Reddy appeared to be out of shape and told the press that traveling from place to place and meeting all comers whether he wanted to or not did not agree with him.[439]

Left to right – Link Pope, Billy Myer, and Sam Myer

During this trip Reddy developed a friendship with Muldoon, and their friendship continued throughout their lives. In addition, Reddy met Otto Floto, who later played important roles in his life. Floto was a native of Cincinnati and a year older than Reddy. He had been educated by Jesuits. In early 1888, Floto was working for Davies and traveled with the combination during at least part of its tour while Davies was taking care of other business.[440]

Personal Loss and a Cancelled Fight

As the bright lights of the specialty company faded, Reddy returned to Cleveland and scheduled a six-round match with Pete Mannen.[441] On May 22, just a few days before that match, Reddy's mother died of bronchitis at the age of fifty-three. Reddy asked Mannen to postpone their meeting for two weeks.[442] Their match was never rescheduled.

With the death of his mother, Reddy's ties to Cleveland were diminished. His brothers were in constant legal trouble. He had sold his interest in the Frankfort Street gymnasium. He had been on the road with some of the biggest fighters and wrestlers of his era. He had cut his ties with Costello, but also worked with some of the top entertainment promoters, including Davies and Floto.

After his mother's death in May 1888 Reddy hung around Cleveland very little. That summer he had a swimming contest with his old trainer Pank and won. He talked about making a match with Dan Daly of Saint Louis and rescheduling the match with Mannen, but none of that panned out.[443]

In early August, Reddy received a letter from Bat Masterson, who was operating Denver's Cribb Club. Masterson wanted Reddy to come to Denver to meet "Denver" Ed Smith or an English middleweight named Jack McGee for a purse of $500.

Gallagher was willing to go to Denver if Masterson would pay his expenses. He said that he would meet either Smith or McGee.[444] After settling on Smith as the opponent, Masterson wrote that the match was off because Smith weighed 180 pounds and couldn't get down to the required weight.[445] In addition to the overture from Denver, Reddy offered to go to Boston to fight an English middleweight named Toff Wall who had come to America looking for a fight with Dempsey.[446]

Taming Saint Louis – Zachritz, McManus, and Daly

Reddy went west but only as far as Saint Louis. In Saint Louis there were several fighters whom he hadn't fought but were credible opponents. One of the possible opponents was Daly.[447] He was the oldest of the three fighting Dalys of Saint Louis. A year earlier, Daly had defeated Ed Kelly in a brutal sixty-three-round fight and then Daly had retired as a prizefighter.

In late September, Reddy appeared at the London Theater in Saint Louis for several days, offering to stop any local middleweight who would fight him in four rounds or forfeit $50. Reddy indicated that his favored opponent was Daly. Irritated by Reddy's challenge on the Daly family's home turf, Charley Daly, Dan's younger brother, appeared one evening with $100 and offered to forfeit it if any middleweight in the country could stop Dan in six rounds.[448]

Reddy managed to arrange a fight with an experienced local fighter named Will Zachritz. They fought at the London Theater on September 28 with Kelly acting as referee. Gallagher was knocking Zachritz all over the place, but at the end of the third round, Zachritz's second claimed that he had been fouled. Kelly allowed the claim and awarded the fight and $50 to Zachritz. With that Reddy punched Kelly and the two then participated in an un-judged real fight.[449]

Soon after the Zachritz match, Reddy arranged a match with another Saint Louis middleweight, Hugh McManus, who was backed by Ed Kelly.[450] McManus was probably proposed to give Reddy a chance to recover some of the money he had been cheated out of in the Zachritz fight. The fight took place at the London Theater, and Reddy pounded McManus from start to finish. In the second round he knocked McManus down with a hard right to the ear. In the fourth round a smash to McManus' face cut him open under his left eye. This time Reddy was awarded the fight.[451] Reddy still wanted a fight with Daly primarily because Daly had a national reputation and called himself the middleweight champion of the West. Reddy wanted to add that title to his own resume.

While waiting for Daly to agree, Reddy returned to Cleveland and opened a saloon on the corner of Erie and Lake streets on the east side of the river at a place formerly called Schuthelm's Old Garden. This was the second time that Reddy invested his money in a business. The first investment in the Frankfort Street gymnasium had lasted only about a month, and a saloon looked like a good investment.

Reddy finally arranged a match with Daly.[452] He left Cleveland on the morning of December 21 and arrived in Saint Louis the next morning. Their six-round fight was supposed to take place at the Masonic Hall as part of a benefit for Daly. The press said that Reddy was planning to go west after the holidays to do some fighting in California.[453] Reddy also planned to return to Saint Louis to spar with the lightweight champion Jack McAuliffe, but that match was never arranged.[454]

The biggest show planned for Saint Louis before the end of 1888 was supposed to be an exhibition between Kilrain and Mitchell under the management of Davies, who was taking those two heavyweights on the road as part of a build up to a world heavyweight championship bout between Kilrain and Sullivan. On the night of the Daly-Gallagher fight, Kilrain and Mitchell were in Chicago. Their trip was to take them to Fort Wayne, Cleveland, Columbus, and then Saint Louis at year end. Saint Louis authorities later prevented the Kilrain-Mitchell show, but the Daly-Gallagher benefit was not prevented, and Reddy showed that he was clearly the superior fighter in his match with Daly although no decision was rendered.[455]

Saving Charlie Mitchell's Bacon

Reddy returned to Cleveland after the Daly benefit, and in a short time Davies, Mitchell, and Kilrain arrived to appear at the Academy of Music. Gallagher knew these men. He had been with the Mitchell and Kilrain show in 1887, met Mitchell in the ring, and worked for Davies.

Neither Mitchell nor Kilrain was popular with the American public. Kilrain had designated the heavyweight champion, but had never defeated Sullivan. In the public's opinion there was a cloud over Kilrain's title. Sullivan had failed to knock out Mitchell and was consequently in semi-disgrace. However, the issue for Kilrain was not whether Sullivan had lost face, but whether Kilrain would be accepted as champion without defeating Sullivan. Mitchell was a loud-mouthed Englishman who had done everything to avoid fighting Dempsey. He was always on the wrong side of American public opinion.

On December 26, Davies, Kilrain, and Mitchell were in Cleveland. Rotten eggs were thrown at Kilrain and Mitchell when they appeared on stage. Davies stepped forward and tried to calm the audience, but was greeted with howls and hisses. Only the presence of the police prevented a riot. After their exhibition, Mitchell and Kilrain went to the Kennard House barroom with a number of friends, including Reddy.

The Kennard House was on Saint Clair Street on the east side of the river at the southwest corner of west Sixth Street not far from Cleveland's Union Depot. Five stories high, the Kennard was the home for sportsmen visiting Cleveland. It ran south along Bank Street to the Academy of Music where Kilrain and Mitchell had just appeared. A favorite feature of the Kennard was the Alhambra room with a Moorish motif and several multisided fountains with pools full of goldfish.[456]

When they arrived, Costello was in the bar with a gang of Sullivan supporters. Mitchell ordered wine for everyone in his group including Kilrain, Reddy, Davies, and two English sprinters who were competing in international track-and-field events. An English middleweight named Hugh Burns was in the bar with Costello's crowd. Mitchell knew Burns and invited him to join the festivities.

Burns was not in a friendly mood and swore at Mitchell, threatening to slug him. Burns then walked over to Mitchell and took a swipe at him as Mitchell ducked. One of the men in Mitchell's party told him that Burns was packing heat and would shoot him given a chance. Mitchell began backing away and accidentally stepped into one of the fountains in the center of the room, spraining his right hand. As Mitchell fled upstairs, Burns pursued him. Meanwhile Reddy held Costello in a chair to prevent him from interfering and then went after Burns to bring him back downstairs.

On the way back to the bar Gallagher and Burns got into a hot fight on the stairway. A call went up saying that the police were there. Costello and his crowd quickly disappeared. Because Mitchell had injured his hand, Reddy took his place and appeared with Kilrain at the show in Cleveland on December 27, 1888. Later Costello said, "When Americans go to England they get no show, and I believe in serving them as they serve us. These men, Mitchell and Kilrain, are not gentlemen and ought not to have been allowed to give an exhibition of sparring here at all, but as long as the police did not interfere I wanted revenge and that is the way I got it. We drove those fellows to their rooms and made them run like whiteheads."[457] Gallagher set himself against many of Cleveland's local sports by siding with Davies, Kilrain, and Mitchell during this incident, and this was the second time he had crossed Costello.

1889 – A Time for Changes

Reddy began the year with a wrestling match at the Academy of Music on January 2, 1889. His opponent was the professional wrestler Captain J.W. Graham. In December, just before he left for the Daly benefit in Saint Louis, Reddy acted as the referee when Graham wrestled Major John McGuire at the Academy of Music. Graham was known as the horseback wrestler. He favored an odd style where each man appeared on the back of equal-sized bareback horses and tried to unhorse the other. If no man hit the ground within the first two hours then the men would dismount and wrestle on the ground.[458]

With no pugilistic opponents at hand, Reddy agreed to another wrestling match with Johnson, who had taken him in their November 1887 match. This second match took place on February 21, and Reddy won $25 when Johnson was unable to gain a fall within fifteen minutes.[459]

The problem for Reddy was that his career was bogged down. He did not work with a promoter or manager. He was not fighting for a club such as those that were popular in New York, New Orleans, and San Francisco. He had the credentials of a top middleweight contender but was stuck in the mud. A fighter named John Herget of California and popularly known as Young Mitchell was rapidly moving up the middleweight ranks. Dempsey and La Blanche were two others who could claim to be the best in their class. Reddy finally wrote to San Francisco's California Athletic Club offering to meet any middleweight of that club's choosing.

In mid-March the C.A.C.'s president, L.R. Fulda, responded to Gallagher's letter asking for a detailed record of his work in the ring and his measurements. Reddy complied with Fulda's request.[460] He wanted a match with Young Mitchell but learned that the C.A.C. wanted him to meet La Blanche on May 28 for a purse of $1,500 with the fighters to weigh less than 158 pounds. Reddy responded that he could not get in shape for a match with La Blanche and make it to California by the date specified. Carroll was then substituted as La Blanche's opponent.[461] Undeterred by Reddy's response, the C.A.C. offered him a salary of $100 a month and fare to and from California if he would come there to prepare to fight a leading middleweight.[462]

For a second time Reddy's departure for California was delayed. After purchasing his saloon Reddy had hired a young woman named Clara ("Carrie") Tripp Brown to work as his housekeeper. Carrie was born in Warrensburg, New York, but grew up on the west side of Cleveland where she lived with her father and younger brother Nathan. At sixteen Carrie married a saloon keeper named Harry Brown. He left her destitute and Reddy then gave her work as his housekeeper. This was probably a platonic and charitable act on Reddy's part. Nevertheless, Carrie was despondent and poisoned herself with an arsenic-based product called "Rough On Rats."[463] Reddy summoned a doctor to try to save Carrie but his efforts proved futile and she died.

A Long Layoff

After Carrie's death a long layoff from the ring ensued. The C.A.C. continued to correspond proposing various fights. In July it appeared that he would be matched with a middleweight from Australia named Billy McCarthy, but Gallagher was again unwilling to accept the money offered. A match in Boston with Joe Lannon was proposed and a fight with Reagan was another possibility.[464] For more than a year Gallagher did not fight or wrestle.

1890 – Back to the Ring—Almost

After trying for about a year to arrange a match, Reddy and the C.A.C. finally reached an agreement. The club proposed that he meet McCarthy for a purse of $1,600 with $1,300 to the winner and $300 to the loser. He was unwilling and countered that he would fight for a purse of $1,800 with $1,500 to the winner and $300 the loser. The club agreed and the fight was made.[465]

This time Reddy started west quickly. As a tune up he appeared at a benefit given at the Detroit Rink on March 31. The benefit was given for James Burns, who was called the middleweight champion of Michigan.[466] Reddy then continued to Chicago where he acted as a second for James Dohony in a fight with Abe Cougle. Their match was held near Shelby, Indiana.[467] Reddy arrived in California on April 14. He went to the C.A.C. and then to Barney Farley's place where he was expected to train for his fight. Reddy also visited Carroll, who was described as "a particular friend."[468]

When he first arrived in California, Reddy was recovering from an illness he had picked up in Cleveland, but it was soon discovered that he had contracted malaria.[469] He could not participate in the scheduled match. As a result the California press began to claim that he was unreliable and lacked "pluck."

While he was in California, Bob Fitzsimmons arrived from Australia, and Reddy was one of the first people to meet him. Fitz was wearing a little cap, and Reddy remembered that Fitz's trousers touched only the top of his boots. Fitz was knock-kneed and told Reddy that he got that way by shoeing horses as a child before his bones had fully grown. Gallagher took Fitz to see Farley, who couldn't believe that Fitz was a real fighter. That opinion was soon put to rest.[470] Reddy left California on about May 29, 1890, headed back to Cleveland.[471]

There is no question that Reddy was riding a bad streak. On his way back to Cleveland he stopped in Denver. Years later he explained that when he passed through Denver in the spring of 1890, he had been on an eastbound train from California where

Chapter 3 - Patrick J. "Reddy" Gallagher (1864–1937) "An ideal middleweight"

he had tried unsuccessfully to secure a match with Dempsey. When the train stopped in Denver, he decided to stretch his "train legs" and began walking around the city.

Denver's Union Depot was located at Seventeenth and Wynkoop streets in the lower downtown portion of the city. Between the depot and Larimer Street where he stopped, there was a commercial area known as the "streets of doom" where a man might get mugged by the thugs and criminals who controlled the area. One of the infamous dives there was the Tivoli Club operated by Soapy Smith. Other joints included the Chicken Coop, Ed's Arcade, and the Bucket of Blood.

Other parts of Denver featured broad streets with horse-drawn trolleys. The streets were lined with some of the finest buildings in America, including the Masonic Temple, the Palace and Windsor hotels, the Broadway Theater, Tabor's Grand Opera House, the Mining Exchange, and the Denver Athletic Club. Thirty years earlier there had been virtually nothing where the city of Denver stood, and the freshness of the place presented a sharp contrast to Cleveland.

During his walk Reddy visited Johnny W. Murphy's place at 1617 Larimer called "Murphy's Exchange." Murphy's was also known as the "slaughterhouse." On the floor above Murphy's bar a fellow named Gavin ran a house of prostitution. Murphy's had been a favorite place for such wild-west personalities as Bat Masterson and Doc Holliday.[472]

Reddy's visit to Murphy's did not happen by chance. Murphy's was a popular hangout for sports from all over the country. The police were frequently called to Murphy's to clean up the bodies, and in 1892, a prizefighter, John Clow, was killed at Murphy's place by a degenerate son of a former Kansas governor.

Reddy met Murphy, and the two men liked one another. Murphy, a retired prizefighter, had also fought McCoy, but the Murphy-McCoy match took place four years before the Gallagher-McCoy match.

Murphy, who was born in New York about 1848 of German parents, came to Colorado in the 1870s. During his ring career he had defeated Harry Webb, James Kain, Bryan Campbell, McCoy, and had challenged Dominick McCaffrey but had never achieved a national reputation.[473] There are claims that Murphy matched Reddy in a four-round exhibition with Jack Burke in an old hall in California.[474] This probably did not happen because Burke left America in mid-1887 and went to Australia before returning to England. He never returned to the States and could not have had a match with Reddy after Murphy and Reddy met in the summer of 1890.

Reddy decided that he liked Murphy and he also liked Denver. He later claimed that he gave up his train ticket and never went back to Cleveland, but that appears to be an exaggeration.[475]

1890 – Billy Brennan Killed and Reddy Gallagher Arrested

In June 1890, the *Chicago Tribune* reported that Davies was planning a huge night of entertainment on July 3 that would include a match between Frank Garrard and Billy Brennan and another match between Jack Ashton and Frank Glover.[476] Davies invited Dempsey to act as referee for the Ashton-Glover fight. Dempsey was on his own tour in the East with shows planned in Saint Louis and Cleveland among others. When Gallagher learned that Dempsey would be in Chicago, he went there to challenge Dempsey. Davies had probably arranged for Dempsey to referee and told Gallagher to be at the contest to challenge

Dempsey, and Davies would have Reddy referee the Garrard-Brennan match so that Reddy would earn some money for his trouble. All of this planning helped create talk about an event and increased public interest.

The entertainment on July 3 ended abruptly with the death of Brennan. The Garrard-Brennan match was supposed to be a five-round contest with four-ounce gloves. Refereeing this match gave Reddy a chance to make the money to finance his trip. Sailor Brown was one of the seconds for Brennan, and Harry Gilmore was a second for Garrard.[477]

There was bad blood between Brennan and Garrard because Brennan had half-killed Tommy White in an earlier fight on May 21 and Garrard was a close friend of White.[478] White and Garrard had for several years been part of a stable of young fighters from Chicago's north side who were pupils of Gilmore and trained together at McGurn's court at 206 Division Street near Goose Island. Brennan was not part of that group but fought at other gyms in Chicago.

Brennan was no match for Garrard. In the second round Garrard rushed him, hitting him at will. Brennan grabbed Garrard's legs and threw him heavily. No foul was allowed by Gallagher. In the fourth round Brennan came to scratch quickly, but Garrard continued to pound him around the ring. Brennan then rushed Garrard in an attempt to hold on and avoid punishment. Garrard tried to shake Brennan off and in that effort the two fell off balance, and Brennan's head hit the floor. He did not move a muscle and was counted out.[479]

Brennan was carried from the ring and placed on a rug in a parlor off the main room where the fights were being held. Davies summoned Dr. Francis R. Sherwood, and when he arrived,

Brennan was ashen with heavy, labored breathing. The doctor gave Brennan injections of brandy and administered aromatic spirits of ammonia without results. Strong coffee was also administered.

While Brennan was dying, preliminary matches continued, and then the match officials learned that Brennan was dead and the proceedings stopped. The crowd quietly left the building. Garrard and Brown were placed under arrest, and the police stood guard outside the room where Brennan's body was located. Patrick Carroll, who had acted as master of ceremonies, Gilmore, and the wrestler Jack McInerney were all locked up. Captain Lewis of the Chicago police placed Davies under nominal arrest. Dempsey left town quickly and went to Saint Louis. Reddy, however, stayed to face the music.

Frank Garrard
(Photo courtesy of Tracy Callis)

Brennan's body was taken to an undertaker and an autopsy was performed. He had suffered a brain hemorrhage, and an inquest was scheduled. Garrard was locked up at the Harrison Street Station. A coroner's jury was convened on July 5 and concluded that Brennan's death was accidental not intentional.

Davies occupied the front seat at the inquest. He was described as having "a sad smile of resignation" and told reporters that he would consider himself under arrest even though he had not been charged with anything. Gallagher and Carroll at first refused to testify, but after Davies told of the events leading to Brennan's death, they both changed their stance and confirmed Davies' explanation. The autopsy suggested that Brennan had preexisting injuries that contributed to his death. All the defendants were discharged and the charges dropped.[480]

Leaving Cleveland for Good

Reddy had been through a rough period. His mother had died at the age of fifty-three. His housekeeper had committed suicide. He had contracted malaria and that knocked him out of his most important fight ever. Then he was referee for a fight where a contestant was killed. Reddy limped back to Cleveland.

In late July, Dempsey came to the Academy of Music in Cleveland as part of his tour. It may be that Reddy was still following Dempsey to try to arrange a match. He was the master of ceremonies at Dempsey's event in Cleveland. About a month later Gallagher sold his saloon and moved permanently to Denver, leaving the first twenty-six years of his life and the rest of his family behind.[481]

Denver and a New Beginning

Reddy was in Denver by early October when another match with the wrestler Sorakichi was arranged. Their match took place in Denver's Coliseum before 1,500 customers and was advertized as involving "bitter feelings." Reddy won the toss, which allowed him to pick the style for the first bout. He chose collar-and-elbow. He won by a submission in fifteen minutes forty-five seconds. Sorakichi then chose catch-as-catch-can for the next bout. Reddy won applause from the crowd for his clever defensive wrestling. After seventeen minutes he gave this bout to Sorakichi. Because Reddy had won his fall in less time than Sorakichi, he had the right to choose the style for the third bout. Reddy elected collar-and-elbow and floored his opponent in just over five minutes thereby winning the match. Depending on the newspaper account, Reddy won between $1,000 and $3,000. Either amount provided him a terrific stake to start a new life in Denver.[482]

Reddy was soon challenged to another wrestling match. This time his antagonist was W.H. Quinn, who styled himself the champion of the Pacific Coast. Quinn was willing to wrestle for $350 with the terms being that he would have to throw Gallagher three times in less than an hour in the collar-and-elbow format.[483] If this match took place, the result has not been located.

Fight Possibilities

In late 1890s, the chances for good fights seemed to improve. In December the C.A.C. was discussing the possibility of matching Reddy with either Reagan or Young Mitchell, but it was concerned because in the club's opinion Reddy had proved "unreliable" in the past.[484]

In mid-February, Jim Hall, another Australia middleweight, arrived at San Francisco. Hall had whipped Fitz back in kangaroo land and looked like a coming champion. He was managed by an Australia gambler, Joe Harris. In the fight business, making good money required good opponents, and Harris tried to arrange a Gallagher-Hall match. If Hall and Gallagher were not matched, then there was a possibility that a promoter named Louis Livingston would back Gallagher for $5,000 and a match with Fitz.[485] Moreover, the C.A.C. was reportedly thinking of a Gallagher-Dempsey match for a purse of $5,000, and Masterson was assuring the California clubs that Reddy was willing to participate.[486]

Matches were not arranged with Hall, Fitzsimmons, or Dempsey, but by June the Occidental Club at San Francisco matched Reddy with Young Mitchell for a purse of $5,000.[487] Tom O'Rourke, a leading promoter in New York, claimed that he had secured Mitchell to fight Reddy with Masterson as Reddy's backer.[488] The Gallagher- Mitchell match was to take place on September 23, and in early August Reddy went to California to train under Martin Murphy.[489]

Years later a story circulated about how Masterson got involved in the Gallagher-Mitchell fight. Masterson was handling both Billy Woods and Reddy. Masterson wanted Gallagher and Woods to have a trial fight in private so that he could personally appraise their relative merits. Gallagher knocked out Woods. Masterson then matched Woods to fight Jack Davis and Gallagher to fight Young Mitchell. Based on the Woods-Gallagher trial fight,

Masterson bet on Davis and Gallagher. Woods then knocked out Davis and the Gallagher-Mitchell fight followed.[490]

1891 – Young Mitchell Wins

The match with Young Mitchell took place at the Occidental Club and was the biggest prizefight of Gallagher's career. The $5,000 purse offered included $750 to the loser. Many of the leading figures in prizefighting were present. Mitchell's seconds were Dempsey and Sam Fitzpatrick, who was Peter Jackson's trainer. Gallagher's seconds were Masterson and Carroll. The great heavyweight Peter Jackson was the referee.

The match began just before 9:00 p.m. and lasted thirteen rounds. Gallagher had the upper hand through the first eight rounds of the fight. He hit Mitchell freely with his left on the head and body. Through these rounds Reddy took the middle of the ring and Mitchell moved around him looking for an opening. Each time Mitchell came forward he caught hard left hands. After the fight Mitchell admitted that Reddy gave him the hardest fight he ever had. He said that Reddy had the best left hand he ever encountered and had lost only because he lacked experience. Mitchell further said that Reddy could whip either La Blanche or Reagan.[491]

From the eighth to the twelfth round the fight was about even, but Mitchell appeared to be the more confident fighter and Reddy was bleeding freely from his eye. As the thirteenth round started, Reddy appeared to be a little dazed but landed two straight lefts on Mitchell's chin. Then it happened. Mitchell came back with a hard right to Gallagher's neck and a left to his chin. Gallagher reeled and went down on his side. He made an effort to rise, but fell back and was counted out.

Reddy left for Denver on September 27, 1891.[492] This ended Reddy's best chance to become the top middleweight contender for the title.

A Complicated Subplot and Romance

While Reddy was in California, he met an actress whose stage name was Florence Chester. At the time they met, Florence was supposedly involved in an affair with Peter Jackson, who had been the referee during the Gallagher-Mitchell match. Miss Chester returned to Denver with Gallagher, but there she fell in love with a cowboy. The story of Chester is complicated and tied into another notorious Denver romantic affair.

Chester claimed to be the sister of an actress whose stage name was Millie Price. Records exist showing that Chester and Price both arrived in New York from Liverpool, England, on September 13, 1888. They had supposedly grown up on the Strand in London, and Price claimed she had been an actress in Europe from the age of six. While playing the part of Rosebud at the Star Theater in Wolverhampton, England, she came to the attention of an American manager named M.B. Leavitt. Leavitt persuaded Price to come to America, and Chester came along with her sister.

By December 2, 1888, Price was appearing at Chicago's Haymarket Theater in "My Aunt Bridget." This job was followed by a nine-month engagement with the producers Koester & Bial and then by an engagement with Hallen & Hart in a play entitled "Later On."[493]

Following a trip back to England, Price returned to the States. Chester and Price then took roles in Frank Dumont's comedy and dance production "Natural Gas" being staged by the promoters Donnelly & Girrard. Chester played Daisy, and Price was a high-kicking dancer in the role of Jimpsy. In 1890, Chester married George Pierce, known by his stage name George "Dutch" Murphy. Murphy was a German dialect comedian and another member of the cast of "Natural Gas."[494]

After its run in Kansas City, "Natural Gas" came to Denver to open at the Tabor Grand Opera House at the corner of Sixteenth and Curtis on New Year's Day 1891. Following morning rehearsal Price met Merrill Clarence Dow, the nineteen-year-old son of C.H. Dow, a wealthy Denver banker who was the president of Denver's Commercial National Bank. The next day, Miss Price and Dow were married by a justice of the peace at Denver's Windsor Hotel at the corner of Larimer and Eighteenth almost next door to the theater.

Price's marriage to Dow became a national scandal. Dow followed Price and the "Natural Gas" company to their appearances in Colorado Springs on January 5, 1891, and then to Pueblo, Colorado. Cut off from financial support by his angry parents, Dow went back to Denver, and "Natural Gas" went on for its scheduled appearance in Salt Lake City and Ogden before the show opened at the Bush Street Theater in San Francisco on January 19.[495]

In 1891, Peter Jackson was the best-known athlete in San Francisco. Jackson also had a reputation for being fond of the ladies. While she was in San Francisco, Chester began an affair with Jackson. English women generally did not share the racial prejudices common among Americans. By June Murphy filed legal proceedings to divorce his wife.[496] He was granted a divorce in New York in October 1892. The respondent named by Murphy was a black minstrel known as John H. Carlton and not Jackson.[497]

Reddy probably knew Chester before he left for California to train for the Young Mitchell fight. He probably saw her perform in January 1891 in the Denver production of "Natural Gas." Whether he knew that Chester was having an affair with Jackson is another matter.

It seems probable that Reddy met Chester in Salt Lake City on his way to California for some type of assignation. A Mrs. George Murphy of London was registered at the Templeton Hotel in Salt Lake on July 27, but on the following day she had moved to the Valley Hotel and registered there as Miss Florence Chester of London. She may have been in Salt Lake to meet Reddy.[498] However, that Chester was in Salt Lake on the main route of the railroads to San Francisco at about the time Reddy was going to San Francisco might have been a mere coincidence. Nevertheless, Chester did return from San Francisco to Denver with Reddy.[499]

Between Reddy's return to Denver at the end of September 1891 and January 1892 there seems to have been a liaison between Reddy and Chester. Whatever happened cooled down by January when articles appeared reporting that Chester had fallen in love with a cowboy named James Everett and that Reddy had kidnapped Chester to keep her away from Everett.[500] At this point one is left to guess that Reddy's relationship with Chester was always a dead end and he was simply slow on the uptake in matters involving this pretty young actress.

Football Over Fights

After a strong showing with Mitchell, Reddy was in demand. In early October 1891, the Olympic Club in New Orleans contacted Gallagher proposing a fight there with Alex Greggains, who had already said that he was willing to participate.[501] No match was arranged and instead Reddy accepted the position as boxing instructor at the D.A.C. and took up the new sport of football. He held his position at the D.A.C. for thirty years.

Several articles reported that Reddy continued fighting, but ultimately he was content to work at the club. He also organized the club's professional football team. Reddy played right guard on the team and was elected its captain.[502] Their team played college and university teams in the West and were considered a brutal bunch on the gridiron.[503]

A Mixed Bag

The D.A.C. was formed in 1884, and in 1890 it constructed the first part of a new Romanesque facility designed by Sterner & Varian architects. Their building at 1327–1331 Glenarm featured stone arches over the front entry and above garden-level windows. In 1892, the D.A.C. doubled the size of its facility. The club featured reading rooms, parlors, and cafés in luxurious oriental motifs. The athletic facilities included a large gymnasium with a gallery at the second-floor level that supported a running track with a corked floor. The club also included fencing, wrestling, and boxing rooms where Reddy was in charge. He was a popular instructor with his ruddy face and a big smile.[504]

Chapter 3 - Patrick J. "Reddy" Gallagher (1864–1937) "An ideal middleweight"

His job at the club provided Reddy with the first steady work of his adult life and he loved the work. He also met and interacted with the gentlemen of Denver's upper class, and this later provided him contacts and business opportunities that did not exist in places like Murphy's Exchange.

In other respects Reddy's boxing career was stalled except for his continuing pursuit of Dempsey, who was no longer a dominant middleweight prizefighter. In January 1891, Dempsey had been destroyed by Fitzsimmons in New Orleans. Dempsey had returned to Portland, Oregon, to teach boxing and run a saloon. However, Dempsey still had many loyal fans, and Reddy thought that he too could whip Dempsey.

Gossip was circulating in 1892 that Dempsey would come back to the ring to fight Reddy for a purse of $3,000 before New Orleans' Olympic Athletic Club.[505] Once again Reddy did not think that the purse offered was sufficient. He had already passed up a ten-round fight with Hall for a $1,000 purse because he was unwilling to give up his position with the D.A.C. so lightly.[506] He said that he would not fight for $3,000 when other men of his class were getting $7,000 for such fights.

It was suggested that the Coney Island Athletic Club might meet Reddy's demands. Later articles suggested that Reddy had rethought his demands and would meet Dempsey for the original purse offered by the Olympic. The fight was not made and the money offered was going in the wrong directions when the Butte City Athletic Club offered only $2,500 for the fight.[507]

While the match with Dempsey fell through, a fight with a second-rate fighter named Jess Smith was arranged for Denver's Coliseum hall. Smith was a black fighter. At the time many of the well-known fighters drew the color line and refused to meet black fighters. Reddy had grown up with Thompson in Cleveland and had no scruples against such fights.

The terms of the Smith-Gallagher fight were unusual. Masterson backed Smith, who was described as the "colored" middleweight champion of Colorado. Masterson offered a purse of $1,000; however, Reddy would win the money only if he knocked out Smith within eight rounds. Reddy was seconded by La Blanche and he weighed 164 pounds for this fight. Smith was seconded by Masterson and weighed 175 pounds.

Masterson was familiar with fights made on such terms. He coached Smith to avoid punishment at all costs. Smith went down with the first swing from Gallagher and he repeatedly went down whenever hit and sometimes when he just thought he was going to be hit. In the second round Gallagher argued with referee Billy Thompson contending that Smith's conduct amounted to a foul. While he was talking to Thompson he was hit by Smith, and this caused a near riot.

When Reddy resumed fighting, he rushed Smith, who promptly went down to avoid punishment. He told Smith to get up and fight, and Masterson made a remark that irritated Reddy, who then hit Masterson in the face. Masterson jumped into the ring and swung at Reddy and they exchanged blows. At that point about a dozen policemen stopped the fight, and it was awarded to Reddy by the referee.[508]

While Reddy went into training for the Smith fight, his duties at the D.A.C. were filled by one of his brothers. This was probably his younger brother, Jack Gallagher, who was fighting professionally in Ohio at the time.[509]

Shortly after the Smith fight, Reddy purchased Denver's Coliseum hall at 1812 Champa.[510] The Coliseum was the largest venue of its type in Denver and hosted a variety of significant events.[511] That he could afford to purchase this venue is remarkable. However, he was always known to be a thrifty person who still had the first dollar he had ever earned.

Not long after the Smith fight another multi-sport athlete visited Denver. James J. Corbett had been heavyweight champion of the world for a year when he stopped in Denver in April 1893. During his visit he played handball with Gallagher at the D.A.C. but quit the game after about fifteen minutes. Jim was ill and nearly collapsed. A carriage was ordered and he was taken back to his hotel room where he was treated by a local physician. Corbett said he had caught a severe cold while visiting in Minneapolis, and his friends were afraid that he might have pneumonia, which was a deadly proposition in the 1890s.[512]

1893 – Reddy and "Denver" Ed Smith – the Last Fight

One of the toughest heavyweights in the 1890s was Edward Corcoran, whose ring name was "Denver" Ed Smith. Smith had learned to box from the great Jem Mace in England before immigrating to the States in 1884. He was a tough customer who had given Peter Jackson a rough time of it in Chicago in 1890 and had also defeated several well-known fighters, including John Clow and Mike Cleary. Masterson had backed Smith as early as 1888.

In March 1893, Smith knocked out the Australian heavyweight Joe Goddard in New Orleans in eighteen rounds. Masterson had done the leg work to put together the Goddard-Smith fight, and both Masterson and Reddy made a lot of money betting on Smith when the odds heavily favored Goddard.

Masterson was a second for Smith during the fight. When the match was going Goddard's way, Masterson had told Smith that if he tried to quit, Masterson would kill him. This threat apparently served a good result for Masterson and Reddy.[513]

Smith was three inches taller and weighed about fifteen pounds more than Gallagher. Fourth of July entertainment in Denver featured the Smith-Gallagher match at the Broadway Theater for the gate receipts. The special terms of their fight were that Smith had to knock out Reddy in four rounds or lose the gate. Reddy won the money by keeping away from Smith for the four rounds. He was credited with being too clever for the big man. Taking home the money seems to have been the primary goal for Reddy in most of his matches.[514]

The Smith-Gallagher match was Reddy's last prizefight. On October 28, 1894, he married Mary McSheehy and had promised her before their marriage that he would fight no more.[515]

1894 – Gallagher and Masterson

Despite their confrontation during the Jess Smith fight, Reddy and Masterson buried the hatchet and began working together to promote prizefights in Denver. Masterson had a reputation as a lawman and gunfighter; however, he had put most of that behind him by the time he went into business as the owner of Denver's Palace Variety Theater and in November 1891 married an actress named Emma Walters.

As young businessmen in Denver, Masterson and Reddy worked together to promote fights. One of their early ventures was a match between "Denver" Ed Smith and Lawrence Farrell. This match took place on October 3, 1894, on the open prairie near a railroad line and about twenty miles from Denver to avoid police interference. A special railroad train was chartered for about 250 high-paying Denver sports who witnessed the fight. A purse of $5,000 was offered. Gallagher acted as referee and awarded the fight to Smith after repeated fouls by Farrell, including his last, which was to throw Smith over the ropes.[516]

Ten days after the Smith-Farrell match, Gallagher and J. McCormick gave a wrestling exhibition at the Columbia Theater in Denver. The exhibition was given during intermission of the romantic play "The Gladiator." Presumably it was supposed to demonstrate that there were still American gladiators even in the 1890s.[517]

Reddy Marries Mary McSheehy

There is not much information about Reddy's marriage to Mary McSheehy.[518] Both of them had experienced a lot of the world in their short lives. After their marriage they both settled down and enjoyed forty-three years of a loving and respectable life in Denver.

Mary was a native of Tralee, County Kerry, Ireland. Her mother, Honorah O'Connor, had married Edward McSheehy in Ireland before 1863, when Mary was born. Two other children of this union were born in Ireland: John in 1865 and Roger in 1871. Before her marriage Mary had been educated in a Catholic convent.[519] This suggests that Mary's parents had some wealth because most Irish-Catholic children at the time received little or no education.

McSheehy died in Ireland and Honorah married a man named Timothy Allman before she immigrated to the States in October

1873. Apparently the Allmans stopped in Chicago for a while, but they were in San Francisco before their daughter Margaret's birth in 1877.

Mary's mother worked hard to make a living in San Francisco. In 1879 and 1880 she lived near the waterfront and sold fruits and vegetables. She gave her occupation to the census enumerator as "huckster." By 1881 she was selling groceries and liquors on Folsom Street. Later she had a restaurant at 272 Brannan in San Francisco. Before 1890, Honorah was a widow for the second time. By 1920 she lived with her daughter Mary and Reddy at their home in Denver. None of this sheds light on how Mary and Reddy met, but they might have become acquainted in San Francisco during one of his several long stays in that city.

The Rest of his Life Begins

After his marriage, Reddy did not compete in the ring, but he remained a primary figure on Denver's sporting scene and continued to wrestle.[520] He often acted as a second or referee in boxing or wrestling matches.[521]

In 1895, Reddy tried to arrange a match in Denver between Fitzsimmons and Corbett. Corbett had defeated Sullivan in New Orleans in 1892, and Fitzsimmons had nearly killed Dempsey to claim the world middleweight title. Fitz had then moved up to the ranks of the heavyweights.

Fitz had been on Corbett's trail for two years trying to shame him into a title match. Matches had been arranged in Florida and Louisiana, but legal actions had scotched them. In May 1895, acting for two of Denver's leading bankers, Reddy wired Corbett's manager, Joe Vending, offering a purse of $25,000 for the two men to fight in Denver. Reddy had a written promise of backing up to $40,000 to make the match, but other cities outbid the Denverites. Nevertheless, the fact that two Denver bankers used Reddy as their agent in attempting to arrange the Corbett-Fitzsimmons fight illustrates the new status he had attained in Denver.[522]

In addition to these activities, Reddy sparred with some of the leading prizefighters when they visited Denver. His opponents included Corbett, Joe Choynski, and Tom Sharkey. These were not real fights but simply demonstrations of scientific sparring that apparently did not violate the pre-nuptial promise he had made.[523]

Caught and Squeezed Between Floto and Masterson

Reddy knew Floto and Masterson long before he came to Denver. For several years Floto had worked in Chicago as Davies' secretary and had learned the ropes of the sports entertainment business from Davies. In early 1888, Floto had traveled with the Davies' Specialty Company when Gallagher and Martin Snee had joined Muldoon and Lewis on their three-month tour. Masterson was also a long-time friend of Davies and had good contacts with other big name sports promoters in both New York and San Francisco. He had tried to induce Gallagher to come to Denver as early as August 1888. It seemed that Floto and Masterson would be the perfect partners in cornering the professional prizefighting business in Denver, and in late 1898 they both wanted Gallagher to be part of their efforts.

The possibility of such a venture was made possible by a statute known as the Cannon Law ("An Act in Relation to Prize

Fighting and Sparring Exhibitions") that was working its way through the Colorado legislature and became law in April 1899. The bias in favor of prizefighting held by the Colorado lawmakers was demonstrated in March 1899 when that assembly adjourned so that its members could attend a fight between Kid Parker of Colorado and Jack Carrig of Buffalo, New York. Floto was the referee for the Parker-Carrig match.[524] While prohibiting prizefighting, the Colorado law included a provision permitting sparring exhibitions with gloves of not less than five ounces when held in a facility operated by a domestic athletic association in building leased for such purposes.[525]

There were inherent problems in a Floto-Masterson partnership. Both men had huge egos, and it was inevitable that their egos would come into conflict. Moreover, they both had different goals when it came to promoting sports. Floto's goal was to produce world class sporting events attracting the biggest named athletes available. Big shows equaled big money if they were properly handled. Masterson wanted the biggest shows available, but his primary goal was to win money by gambling on sporting events. Producing shows gave Masterson a chance to influence outcomes and thereby improve his odds when gambling. The competing goals of Floto and Masterson were inherently inconsistent.

Soon after their plans to corner Denver's sports entertainment business started, their partnership fell apart. In the spring of 1899, Floto organized the Colorado Athletic Association and spent $10,000 to build a new steel structure with a seating capacity of 5,000. His facility was to be the jewel of Denver that would enable him to crowd out Masterson.[526] Floto wasted no time trying to book big fights. While his new building was being constructed he tried to book a match between Fitzsimmons and Jim Jefferies for a purse of $20,000 in Denver.[527]

Masterson organized the Olympic Athletic Club and renovated the Haymarket Theater at Sixteenth and Market streets. He booked George Dixon and Tommy White to fight at the Olympic. Dixon was the featherweight champion of the world and White was a tough featherweight from Chicago's north side who had a terrific ring record. Many of the leading lights of sports attended the Dixon-White match along with 2,500 paying customers. O'Rourke was Dixon's manager and was in his corner. Masterson acted as the referee and gave the match to Dixon at the end of the twenty rounds.[528]

Supposedly during 1899, Reddy gave his support to Masterson and the Olympic Athletic Club and then in 1900 switched his allegiance to Floto. If Gallagher left a business association with Masterson, this was probably motivated by disputes over money. From the days of Costello forward it had become apparent that Gallagher's interest in business propositions focused on money and getting paid for his work. The split between Reddy and Masterson resulted in Masterson attacking Reddy in the press and physically attacking Floto on the streets of Denver. Not long after these events, Masterson left Denver and turned over the Olympic to another partner, Gus Tuthill.[529]

Gallagher's Success

The image of the typical prizefighter is a man who ends up penniless and on skid row. That was not the case for Reddy. In 1906, Jack Root was an ex-light heavyweight champion turned sports writer. He wrote that Gallagher was already one of the wealthiest citizens in Denver.[530] A year later Gallagher was described as the richest prizefighter in the world. He had made his fortune by saving his money while a fighter and successfully promoting boxing in Denver. He had also sold Coliseum Hall in Denver for "something like $150,000."[531] The United States government purchased the hall to use it as part of the site for a new Denver post office, and Reddy leased it back for use as a skating rink.[532] The equivalent value of this sale in 2010 would have been about $3.5 million. Later in 1907 Reddy purchased the three-story Lewiston Hotel at Eighteenth and Stout streets in Denver for $135,000.[533]

Reddy continued his work as the boxing instructor for the D.A.C. until the 1920s. He was later awarded a life membership in that club. He was also active in the Knights of Columbus and held the rank of fourth-degree knight. Toward the end of his life he was described as a political power in Denver.[534]

Reddy was proudest of the athletic training and boxing instruction he gave to many young men from Denver. A few fighters who received their first training from Reddy were: George Manley, a light-heavyweight fighter who fought professionally from the early 1920s into the 1940's; Eddie Mack, a junior lightweight from Denver who fought in the middle part of the second decade of the twentieth century and was later the boxing promoter at the Boston Garden; Mickey (David) Cohen, who fought at about 137 pounds between the mid-1920s and into the 1930s; Jimmy Hanlon, a junior lightweight from Denver; "Fighting" Dick Gilbert, a light-heavyweight who fought the second Jack Dempsey; and Eddie Egan. Reddy considered the last of these to be his prize pupil. Eagan was an amateur boxing champion and later a district attorney in New York and then chairman of the New York State Athletic Commission. He also employed Edward Pitts, who became a noted fight promoter.[535]

Gallagher also operated a very successful real estate agency, and when Floto died in 1929, succeeded him as the sports editor of the *Denver Post*. About two weeks before he died he attended a wrestling match in Denver although he had a bad cold. His cold turned to pneumonia. Two days before his death he was rushed to the hospital where he succumbed on November 13, 1937.[536]

Funeral services were held at Denver's Immaculate Conception cathedral. A nephew, the Rev. Francis T. Fergus, sang a requiem mass. Father Fergus was the son of Reddy's sister Ellen and her husband Michael J. Fergus and was later the director of radio and television for the Archdiocese of Cleveland.[537] There were more than sixty honorary pallbearers at his funeral.

His estate was estimated to be about $375,000 after his death, which would be equivalent to about $4.5 million in 2010.[538] His wife, Mary, died in 1944 while visiting her sisters in Pasadena, California.

After Reddy died, a Denver reporter wrote that he was "a great Irishman, tough, thrifty, he did a lot for old-timers who were less fortunate than he. Most of his charitable deeds were never known, for Reddy was not the kind of man to brag about that sort of thing. You couldn't borrow a cent from him to gamble or drink with, but a friend who needed money could get any amount from him."[539]

Reddy's widow donated the Gallagher Memorial, which is used as a mausoleum for the bishops of Denver and to honor her husband. The mausoleum is in Mount Olivet Cemetery and includes the Gallagher Memorial Chapel and altar. It is located in Section 21, Block 7, in Wheat Ridge (Jefferson County),

Colorado. The structure has an arched entry supported by marble columns. It was a long trail for Reddy from Clarksville, Tennessee, to Denver, Colorado. The footprints he left along the way have been washed away so that only a few shadows remain.

Chapter 4
Herman Arthur Macziewski
aka Herman Arthur Magesky
aka Arthur Magesty
aka Arthur Majesty
aka A.B. Tracy
(1859-1891)

Arthur Majesty

Arthur H. Majesty was born Herman Arthur Macziewski in 1859 in Toledo, Ohio. His father, Herman, and his mother, Anna, were born in Germany, but were of Polish ancestry. The family was well-off in Germany, but fell on hard times before immigrating to the United States and locating in Toledo. Arthur had a younger sister, Addie. The Macziewskis' financial circumstances did not improve in Toledo, where over a period of four decades Herman worked as a janitor in commercial buildings in Toledo's business district.

Majesty's Background

Majesty, a good student, graduated from elementary and high school. He was small, but a natural athlete. As an adult he was five feet four inches tall and weighed between 110 and 135 pounds. After high school he worked as a stenographer for A. Backus & Son, a grain dealer in Toledo, before leaving town and striking out on his own.[540]

Majesty bounced around the Midwest before settling in Peoria, Illinois, where he trained at Charley Flynn's gymnasium. Peoria had strong financial ties with Toledo because the Toledo, Peoria and Western R.R. connected the communities, and Peoria grain traders shipped substantial quantities of grain to Toledo for shipped east on the Great Lakes.

Majesty's initial stay in Peoria was short, and in 1885 he was living about forty-five miles southeast of Peoria in Bloomington, Illinois, where he boarded in a home at 206 East Chestnut Street in the most upscale part of town.[541]

In Bloomington, Arthur opened a school where he taught the art of self-defense and attended Illinois Wesleyan University's College of Commerce. Wesleyan offered courses in the new Eclectic shorthand method that had been created and taught by Dr. Jesse George Cross. The university was two blocks north of Majesty's residence. He also worked part-time for George L.

Hutchin, the editor and proprietor of a high-quality, multi-color weekly newspaper known as *The Eye*.[542]

Virtually every Central Illinois town of any size had a room where boxers, wrestlers, club swingers, and gymnasts trained, and there was healthy competition between athletic clubs in those cities. Bloomington had a good boxing community, whose leading figure, Lee Cheney, was the owner of a pool room in the Ashley House hotel in downtown Bloomington and operated a horse racing track on the east side of town. The Ashley House was the place where visiting sports normally put up when they were in Bloomington. Both John L. Sullivan and Jack Ashton stayed there during one of Sullivan's grand tours. Majesty's boxing school had a student body that included policemen, iron moulders, a local barber, several young men, and Abe Williams, the black welterweight champion of Illinois who worked as a cook at Kadigan's restaurant on Main Street in downtown Bloomington.

The Promoter, Charles E. "Parson" Davies

The leading boxing promoter in the Midwest in the 1880s was Charles E. "Parson" Davies of Chicago. Davies began using Bloomington fighters in his Chicago boxing carnivals as early as September 1881, when Williams won a cup for defeating Charles Saunders in a three-round scientific fight as part of the preliminary matches given before John L. Sullivan's first appearance in Chicago.

Davies' relationships in Bloomington were well-established in the mid-1880s. In 1884, he was promoting two heavyweights: Jem Goode of England, who had a good reputation and substantial fighting experience, and Patsey Cardiff, a young heavyweight who had learned to fight in Toledo. Cardiff had lived in Toledo in 1882, where he worked as a carriage maker before coming to Peoria to train at Flynn's gym. Cardiff had already appeared in Bloomington to fight one of Majesty's pupils, Richard T. Dunn.[543] Cardiff and Majesty had similar backgrounds in Toledo and then later with Flynn in Peoria, and it is likely that they knew one another.[544]

In June 1884, Davies sent both Goode and Cardiff to appear in a sparring match at Bloomington's fair grounds and then on December 22 sent a combination of boxers and wrestlers, including Cardiff, to put on an evening of entertainment at Bloomington's downtown Durley Hall.[545] All of these activities built relationships between Bloomington's sporting men such as Majesty and Davies and opened opportunities for local athletes to compete at higher levels in their professions. Davies knew and used many good fighters from Chicago, but it was always good to bring in some fresh faces to keep the interest of local fans.

1885 – Tommy Warren

Tommy Warren

In the spring of 1885, Tommy Warren, known as "Little Casino" and a promising young featherweight fighter from the West, came to Chicago and asked Davies to manage his interests. Davies sent Warren with a combination of other fighters to Danville, Illinois, to put on a show. The combination included Alf Greenfield, an English heavyweight fighter under Davies' management, One-Eyed Jimmy Connolly, and Harry Franks.[546]

Davies arranged a private fight between Warren and Andy Hanley, a well-known but over-the-hill featherweight from New York. The fight at the Chicago Athletic Club was stopped by the police, but Davies intervened, and after most of the spectators had left, the fight did take place. It was brief because Hanley broke his right forearm during the first round of the match.[547]

Davies next matched Warren with a featherweight named Chris Sommers from Saint Louis. Four cowboys from the Buffalo Bill Wild West Show who were friends of Warren's attended that fight in full cowboy regalia, and Tommy put on a terrific show punishing Sommers throughout the fight. In the fourth round, when Sommers was covered with blood, he rushed Warren, and Tommy took a knee to show his knowledge of ring tactics. At that point Sommers hit Warren twice while he was kneeling down, and the referee awarded the fight to Warren.[548]

Davies was so sufficiently impressed with Warren's performance that he decided to put him in the final preliminary match before the greatest prizefighting event in Chicago up to 1885. The featured event was a non-championship heavyweight fight between Jack Burke, "The Irish Lad," and John L. Sullivan.

Majesty-Warren No. 1 – Majesty Hits the Big Time

Davies needed to find a credible and talented featherweight opponent to meet Warren. Hanley was not available because of his broken arm and Sommers was not the answer, having failed to show well in his earlier match with Warren. Davies then contacted Arthur Majesty in Bloomington and asked to appear with Warren. The preliminary fights were announced on June 11.[549] Davies probably did not want a fighter who would beat Warren, but he did want a man who knew how to fight and would make a good show and not just hold on, fall down, and roll over.

The big show was held at Chicago's Driving Park on June 13. The park had a horse racing track. A raised twenty-four-foot platform and ring were set up in middle of the track in front of the judges' stand. The grandstands at the park were full from end to end with several thousand men from business circles, young professionals, sporting men, and a fair sprinkling of women. There was a twenty-piece brass band to provide entertainment between events.

Majesty and Warren were the last of seven preliminary wrestling and boxing matches held before the Sullivan-Burke match, and therefore the entire crowd was present during their match. After the Majesty-Warren fight, the two contestants were uniformly praised. The *Chicago Tribune* described their match as "just warm enough to catch the crowd, and young Warren, who is a mere boy in appearance and stature, was heartily cheered as a reward for the hard punishment he had inflicted upon his adversary." The *Chicago Herald* wrote that "Tom Warren, the featherweight champion of Wyoming, and Arthur Kenzie [sic Majesty] made the only creditable match of the afternoon. Four lively rounds were fought in which Warren proved himself a game little man."⁵⁵⁰ This preliminary fight was a pivotal event in launching Tommy Warren's long boxing career and put him on the map of great young featherweight fighters.

Majesty-Warren No. 2 – a Show for the Bloomington Fans

Five weeks after their preliminary fight, Majesty and Warren had a rematch in Bloomington. Their rematch may have been part of the original consideration for Majesty to appear in Chicago or it may have been suggested by Davies who liked to keep his fighters working and knew that they would draw a big crowd in Majesty's home town. Warren fought Joe Morris, a featherweight from England, at the Park Theater in Chicago on Friday, July 17. The terms of the fight were that if Warren failed to knock out Morris within four rounds, then Morris would win $100. Warren punished Morris throughout the fight but lost the match on a foul in the fourth round. He lost the $100 but cleared $315 as his share of the gate receipts.

The following morning Warren took the Chicago & Alton R.R. down to Bloomington. He was scheduled to give a four-round exhibition there with Majesty at the Opera House, which also happened to be the home of *The Eye* where Majesty worked. The local press said their match was to "settle the vexed question of pugilistic superiority, arising out of Majesty and Warren's set-to in Chicago on the occasion of the Sullivan-Burke 'knock out.'" Warren was described as a twenty-year-old "midget" who weighed about 110 pounds but was the champion featherweight of the Pacific Slope. He was also described as "neat and elegant" with a slight "dude appearance." Majesty also weighed 110 pounds, but he was "a trifle taller and wider across the chest than Warren." Majesty was also described as a "scientific sparrer" with a fine record.[551]

The affair at Bloomington was under Majesty's management and very successful. A large audience attended, including a large number of sporting men and many of the "highly respected citizens, including a number of city officials." There were several preliminary fights, with two of them featuring Richard Dunn and a local painter named Rudy Schroder and with Dunn then appearing for three rounds with Pat Coyle, a Bloomington policeman. Two fighters from Peoria also put on an exhibition. Entertainment included Indian club swinging, a match with blackened gloves so the audience could see where the punches landed. This was the template for boxing shows at the time. The local public liked to see their local heroes, but they also wanted to see some national talent, and Warren was the national talent.

At the conclusion of the preliminaries, Warren and Majesty appeared for four rounds. The audience was in sympathy with Majesty, but at the finish Warren was a strong favorite and considered an overmatch for the professor. The match was declared a draw—which probably meant that Warren lost another $100— but the gate was excellent.[552] At the end of the match Warren made a little speech to the audience asserting that he had been denied "fair play" in the outcome and offered $500 for a finish fight with Majesty.[553] This result may have been cooked up in advance as a way for Majesty and Warren to promote a third match.

The next morning Majesty spoke to the local press and announced that he would challenge Warren to a hard glove finish fight. Because Majesty was himself a member of the local press it probably wasn't too hard to find a receptive ear. He said that he was aggrieved because Warren had not acted fairly during their exhibition by "casting reflections upon him in the assertion to the audience that he had been treated badly." Majesty said that he personally abhorred slugging matches but that Warren's conduct demanded a manly response.[554]

Someone might have smelled a rat at this point because Majesty and Warren soon began a relationship that lasted for almost a year. During that time they would fight three more times, and it was widely believed that they actually fought many other times in contests where Majesty participated using an assumed name. The speculation was that Warren wanted to build a ring record that was sufficient enough that he would be considered a contender for the featherweight championship but that he wanted to do this without taking real risks. He therefore paid Majesty to appear, put on a good show as a skilled opponent, and then take a dive. After all, who was getting hurt in this format? The public got a good show. Promoters made good money from ticket sales, Majesty made some money, and Warren got the good press and good record that he wanted with the minimum amount of risk.[555]

1886 – Majesty-Warren No. 3 – a "Championship" Match at Louisville

Warren continued to fight other matches in the Midwest. On August 22 he had a rematch with Hanley at the Park Theater in Chicago. Warren had a left hand that was too much for Hanley, and by the end of the third round, Hanley was groggy. No one was the clear winner at the end of the fourth round, and the referee insisted that the fight should continue for a fifth round. After that extra round Hanley was unable to continue and Warren was awarded the fight.[556]

Three days after the Hanley fight, Davies traveled to Cincinnati to watch the Sullivan-McCaffrey fight. He took Warren and several other fighters with him, and when they arrived, Warren was booked for a preliminary match. His opponent was Jack King (the "Humming Bird"), who was described as much bigger than Warren, but King was knocked out despite his size. King angered Warren before the fight began by telling the press that he would rather fight a man than a mere boy.

For reasons that aren't clear, Warren did not return to Chicago with Davies, and their relationship seemed to end, at least temporarily. Davies did not like fixed fights because they undercut the whole boxing profession. He may have figured out that Warren was fixing fights and might not have liked the looks of the Warren-King match. Warren then had another fight in Cincinnati on October 9, but soon turned back to Majesty as his opponent.

Travel for Big "Fights"

On January 15, 1886, word came from Louisville, Kentucky, that Majesty had arrived on the prior day and signed articles of agreement with Warren for a twenty-round finish fight with hard gloves for $500 and the featherweight championship.[557] The loser of the fight received 35 percent of the gate receipts. Their fight took place at the Louisville Athletic Club. Warren weighed 115 pounds and Majesty weighed in at 123 pounds. They fought with small four-ounce gloves. Warren landed five blows for every one that Majesty got home, and Majesty suffered severely during the match. At the end of the fourth round, Majesty was bewildered and unable to defend himself when Warren delivered a hard blow to his ribs. At that point a local justice of the peace tried to stop the fight and was tossed out. It was apparent that Majesty could not go on, and Warren was awarded the fight.

Post-fight articles stated that Majesty had previously defeated some good fighters, including men identified as James Lee and Anton Cristol. The latter was known as a wrestler from Cincinnati, Ohio, who sometimes boxed. However, there appears to be no record of Majesty meeting either a Lee or Cristol.[558] The day after the fight Majesty said that he would challenge Warren to a fourth match.[559] Again, questions might be asked concerning whether this fight was real or the outcome prearranged.

Less than three weeks after the Louisville fight with Majesty, Warren met a fighter named Johnny Murphy of New York at the New Grand Theatre in Louisville. Warren was putting on pounds and weighed 123 pounds for this match—eight pounds more than Murphy. The place was packed. Murphy was beat up badly by Warren. At the beginning of the fourth round he was groggy and his left eye was puffy and closing to a slit. By the sixth round Murphy's eye was totally closed with a big swollen knot, and in the eighth round Murphy's face looked like "beef pudding." After two minutes of the eighth round, Murphy stepped before the footlights and gave up the fight saying that Warren was the best man he had ever fought.[560]

Majesty-Warren No. 4 – a Return to Bloomington

The rematch that Majesty demanded after the Louisville fight was scheduled to take place back in Bloomington, Illinois, on March 10.⁵⁶¹ Again there were several preliminary matches, and one of them included Abe Williams against a local man named Mike McHugh who had a nice little criminal record. This fourth match took place before five hundred patrons and was for four rounds for "scientific points." Essentially this meant that Majesty would not have to take as much punishment as he had in Louisville to make some money.

In Majesty-Warren No. 4, Majesty did some "clever sparring" during the first two rounds and landed some decisive blows on Warren's face. In the third and fourth rounds, Warren began to punish Majesty as he had at Louisville from the beginning and was awarded the decision.⁵⁶² Warren returned to Louisville, where he met Tommy Barnes of New York on March 23 at Mill Creek, Kentucky. This fight appears to have been real. It lasted forty-five rounds with Warren knocking out Barnes to end their fight.⁵⁶³

In April Warren went to Indianapolis. During the next four months of 1886, Warren participated in fights in Saint Louis and Chicago, but he was fighting primarily in Indianapolis and Grand Rapids, Michigan. On April 2 he was advertised to participate in a fight at the Zoo in Indianapolis with a fighter identified as Pat Carroll of Buffalo. The Zoo was a famous sporting establishment that featured vaudeville and athletic events. Fighters such as Burke and Pat Killen fought there, and other acts such as Rice & Barton, "The Kings of Black Face Comedy," Toothless Murphy, the 4-Brilliants, an instrumental and comedy team, Miss Dolly Davenport, the comic queen, and the Silver Toned Quartette all appeared at the Zoo.

Warren dominated Pat Carroll (sometimes identified as Patsy Cahill), and at the end of three rounds their match was stopped by the police. No arrests were made.⁵⁶⁴ Five days later he met Joe Wehrle in Cincinnati and knocked him out in three rounds. He then met Pierce Murphy in Saint Louis on April 23 and finally went back in Chicago for a fight with Harry Nolan on May 10. This last fight was arranged by Davies as a preliminary to a match between Charley Mitchell and Burke.⁵⁶⁵

A few weeks later, Warren was fighting in Grand Rapids, Michigan. On May 31 he fought a man named Jim Johnson, a so-called "unknown" of Cadillac, Michigan. This man was sometimes called Pike Johnson, Pug Johnson, Jim Johnson, or John C. Johnson.⁵⁶⁶ Then in mid-June Warren went to Grand Rapids for another match where his opponent was not known.⁵⁶⁷ Warren's fights with Pat Carroll (sometimes called Pasty Cahill), the unknown from Cadillac, and the second unknown who he fought in Grand Rapids were most probably additional fights that he had with Arthur Majesty with Majesty fighting under an assumed name and being paid by Warren to appear.⁵⁶⁸

Majesty Works with Billy Myer and Streator Fighters

In mid-1886, a young lightweight fighter from Streator, Illinois with terrific promise appeared. William ("Billy") Myer would later be known as the "Streator Cyclone" and would fight twice for the lightweight championship of America. Myer was born February 23, 1860, in Blackstone, Illinois. In his prime he was five feet six inches tall and weighed about 135 pounds. Billy was of Prussian descent. His father was a carpenter, and Billy was also skilled in that profession.

Before 1885, Myer has a short record of fights that were of no particular note. However, in September 1885 his career began to take off when he knocked out a good lightweight fighter named Paddy Welch (sometimes called "Welsh") at Streator in the first round of a fight presented as part of a veterans' reunion. At that time Welch was considered a coming fighter and had been used by Parson Davies to fight Ed Crook in a preliminary match before a heavyweight fight between Jack Burke and Alf Greenfield and another match where Welch met Crook before 8,000 in a preliminary match before a fight between Tommy Chandler and Frank Glover.

After a long layoff, Myer was scheduled to fight another promising lightweight named Frank Ware, who had been declaring his own abilities and had been called the best lightweight fighter in Illinois. Ware failed to show up for the fight. His failure to appear for his match with Myer had the effect of enhancing Myer's reputation.

In June, Majesty was still living in Bloomington, but he often worked in Streator, Illinois, with fighters including Myer, his young brother Eddie Myer, Link Pope, and Charles Lomasney, a good Streator heavyweight. Myer's backer was a Streator saloon owner named Alf Kennedy. On June 10, Majesty and Kennedy took the short trip from Streator to Braidwood, Illinois, to arrange a fight there for Lomasney.[569] Then on June 18, Majesty went to Chicago and fought Paddy Welsh.

Majesty had agreed to fight Welch with kid gloves for $500 a side and the gate receipts. He may have accepted this fight so that he could help Myer prepare for an upcoming rematch with Welch. By fighting Welch he would be well-equipped to coach Myer. There was a lot of money at stake, and Majesty was probably paid a little extra from Myer's backer to participate in this match. The Majesty-Welch fight took place in a cellar on the north side of Chicago and was witnessed by about sixty sporting men. Welsh put Majesty down four times in the first round of their match. In the second round he was knocked down almost immediately and was bleeding profusely. He was put down seven more times during that round before he crawled on all fours to his corner and gave up the battle.[570]

A few days after the Majesty-Welch fight, Billy Myer signed articles of agreement to fight Welch at Braidwood, Illinois, on July 6 for $1,000. That same day Majesty denied that he was the person who had fought Welch. He claimed that he had only attended the match as an observer, but no one believed him, and his own subsequent statements seemed to belie his assertion.[571] The best bet was that Majesty had met Welch, picked up a few dollars in the process, and brought valuable information back to Myer.

On July 6, Majesty was still considered a resident of Bloomington, but was again working in Streator. That day he traveled from Streator to Braidwood, Illinois, with Myer for Myer's fight with Welch.[572] Three railroad carloads of Streator fight fans made the trip to Braidwood. Majesty acted as Myer's second during the fight, and Lee Cheney of Bloomington was the master of ceremonies for the match. The Streator man dominated Welch and knocked him out in the third round. The blow he delivered knocked Welch through the ropes, and during his fall, Welch's shoulder was also dislocated. After the fight Majesty offered to back Myer for a fight with Warren. Part of the post mortem contended that during his earlier match with Welch, Majesty had intentionally taught Welch to overestimate his ability and this worked to Myer's benefit.[573]

1887 – Majesty Returns to Peoria

Majesty continued to associate with Myer. In February 1887, Myer and Majesty worked as seconds for a fighter named Johnny Conners during a fight in Decatur, Illinois.[574] Sometime about 1887, Majesty left Bloomington and moved back to Peoria. He probably relocated because the growing opposition of Bloomington authorities to prizefighting made operating a successful business difficult. He may have also learned all that he could about the new Eclectic method of shorthand and thought he could market that knowledge outside of Bloomington.

When he went to Peoria, Majesty originally opened a school to teach shorthand. He was probably teaching the Eclectic method he had learned at Wesleyan. Soon after arriving he also opened a gymnasium in the one hundred block of Adams Street where he taught the art of self-defense. Majesty had a large class at his gym. His students included merchants, professional men, and clerks. His reputation was well known because of his work with Bloomington fighters, four matches with Warren, and his work with Myer. Majesty soon outgrew the Adams Street location and moved to rooms over the First National Bank at the corner of Main and Washington, a block west of the levee and railroad tracks on the west side of the levee. Majesty made many friends in Peoria and was considered a consummate gentleman.[575]

While living in Peoria, Majesty occasionally engaged in prizefights. On May 25 he fought a man named Fooler from Pekin, Illinois. This may have been Charles Fooler, who was born in Kentucky in 1866 and lived in Pekin. The fight was described as a "very lame affair" in which Majesty had it all his own way.[576] On Christmas Day 1887 he fought a man named Shea at Peoria for $250 a side. Shea was described as the lightweight champion of Indiana.

Between the dates of his matches with Fooler and Shea, an old penny turned up. On June 10 it was announced that Majesty had finished the preliminary arrangements for a fifth match with Warren, this time to take place in Peoria for a stake and gate receipts.[577] This fifth match was substantially delayed because Warren did not fight anyone between May and October. He had a good excuse for not fighting. In mid-July Warren was nearly killed. About sixteen miles south of Saint Paul on the Mississippi River, Warren fell off a boat and was trapped under it. At the time he was traveling to a fight between Billy Edwards of Chicago and Danny Needham. After ten minutes he was fished out of the water in poor condition.[578]

1888 – Majesty-Warren No. 5 – a Fizzle at Peoria

The fifth Majesty-Warren contest finally took place on January 21, 1888, at Peoria's Standard Theater. Parson Davies was present for the fight and acted as referee. Fighting in Chicago had been virtually closed down at that point, and Davies had been making his money promoting Evan "the Strangler" Lewis. Three nights before this match most of these men had probably seen each other in North Judson, Indiana, to watch the rematch between Myer and Harry Gilmore. From a spectator's standpoint their match had been a dud because Myer knocked out Gilmore in the first round, and it had taken hours on a night that was only six degrees for people to reach the site of that fight.

Warren had put on weight and now outweighed Majesty by twelve pounds. The affair was generally another dud with

Majesty keeping out of Warren's reach. One account said that Warren pounded Majesty all over the stage with Majesty keeping busy trying to dodge the blows. No result was announced.[579] This seems to have been Majesty's fifth reported meeting with Tommy Warren and Majesty's second-to-last professional fight. He did not fight again for almost three years and that would be his last.

1889 – Majesty Returns to Toledo

In about 1889, Majesty moved from Peoria back to Toledo. His sister, Addie, had married in 1888 and moved to Buffalo, New York. Majesty may have returned to help out his parents because his sister had moved away. Whatever his reason for moving back home, he did live with his parents at 564 Oakwood Avenue.[580]

One account states that in Toledo he was in charge of the physical culture department of the Toledo public schools.[581] He also opened his own gymnasium in Toledo in Room 7 of the Chamber of Commerce building on the Findlay block at the corner of Summit and Madison streets. His gym was across the street from the Hough & Barber business college and it seems possible that he taught shorthand at that college part-time just as he had in Peoria.

Majesty's physical education business was successful, and he moved to a larger facility on the Ketchum block in downtown Toledo. He had a large enrollment of young and middle-aged men. His students were prominent citizens of Toledo and included John H. Hall, a clerk at Toledo's Madison Hotel; Dr.

W.W. Coldman, a Toledo physician whose office was on Madison Street four blocks from Majesty's gym; J. Frank Zahm, a commission merchant and owner of a wholesale produce business who lived on Collingwood Avenue near Majesty's home; Will P. Tyler, a deputy collector for the Internal Revenue Service; and Valentine H. Ketcham, who ran a real estate and loan business on Summit Street and whose family had founded the Ketchum National Bank in downtown Toledo. At the time Ketcham was about thirty-five years old and known as a local sportsman.[582] In addition to his regular students, Majesty was also coaching professional aspirants Frank Kelly of Toledo and another man from Saginaw City.[583]

Majesty did not cut his ties with professional prizefighting nor with Peoria. At the end of December 1890, he started for Peoria where he acted as a second for George Siddons of Peoria in a match with Robert Raymond of Louisville, Kentucky. "Sparrow" Lewis of Troy, New York, was Raymond's second. Siddons was a good fighter who had been in the ring with some of Chicago's top young fighters. In this case he had agreed to stop Raymond in eight rounds, but failed in that task and was severely punished by Raymond.[584]

Lewis then signed articles of agreement to meet Siddons in a finish fight for $400 a side and gate receipts. Majesty was designated to act as referee for this match to take place on the evening of January 9, 1891.[585] Their match was postponed because of close police surveillance.[586] While he was in Peoria for the Siddons matches, Majesty renewed friendships there and told some acquaintances that he intended to return to Peoria and make it his home.[587]

1891 – Majesty Agrees to a Fight

Majesty's work with professional fighters in Peoria during the first two weeks of January 1891 may have tempted him to return to the ring. Giving in to that temptation ultimately proved fatal.

A young man lived in Columbus, Ohio, named David F. Seville, who was born in New Albany, Indiana, on June 7, 1870. By 1891 Seville had been a resident of Columbus for more than ten years. Seville's father was fifty-two years old when David was born. His mother, Lisa, was thirty-two years younger than her husband.

Seville worked at the Columbus shops of the Pittsburgh, Cincinnati, Chicago and Saint Louis R.R., which were commonly called the Panhandle machine shops. He was known as a scrapper, but participated in his first professional fight in January with another Columbus fighter named "Punk" Evans. Seville also had a relationship with a Columbus heavyweight named Tom Macy who apparently saw great promise in his young pupil.[588] Seville may have had promise, but his skill was not in balance with his character.

Nelsonville, Ohio, was a small town about fifty miles southeast of Columbus. David Nelson operated a hotel in Nelsonville, and Emil Rosser had a liquor store there. Nelson and Rosser were sporting men and apparently cooked up an idea about how to make some good money at Seville's expense.

In late January, Nelson and Rosser met with Seville to lay out a proposition for a match in Nelsonville. It is likely that Tom Macy was part of that discussion. About February 1, Nelson and Rosser made final arrangements for Seville to appear at Nelsonville to engage in a finish fight with a person to be named later for $200 a side, to be paid by the loser to the winner. February 7 was fixed as the final date to sign the agreement to fight.[589]

It seems likely that Nelson and Rosser had lined up Majesty as the person to be named later before they went to Seville with their proposal. It is possible that Nelson, Rosser, and Majesty had all attended the Seville-Evans fight and had an idea about Seville's fighting ability.

Nelson and Rosser had made additional arrangements for the fight. They formed an athletic club known as the Nelsonville Athletic Club that was to exist for one day only. The Ohio criminal law prohibiting prizefighting included an exception for sparring matches held in athletic clubs that were open to the public. Nelson and Rosser also obtained a license from the mayor of Nelsonville to further protect those involved from criminal prosecution.

Majesty went to Valentine Ketcham and induced him to act as his backer for the $200 in prize money. This took Nelson and Rosser off the hook for that expense. Majesty also agreed to appear under the assumed named of A.B. Tracy. It is likely that he assumed this name for several reasons. First, he wanted to protect himself from possible prosecution in the event something went wrong. Next, Nelson and Rosser wanted to take private side bets on the fight with the knowledge that Seville's opponent was a long-time professional prizefighter and boxing instructor while those betting on Seville thought that Seville's opponent was a little-known man named A.B. Tracy.

Before he traveled to Nelsonville, Majesty visited the editor of the *Toledo Daily Commercial* and asked him to include a personal item in the newspaper saying that he was going south in Ohio to act as a referee in a fight. Before he left the newspaper, he asked the editor not to include the personal item and whispered that he was actually going to fight himself, but that should be kept quiet. Majesty's friend John Hall traveled with him to help train him for the match.[590]

Majesty was in Nelsonville by February 15, when he wrote the first of two letters to his friend, Alfred Stephens:

Nelsonville, O., Feb'y 15, 1891.
Friend Alfred:

Would like to have you come to Nelsonville, O., where I am matched to fight Seville, of Columbus, for a purse of $200.00, to a finish, with 2-oz. gloves. You can call on Keere Bros., in the saloon business; they will be down here. Do not tell them who I am or that you know me, as I go under the name of A.B. Tracy. Our protection is good as we have a license. Come if you possibly can. We fight Feb. 24th, in the evening. Will see you all right. Am in training here. If you come this way, stop and see me. Yours truly, Arthur Majesty. Address A.B. Tracy.

Two-ounce gloves amounted to little more than a modern golf glove. Fighting in two-ounce gloves could be more dangerous than bare-knuckle fighting because the gloves held the fingers together and tended to avoid broken hands. A blow with two-ounce gloves was a harder blow than with an unprotected fist. A finish fight with two-ounce gloves was a dangerous proposition.

Majesty wrote a second letter to Stephens on February 20:

Nelsonville, O., Feb'y 20th, 1891.
Friend Alfred:

The man I meet is Seville, of Columbus, and we fight at 120 pounds for a purse of $200.00, all to go to the winner. Nelson and Rosser of this place are handling me. I don't anticipate any trouble in disposing of him. John Hall, of Toledo, is with me. You have met him before. Tickets are $3.00 per head, but I will place you all right; but do not let those people of your town know of it. If you can induce them to come and see the fight. It is to a finish with two-ounce gloves, in a large hall, with a seating capacity of 800 on elevated seats around the ring, same as all first-rate clubs.

Yours truly,
Arthur, *alias* A.B. Tracy

Majesty is Killed

At least two men from Toledo were present at the fight with Majesty. Ketcham, his backer, was there along with John Hall, his trainer and second. Majesty, under the alias of A.B. Tracy ("Hank" Tracy), was represented to be a miner or mule tender. Seville was seconded by Tom Macy and Reddy Hennessey, a middleweight from Troy, New York. Frank McHugh, a well-known featherweight fighter, was also present and chosen as the referee for the match.

The gate receipts for the fight were over $1,000, which was good news for Nelson and Rosser, who had hatched the scheme in the first place. The Nelsonville promoters took all bets from the Columbus fans at odds of ten to eight and undoubtedly thought they would clean up in every way. They probably thought the Columbus men were like fish running upstream to spawn and just waiting to be reeled in.

The fight began at about 12:24 a.m. on February 25. It went Seville's way from the beginning. The Nelsonville crowd must have seen what was happening from the start. He attacked and used an uppercut, which was a relatively new punch at the time. Accounts say that Seville ran Majesty around the ring "like a game cock pursuing a runner." Majesty appeared to be in the fight only during the seventh round. In the eleventh round Seville caught Majesty on the nose and knocked him dizzy. From the thirteenth to seventeenth round Seville pounded Majesty at will. Accounts of the final and fatal round vary widely.

An early account states that the final round was short and decisive. Seville knocked Majesty out with a right hand, swinging uppercut to the nose, and at the call of time for the next round Majesty was unable to respond. Another account said that at the beginning of the eighteenth round Majesty arose with an effort and advanced to the middle of the ring. Seville swung, and Majesty swayed backward out of reach. Seville then caught him with a right to the neck, and Majesty fell backward against the ropes and through them onto his face unconscious. Yet another account that was widely repeated said that in the final round Majesty came forward and said, "I can't see, hit me, if you want to." Seville then slammed Majesty in the jaw, breaking his neck. A final account modified the last story by saying that the final blow was a smash between the eyes that dropped Majesty unconscious.[591]

After the Fight Ended

When the fight ended, Majesty was carried upstairs into a club room and put on a bed where he was attended by a Dr. Edward Butt. As he was carried away, the prize money was paid to Seville, and he departed on the fast train for Columbus.

Imagine the difference in treatment that a person would receive today. He would not be moved immediately. His head and neck would be stabilized and he would be put on a stiff board to prevent movement. Immediate steps would be taken to assist breathing and attempt to limit swelling, and the patient would be rushed to an emergency room where highly trained medical personnel would assess and treat the injury. None of that happened.

Dr. Butt dressed a scalp abrasion and set Majesty's broken nose and then departed. Seville and Macy were already on their way to Columbus and McHugh went in a different direction. Majesty remained unconscious for several hours, rallied briefly, and then died between 2:00 and 3:00 a.m. on February 25.[592] A post mortem examination was undertaken, and it was determined that Majesty's skull was fractured by one of the blows and an artery of the brain ruptured, which caused his death. Majesty's head, neck, one arm, and his body all showed severe punishment. One of his eyes was black, his nose was cut, and his mouth and lips were swollen.[593]

After Majesty's death a telegram was sent to his father. It was not a thoughtful communication. It read: "Arthur is dead at the hotel here. What shall we do with the body?"[594] The next morning around 9:00 a.m. a train with the body of Majesty passed through Columbus. Ketchum and Hall had stayed with the body. Telegrams were also sent to the superintendent of the Columbus Police Department to arrest Seville and Macy and return them to Athens County, Ohio, to be held on charges of engaging in an illegal prizefight and murder. A similar telegraph was sent to Lancaster, Ohio, where McHugh was living to secure his arrest and return to Athens County. Seville and Macy were arrested about 10:40 a.m. on February 25 and taken to jail at Columbus.[595] Reddy Hennessy was also arrested.

Interviewed at the jail, Seville denied that he had participated in a prizefight and asserted that the match was for points with six-ounce gloves and was a licensed show. He claimed that after a clinch Majesty's body fell and struck a stake. Macy said that he had talked to Majesty after the fight and had been told that Seville was the best man he had ever faced and that he had no complaints about the fight in any way.[596] Given the conclusive post mortem evidence that Majesty had a fractured skull and a ruptured artery of the brain, it seems likely that Macy was lying when he said he had talked to Majesty after the end of the match.

Majesty's body reached the Pennsylvania R.R. depot at Toledo about 2:35 p.m. on February 26. His father was there to meet the train. John Hall met Majesty's father as the casket was removed from the train. An undertaker was on hand and the family was able to view the body. A lawyer also met the train and apparently told Hall not to talk to the press or to answer any questions. The following day a funeral was conducted at the home of Majesty's parents by an Episcopal minister, and Majesty was buried at Woodlawn Cemetery on West at 1502 West Central Avenue in Toledo.

The Legal Proceedings

The sheriff of Athens County picked up Macy, Seville, and Hennessy at the Columbus jail on February 26 and transported them to Athens, the county seat. The preliminary hearing was delayed for a few days because the, defendants' attorney had not been able to obtain a copy of the autopsy. Seville's bond was set at $3,000 on condition that he would appear before the Athens County grand jury. McHugh, Macy, and Hennessy's bonds were set at $800 on like conditions. None of the men were able to post the necessary amounts, and they were returned to jail. An indictment was soon returned, charging Seville with engaging as a principal in an unlawful and premeditated fight commonly called a prizefight. A separate indictment was also obtained charging Seville with murder, but that charge was later reduced to manslaughter.[597]

The trial in the case began in Athens on April 3.[598] To help prove that Seville had engaged in a prizefight, the letters that were written by Majesty to his friend Alfred Stephens were offered into evidence by the prosecution and admitted over the objections of Seville's attorneys. The defense introduced the license for the fight and the articles incorporating the Nelsonville Athletic Club. They also called a professional prizefighter as a witness to testify that he had participated in fifty-two prizefights and had attended the Majesty-Seville match.

This witness testified that in order for the contest to be a real prizefight, the rounds could not be limited in time, the contestants had to be permitted to wrestle or throw each other, the fight could not be of limited duration but not to a finish, and the fighters could not wear gloves. After this testimony the witness was asked to express his opinion as to whether the Majesty-Seville match was a prizefight. The prosecution objected, contending that this question called for the witness to express an opinion of law which was the province of the jury to decide following jury instructions that would be given by the court. That objection was sustained and the witness was not allowed to give his opinion on the ultimate issue.

The jury was instructed on the applicable law and returned a verdict of guilty. Seville was thereupon sentenced to one year in prison at hard labor. In late June, Seville filed a petition with the Ohio Supreme Court asking it to review his conviction.[599] The petition was allowed.

While waiting for the review of his conviction, Seville's problems multiplied. In October 1890, he had married Lena C. Baltzer, who was only eighteen years old at the time of their marriage.[600] In August 1891, Lena went to court in Columbus and obtained an injunction prohibiting her husband from disposing of property in Athens County valued at $3,000. The property held in Athens County was undoubtedly the cash Seville had posted to bond out of jail. Her action was taken as preliminary to a suit for alimony in which she charged that Seville had not supported her since they were first married.[601]

On March 2, 1892, the Ohio Supreme Court issued its opinion affirming Seville's conviction. Its decision was widely reported and even made the *New York Times*.[602] This decision set an important legal precedent and was frequently relied upon in other jurisdictions by courts trying to put an end to prizefighting.

After the decision, Seville went to the Ohio state prison and was turned away. He was told that he first had to go to Athens County and get a writ of *mittimus* from the county sheriff before he could begin his imprisonment.[603]

After he had been in prison for several months, Seville submitted an application for a pardon to the Ohio pardon board. About six weeks after, his application was rejected and he had to serve his full one-year imprisonment.[604] He was never tried for manslaughter, which was a harder case to prove.

Seville's Dissolute Life

Nothing very positive seemed to happen during the rest of Seville's life. In June 1894, he was arrested on charges of stealing a quantity of clothing from a man named Rosenfeld of Marion, Ohio.[605] Two years later when he was being arrested for public drunkenness, he got into a fist fight with the policeman who was trying to arrest him.[606] In November 1896, he announced that he was going to return to the ring and was willing to take his chances with the law.[607] In August 1897, Seville secured a fight with Johnny Van Heest who had been fighting professionally for ten years. Van Heest had been in two fights with Tommy Warren and had fought many other well-known fighters, including Tommy White, Danny Needham, Dan Daly, Young Griffo, Solly Smith, George Siddons, and Oscar Gardner. Van Heest whipped Seville in twelve rounds.[608] Seville also secured a fight with Dennis Gallagher that ended in a twenty-round draw that didn't amount to much because of police presence throughout the match.[609]

In 1901, Seville incorporated an entity known as the Manhattan Athletic Club. Somehow word reached Ohio's governor that Seville was the same man who had killed Majesty ten years earlier. The governor then ordered the Ohio attorney general to initiate legal proceedings to revoke the club's charter.[610]

After his unsuccessful attempts to become a prizefighter, Seville opened a saloon in Columbus. In that capacity he was arrested in connection with the murder of an unknown man whose body was found in the doorway of Seville's saloon. The man was believed to be about forty years old. A bar apron covered with blood was found near the body, and Seville admitted that the apron was his. Ultimately Seville was not prosecuted.[611]

Seville seems to have disappeared from the records after 1910. He had two additional failed marriages, but was living alone when he died in Columbus on June 11, 1944. He had lived fifty-three years after killing Arthur Majesty, an event that probably haunted him over all those years.

ACKNOWLEDGEMENTS

I have found in writing a book that no author can produce a credible work without the help of a great many people. The problem is remembering to give credit to all those who helped. The list of those who helped with this book must include the greatest boxing historian of our time Tracy Callis who has been so supportive and encouraged my efforts. Others who helped include the staff at the McLean County Museum of History and in particular Bill Kemp and George Perkins who helped with research about Arthur Magesty. I received additional important help from the Local History and Genealogy Department of the Toledo-Lucas County Public Library.

Susan Malone provided the highest quality research in helping confirm information relating to the McGurn family, which played an important role in Jimmy Barry's life. Tim McGurn gave me access to a family scrap book kept by his grandfather Charles G. McGurn that included information about Jimmy Barry that I could not have obtained from any other source. Pam Ackermann, another McGurn descendant also provided some information about McGurn's court from her great aunt which helped with the story of Jimmy Barry. The Ronald Williams library at Northeastern Illinois University also gave me access to its generous resources.

Jill Baker provided help with Reddy Gallagher as did James Rogers, Senior Librarian of the Western History/Genealogy Department of the Denver Public Library. The staff of Chicago's Newberry Library provided professional services and quick access to its world-class collection of books, manuscripts, and maps, that was significant in developing the chapters about Captain James Dalton and Jimmy Barry.

Finally, I want to thank my wife Martha who lived through the entire process, proofreads my early efforts, and listened to me talk about the disparate parts of each biography without complaint and with a great deal of patient encouragement.

ENDNOTES

Chapter 1

1   Illinois Statewide Death Index, Pre-1916; Name: Barry, Mary, date of death 1899-02-09, Chicago, Illinois, age at death 73 years, Cook County Certificate 00001170, Microfilm Roll 1033059 Item 2; "Jimmy Barry's Mother Dead," *Chicago Tribune*, Feb 2, 1899, 4.

In 1858 a tailor named John Shields lived at 91 North LaSalle, which was across the street from the home of Garrett and Mary Shields Barry. See Chicago City Directory, 1858 (John Gager & Co.), 266. In 1860 Anne Shields, who was born in Ireland in about 1798, was living at 137 Townsend in Chicago's 7th Ward and she was listed as the widow of John Shields. See D.B. Cooke & Co.'s Chicago City Directory for the year 1860-1861 (T.M. Halpin & Co. 1861), 327.

The Anne Shields who lived on Townsend had the following children living with her according to the 1860 census: James Shields, 17; Patrick Shields, 15; Michael Shields, 13; and Kate Shields, 10. See U.S. Census 1860; Census Place: Chicago Ward 7, Cook, Illinois; Roll: M653_167; Page: 822; Image: 128; Family History Library Film: 803167. There was a second Anne Shields who in 1860 was twenty-nine years old and also living nearby in Chicago's 7th Ward. A John Shields who was only four years old was living with this Anne Shields. See U.S. Census 1860; Census Place: Chicago Ward 7, Cook,

Illinois; Roll: M653_167; Page: 949; Image: 255; Family History Library Film: 803167.

Ten years later at the time of the 1870 census and Jimmy Barry was only nine months old there was a John Shields age thirteen living with his family. It seems probable that Mary Shields Barry was the oldest child of John and Anne Barry and that the younger Anne Shields listed in the 1860 census was another daughter of Anne and John Shields and a sister of Mary Shields Barry. It seems probable that the John Shields who was living with the younger Anne Shields in 1860 is the same person who was living with Mary Shields Barry in 1870. By 1870 the rest of the Shields children would have been old enough to be on their own. See U.S. Census 1870; Census Place: Chicago Ward 18, Cook, Illinois; Roll: M593_210; Page: 96A; Image: 195; Family History Library Film: 545709.

2 Illinois Statewide Death Index, Pre-1916; Name: Barry, Garrit [sic Garret], date of death 1885-11-06, Chicago, Illinois, age at death 67 years, Cook County Certificate 00072405, Microfilm Roll 1030912.

3 Chicago City Directory, 1858 (John Gager & Co.), 15; Chicago Business Directory and Commercial Advertiser, 1859, (S.C. Griggs & Co.), 36; Chicago City Directory for the Years 1860-61 (D.B. Cooke & Co.), 31; Chicago City Directory for the Year 1861-62 (Halpin & Bailey), 33; Chicago City Directory for the Year 1862-63 (Halpin & Bailey), 34; Chicago City Directory for the Year 1863-64 (Halpin & Bailey), 36; John C. W. Bailey's City Directory, Vol. X, for 1867-68 (John C. W. Bailey), 72; City Directories for Chicago, Illinois Year: 1872 (Richard

Edwards and Co.), 110; City Directories for Chicago, Illinois 1874 (Williams Donnelley and Company), 154; City Directories for Chicago, Illinois 1875 (Donnelley Loyd and Company), 151; City Directories for Chicago, Illinois 1890 (The Chicago Directory Company), 236; The Lakeside Directory of the City of Chicago 1893 (Reuben H. Donnelly & Sons Co.), 180 (Barry, Mary, 1106 Bonney Ave.); [See Thomas Barry] and intervening and following directories.

4 Selah was a north-south street that ran between Division and Wendel. It was located one block east of Judson and was only two blocks long. The first street that was south of Division was Elm Street, which intersected with Selah and ended at Judson. Elm was two blocks east of the ship canal off the North Branch of the Chicago River. The canal was the eastern border of Goose Island. The west side of Goose Island is framed by the North Branch of the river. The east side of Selah was the west side of Chicago's 18th Ward. See U.S. Census 1870; Census Place: Chicago Ward 18, Cook, Illinois; Roll: M593_210; Page: 96A; Image: 195; Family History Library Film: 545709; Peltzer's Atlas, Chicago, Illinois, Vol. 1; and Greeley, Carlson & Co's, Atlas of the City of Chicago (1884).

5 "Barry's Mother Is Hopeful," *Chicago Tribune*, Dec. 8, 1897, 6. Some sources assert that Dave Barry (aka "long count" Barry) was a brother of Jimmy Barry but this is not correct. The two fighters were not related.

6 Miller, Donald L., City of the Century, (Simon & Schuster Inc., 1996), 153; Chicago – The Great Central Market, (R. L. Polk & Co. 123), 24; Winslow, Charles S., Historic

    Goose Island, (Typescript, Oct. 10, 1938 – Newberry Library, Chicago).

7   Johnston, J.J. and Curtin, Sean, Chicago Boxing, (Arcadia Publishing, 2005), 15; City Directories for Chicago, Illinois 1874 (Williams Donnelley and Company), 154.

8   "Criminal," *Chicago Tribune*, Jun. 6, 1876, 8 (Michael Barry and Matthew Brennan entered a saloon on North Market where they drank and then refused to pay. They were ejected and began throwing stones at the saloon. When the owner tried to stop them he was attacked but shot Barry in the left arm before Barry was arrested); "Criminal Court," *Chicago Tribune*, Sep. 23, 1876, 3 (Michael Barry and John Mahoney guilty of larceny and given twenty days in the county jail); "Criminal," *Chicago Tribune*, Oct. 23, 1876, 8 (Michael Barry, Michael Fenton and Patrick Malloy assaulted a Chicago policeman at Larrabee and Division and taken to jail); "Criminal," *Chicago Tribune*, Aug. 15, 1877, 8 (Michael Barry fined $100 for whipping his mother); "Criminal," *Chicago Tribune*, Mar. 4, 1878, 8 (Michael Barry ejected from a saloon. He tries to reenter the saloon and stabs a patron in the shoulder with a pocket knife. In September 1877 he reportedly hit a police officer over the head with a brick); "Criminal," *Chicago Tribune*, May 30, 1878, 8 (fined $600 for the March 1878 stabbing incident and $500 for hitting his mother with a chair and breaking out her front teeth); "Criminal," *Chicago Tribune*, Feb. 10, 1879, 8 (charged with theft and threatening to kill his mother, he is reported to have served a dozen terms in Reform School or the House of Corrections); "Criminal," *Chicago Tribune*, Jan. 3, 1880, 3 (Barney Geary

and Michael Barry charged with burglary and assaulting Barry's mother); "Bad, Very Bad Barry," *Daily Inter Ocean*, Jan. 3, 1880, 2; "Police Negligence," *Chicago Tribune*, Jan. 4, 1880, 5 (Michael Barry being held in lieu of a $2,000 bond escapes but is recaptured trying to leave town); "The Brute Will Toil Long," *Daily Inter Ocean*, Dec. 16, 1881, 8 (charged with strangling his "step-mother" he attacks her lawyer in open court); "Miscellaneous," *Daily Inter Ocean*, Apr. 19, 1889, Part 1, 7 (burglary of home); "Daring Robbers. They Hold up a Man in the Back of a Saloon and Escape," *Daily Inter Ocean*, Feb. 12, 1892, 6; "Refused to Say Who Shot Him," *Daily Inter Ocean*, Dec. 31, 1894, 2. A few of these articles refer to Mary Barry as Michael's step-mother.

9 Illinois Statewide Marriage Index, 1763–1900, Groom: Flynn, James F., Bride: Margaret L., Date: 1883-10-15, License No. 00075946, Cook County, Microfilm Roll No. 1030135.

10 "Man Dead: Wife Is Accused," *Chicago Tribune*, Feb. 7, 1903, 11; "Causes Scene At Funeral," *Chicago Tribune*, Feb. 10, 1903, 14; "Murder Charge," *Dubuque Telegraph-Herald*, 6.

11 1Illinois Statewide Marriage Index, 1763–1900, Groom: Barry, Thomas J., Bride: McHenry, Mamie, Date: 1890-09-24, License No. 157858, Cook County, Microfilm Roll No. 1030194. Thomas J. Barry's employment is documented in Chicago city directories from 1886 through 1916.

12 "Sporting Notes," *Daily Inter Ocean*, Mar. 7, 1895, 4; "Barry Popular In Chicago," *Chicago Tribune*, Dec. 8, 1897, 6; <u>City</u>

Directories for Chicago, Illinois 1890 (Skinner William Mfg. Co.), 2854.

13   U.S. Census 1870; Census Place: Chicago Ward 18, Cook, Illinois; Roll: M593_210; Page: 96B; Image: 196; Family History Library Film: 545709; U. S. Census 1880; Census Place: Chicago, Cook, Illinois; Roll: 198; Family History Film: 1254198; Page: 14C; Enumeration District: 176; Image: 0323; U.S. Census 1900; Census Place: Chicago Ward 23, Cook, Illinois; Roll: T623_272; Page: 4B; Enumeration District: 686; "Old Handball Player is Dead," *Chicago Tribune*, Aug. 5, 1908, 11.

14   In October 1887 the Toronto newspaper still considered Gilmore to be living in Toronto. "The Ring. Gilmore Knocked Out in Five Rounds," *The Toronto Daily Mail*, Oct. 19, 1887, 10. Other newspapers considered Gilmore as being from Canada up to the end of 1887. "Gossip at Ringside," *The Philadelphia Record*, Dec 25, 1887, 2.

15   "General Sporting Notes," *Plain Dealer*, Feb. 4, 1888, 5; "Parson Davies' Big Scheme," *Chicago Herald*, Feb. 5, 1888, 3; "Evans and Muldoon. To Start out under Parson Davies Auspices with Special Offers to All Comers," *Cincinnati Commercial Tribune*, Feb. 6, 1888, 2; "Muldoon on Wrestlers," *Chicago Tribune*, Feb. 5, 1888, 14; "Miscellaneous Notes," *Chicago Herald*, Feb. 5, 1888, 14 "Lewis Downed McMahon," *Chicago Tribune*, Feb. 15, 1888, 6; "Will Settle Down Here," *Daily Inter Ocean*, Feb. 21, 1888, 2; "The Sporting World," *Plain Dealer*, Feb. 22, 1888, 5; "Sporting Notes," *Daily Inter Ocean*, Feb. 23, 1888, 10 (Gilmore telegraphs that he will return to Chicago this day apparently having failed to obtain backing for another

match with Myer); "Sporting. Gilmore Still Sanguine," *Daily Inter Ocean*, Feb. 23, 1888, 7; "Sporting Notes," *Daily Inter Ocean*, Mar. 2, 1888, 3 (Gilmore will immediately form a boxing class); "Phillips Confidence," *Daily Inter Ocean*, Mar. 6, 1888, 2.

16 "Harry Gilmore's New Position," *Chicago Tribune*, Oct. 8, 1888, 3.

17 "The City Politics," *Chicago Tribune*, Oct. 2, 1874, 5 (Michael McGurn is the 18th Ward representative to the Democratic executive committee for upcoming election), "A Speedy Trial," *Chicago Tribune*, Nov. 27, 1878, 5 (Michael McGurn charged with violating Internal Revenue Service laws, i.e., failing to collect or pay tax on liquor sold at his saloon); "In General," *Chicago Tribune*, Jul. 19, 1885, 16 (McGurn is a bridge tender at Halsted Street, i.e., a highly paid and political position); "Sporting Salad. The Garden City Athletic Club Begins Its Career with an Entertainment," *Daily Inter Ocean*, Jan. 6, 1888, 3; "Athletic," *Daily Inter Ocean*, Jan. 11, 1888, 6; "Local Politics," *Daily Inter Ocean*, Oct. 5, 1886, 7 (John McGurn is Democratic election clerk for the 17th Ward); "Sporting. Garden City Athletic Club," *Daily Inter Ocean*, Nov. 21, 1888, 2; "Harry Gilmore Benefit," *Daily Inter Ocean*, Dec. 9, 1888, Part 1, 2; "Sporting Notes," *Daily Inter Ocean*, Jun. 14, 1889, Part 1, 6 (Gilmore to meet Dan J. Kelly at McGurn's as part of a series of exhibitions); "The Colored Champion," *Daily Inter Ocean*, Jun. 29, 1889, 6; "Sparring Exhibition," *Daily Inter Ocean*, Jun. 30, 1889, 6: "Glove Contest," *Daily Inter Ocean*, Aug. 16, 1889, 6 (fighters include Ed Bartlett, Con Connors and Billy Young);

"Tommy White's Benefit," *Daily Inter Ocean*, Dec. 9, 1889, 7 (fighters include: Tom Morgan, Joe Rollo, Harry Gilmore, Ben Nolan, Frank Garrard, Artie Cudney, a clever featherweight, and a host of others).

18 "Jack Kelly to go to San Francisco," *Chicago Tribune*, Apr. 24, 1889, 3 (Harry Gilmore benefit at McGurn's); "General Sporting News," *Chicago Tribune*, Apr. 28, 1889, 10.

19 Advertisement, *Chicago Tribune*, Oct. 7, 1894, 23; Advertisement captioned "Instruction," *Daily Inter Ocean*, Jan. 20, 1895, Part 2, 19.

20 "Among the Chicago Gymnasiums," *Chicago Tribune*, Oct. 13, 1889, 6.

21 "Barry's Mother Is Hopeful," Chicago Tribune, Dec. 8, 1897, 6; "Jimmy Barry-Bantam King of '90s, Dies," *Chicago Tribune*, Apr. 5, 1943, 30 (he started boxing when 17 years old and weighing about 90 pounds); "Barry Starts His Boxing Career Early," *Chicago Tribune*, Apr. 6, 1943, 26 (his first lesson in McGurn's handball court…when only 12 years old).

22 "Barry's Mother Is Hopeful," *Chicago Tribune*, Dec. 8, 1897, 6; "Barry Popular In Chicago," *Chicago Tribune*, Dec. 8, 1897, 6; "In My Day – A Champion Didn't Lose," *Chicago Times*, Mar. 21, 1937, 52.

23 "Fought a Bloody Battle. William Brennan defeats Joe Rollo in a Terrific Fight," *Chicago Tribune*, Mar 10, 1890, 5; The Lakeside Annual Directory 1877 (The Lakeside Press), 670 (Michael McGurn had a grocery at Crosby on the northeast corner of Elm and a saloon on the north side of Elm near Crosby); The Lakeside Annual Directory of the City of Chicago – 1887 (The Chicago Directory Company),

1008; <u>The Lakeside Annual Directory of the City of Chicago – 1888</u> (The Chicago Directory Company), 1094; <u>The Lakeside Annual Directory of the City of Chicago – 1889</u> (The Chicago Directory Company), 1151; <u>The Lakeside Annual Directory of the City of Chicago 1889</u> (Reuben H. Donnelly), 1151 (Michael McGurn's saloon was at 206 Division and William McGurn was a bartender at 206 Division).

24 "Handball," *Daily Inter Ocean*, Jan. 7, 1888, Part 1, 3 (Will McGurn among the best handball players in the West); "Handball," *Daily Inter Ocean*, Feb. 16, 1888, Part 1, 2 (Cap Anson and Dennis Cronin in matches with Will and Michael McGurn); "Hand-Ball Tournament," *Chicago Tribune*, Apr. 14, 1889, 36.

25 "Jimmy Barry Whips a Foe and Gains a Lifelong Friend," *Chicago Tribune*, Apr. 7, 1943, 7; "Jimmy Barry's Trip," *Chicago Tribune*, Sep. 27, 1897, 4.

26 "The Contest Before the Olympic Club," *New Orleans Item*, May 31, 1894, 4; "In My Day – A Champion Didn't Lose," *Chicago Times*, Mar. 21, 1937, 52.

27 "Casino Sports," *Daily Inter Ocean*, Apr. 27, 1890, Part 1, 2.

28 "Among the Fighters," *Evening Tribune*, Feb 27, 1890, 4; "Among the Fighters," *Lawrence Daily Journal*, Mar 4, 1890, 4.

29 "Amateur Sporting Notes," *Chicago Tribune*, May 26, 1889, 12.

30 "Sparring and Wrestling Championships," *Chicago Tribune*, Mar. 16, 1889, 3; "Athletics Among the Soldier Boys," *Chicago Tribune*, Mar. 17, 1889, 11.

31 "General Sporting Notes. The Two Tommys Will Fight," *Chicago Tribune*, Aug. 9, 1889, 3 (Tommy White under Gilmore's supervision to fight Tommy Morgan to a finish in skin-tight gloves for $250 a side); "Jack Kelly to Go to San Francisco," *Chicago Tribune*, Apr. 24, 1889, 3 (Kelly to spar Billy Arthur at McGurn's); "General Sporting News. Sport at a Benefit," *Chicago Tribune*, Apr. 28, 1889, 10 (Fighters including Tommy White, Frank Garrard, Dan Kelly and Ben Donnelly to appear under Gilmore's supervision at McGurn's); "Brennen and White Matched," *Chicago Herald*, Mar. 29, 1890, 6 (Tommy White under Gilmore's supervision to fight Billy Brennen to a finish with skin-tight gloves); Corrothers, J. D., In Spite of the Handicap, (George H. Doran Company, 1916), 89–91; "Boxing at McGurn's Court," *Chicago Tribune*, Sep. 1, 1891, 6.

32 "Athletes at Turner-Hall," *Chicago Tribune*, Apr. 16, 1890, 6; "Sporting Notes," *Daily Inter Ocean*, Apr. 16, 1890, Part 1, 6 (describes the Young/Garrard fight as scheduled for six rounds).

33 "Make Believe Fighting," *Daily Inter Ocean*, Apr. 22, 1890, 2.

34 "Manager Whitney's Benefit," *Chicago Tribune*, Apr. 23, 1890, 2 (this article refers to a Billy Swift and Ganard but it seems apparent that the fighters involved were Billy Stift and Frank Garrard); "General Sporting Notes," *Chicago Tribune*, Apr. 27, 1890, 3 (this article correctly identifies Frank Garrard and William Stift but refers to "William" Barry rather than Jimmy Barry); "Casino Sports," *Daily Inter Ocean*, Apr. 27, 1890, 2; "Skill Of Athletes," *Daily Inter Ocean*, Oct. 20, 1892, 6.

35   "General Sporting Notes," *Chicago Herald*, Nov. 15, 1890, 7.

36   <u>The Lakeside Annual Directory of the City of Chicago 1891</u> (Reuben H. Donnelly), 1353 (Frederick Larson, r. 107 Hobbie, sailor); U.S. Census: 1920; Census Place: Chicago Ward 7, Cook (Chicago), Illinois; Roll: T625_315; Page: 8B; Enumeration District: 404; Image: 585; Roberts J. B and Skutt, Alexander J., <u>The Boxing Register: International Boxing Hall of Fame Official Record Book</u> (McBooks Press, 2006), 64; Johnston, A., <u>Ten-And Out! The Complete Story of the Prize Ring in America</u> (Ives Washburn, 1927); "In My Day – A Champion Didn't Lose," *Chicago Times*, Mar. 21, 1937, 52.

37   <u>The Lakeside Annual Directory of the City of Chicago 1891</u> (Reuben H. Donnelly), 462 (Cassidy, Thomas, teamster, h. 112 Sedgwick); U.S. Census: 1870; Census Place: Chicago Ward 7, Cook, Illinois; Roll: M593_202; Page: 148A; Image: 300; Family History Library Film: 545701.

38   <u>The Lakeside Annual Directory of the City of Chicago 1891</u> (Reuben H. Donnelly), 1594 (Miller, John, clk 242 State h. 349 Elm); U.S. Census: 1930; Census Place: Chicago, Cook, Illinois; Roll: 444; Page: 9B; Enumeration District: 659; Image: 442.0; "Was No Match for Tommy White," *Chicago Tribune*, Sep. 27, 1891, 6.

39   Casey, M, "Jimmy Barry. The Toughest Little Tiger," (Cyberboxingzone)("Jimmy Barry would hang 'em up with 70 official fights on his log and not one defeat."); Fleischer, N. and Andre, S., <u>An Illustrated History of Boxing</u> (Citadel Press, 2002), 367 (68 bouts between 1891 and 1897); Johnston, J.J. and Curtin, S., <u>Chicago</u>

Boxing, (Arcadia Publishing, 2005), 14 (KO'd 38 fighters in 60 bouts); Roberts, J.B. and Skutt, A.G., The Boxing Register (McBooks Press, 2006), 65 (59-0-9).

40 "Gilmore's Athletic Show," *Daily Inter Ocean*, Mar. 17, 1891, 6.

41 "Cleveland' Meets Barry. His Backer Throws Up the Sponge in the Fourth Round – Some Lively Set-Twos," *Chicago Herald*, Jun. 9, 1891, 6.

42 "Want To Fight Tommy Ryan," *Chicago Herald*, Jun. 9, 1891, 6.

43 "Blood At Battery D," *Daily Inter Ocean*, Jan. 13, 1892, 6.

44 "Sports Give A Show," *Chicago Tribune*, Feb. 2, 1892, 6.

45 "Ald. O'Brien Makes A Speech," *Chicago Tribune*, Dec. 3, 1891, 3; "Police Stop A Fight," *Chicago Tribune*, Feb. 16, 1892, 7.

46 Barry's reported fights can be found in the following: "Queenan And Baker," *Daily Inter Ocean*, Jan. 3, 1892, 6; "Made Good Guesses," *Daily Inter Ocean*, Jan. 14, 1892, 6; "Bowen And Murphy," *Daily Inter Ocean*, Feb. 10, 1892, 3; "The Ring," *Pittsburgh Dispatch*, Mar. 20, 1892, 6; "Boxing," *Daily Inter Ocean*, Apr. 2, 1892, 6; "Athletic Events," *Daily Inter Ocean*, May 21, 1892, 2; No Headline, *Fort Wayne Sentinel*, Aug. 10, 1892, 3; No Headline, *Fort Wayne Sentinel*, Aug. 18, 1892, 4; "Sporting Melange," *Daily Inter Ocean*, Oct. 14, 1892, 6; "Skill Of Athletes," *Daily Inter Ocean*, Oct. 30, 1892, 6; "Sporting Scraps," *Daily Inter Ocean*, Nov. 7, 1892, 6; "Fought A Draw," *Daily Inter Ocean*, Nov. 18, 1892, 6; "Romeo Where Art Thou?," *Daily Inter Ocean*, Nov. 15, 1892, 6; "Jackson And Lewis," *Daily Inter Ocean*, Dec. 2, 1892, 6; "Is Maher Sure To Lose,"

Brooklyn Eagle, Dec. 5, 1892, 7; "Gossip Of The Fighters," *New York Herald*, Dec. 5, 1892, 8; "Myer vs. McAuliffe," *Daily Inter Ocean*, Dec. 7, 1892, 6; "Won In Four Rounds," *Chicago Tribune*, Dec. 20, 1892, 7; "Fight to be Finished," *San Antonio Daily Light*, Dec. 29, 1892, 1.

47 "In The Tenth Round. Bob Quade Defeated By Jimmy Barry of Chicago," *Chicago Tribune*, Jan. 16, 1893, 12; "Boxers Appear In Public," *Kansas City Times*, Feb. 27, 1890, 2; "A Clever Contest Between Warren and Bobby Quade of this City," *Kansas City Times*, Apr. 23, 1890, 2.

48 "Edward Kelly Knocked Out," *Daily Inter Ocean*, Mar. 9, 1893, 1.

49 It seems unlikely that some of these matches took place. It is improbable that Barry had an exhibition with Jack Hooper in Brooklyn, New York on March 6, 1893 and then appeared with Frank Fitzgerald in Chicago on March 8, 1893. It is also unlikely that Barry fought Jack Levy on December 5, 1893 because the governor of Indiana had closed Roby using the Indiana National Guard and the club's reopening was pushed back to December 16, 1893. Before Roby reopened a receivership was created in Lake County, Indiana. In addition, while this match is sometimes called a match for the championship of America other records show that Levy had been soundly beaten at New Orleans by Jimmy Gorman and a Barry-Levy fight would not have been a championship fight.

50 "General Sporting Notes," *Chicago Tribune*, Jun. 5, 1893, 12.

51 "Will Fight At Roby," *Daily Inter Ocean*, Jul. 3, 1893, 4; "Carpet Sports," *The Morning Call*, Aug. 14, 1890, 7; "The

Sporting Fraternity," *The Daily Morning Astorian*, Sep. 4, 1890, 4; "Bogan Whips Shea," *The Morning Call*, Sep. 6, 1890, 8; "The Bogan-Shea Contest," *The Daily Morning Astorian*, Sep. 6, 1890, 3; "Blather of Pugilists," *Omaha Daily Bee*, Dec. 11, 1898, Part II, 14.

52 "Little Sol Smith Proves A Champion," *Times Picayune*, Jul. 11, 1893, 6; "Settled Him In Four Rounds," *Elkhart Daily Review*, Jul. 11, 1893, 1; "Won By Smith," *The Morning Call*, Jul. 11, 1893, 1; "Smith Wins the Fight," *The Salt Lake Herald*, Jul. 11, 1893, 1.

53 "Dempsey And Dick Burge Matched," *Chicago Tribune*, Jul. 25, 1893, 7.

54 "Pierce Is Particular," *Brooklyn Eagle*, Jul. 26, 1893, 2.

55 "Pugilistic Gossip," *Daily Inter Ocean*, Jul. 29, 1893, Part 1, 4; "The 'Kid's' Oppo-nent," *Saginaw News*, Aug. 28, 1893, 7.

56 In 1931 the *Chicago American* wrote: "Few will forget his historic battle with Johnny Connors for a $1,500 purse on Sept. 4, 1893." "Way Back When," *Chicago American*, Jan. 26, 1931. Few would forget because that match did not happen. "Did Not Materialize," *Bay City Times*, Sep. 5, 1893, 1; "Had a Surprise Party Planned," *Daily Inter Ocean*, Nov. 26, 1893, Part 1, 10 (reopening delayed until December 4, 1893); "Again Postponed," *Daily Inter Ocean*, Nov. 29, 1893; "Roby Managers Are Meek. Opening Again Postponed with Assurances of Peace to the Governor," *Daily Inter Ocean*, Dec. 2, 1893, Part 1, 6; "Governor Matthews Firm. Indianapolis National Guard Likely Again to Go to Roby," *Daily Inter Ocean*, Dec. 8, 1893, 8; "Roby Receivership Argued. Supreme Court of Indiana Has the Case Presented

by Attorneys," *Daily Inter Ocean*, Dec. 16, 1893, Part 1, 6; "Its Glory is Departed. Roby, Ind, Deserted and Forsaken by the Sporting Fraternity," *Daily Inter Ocean*, Jan. 28, 1894, Part 1, 8.

57 "The Ring," *Times-Picayune*, Aug. 18, 1893, 18; "The Ring," *New Orleans Item*, Oct. 12, 1893, 8.

58 "Live Sporting Notes," *New York Herald*, Oct. 28, 1893, 13; "Sporting Gossip," *New Orleans Item*, Oct. 30, 1893, 4; "The Ring," *New Orleans Item*, Nov. 11, 1893, 4.

59 "Fistic Stars Galore," *Daily Inter Ocean*, Nov. 12, 1893, 8; "Are All Boxing Stars," *Daily Inter Ocean*, Nov. 13, 1893, 4; "Good Fistic Exhibit," *Daily Inter Ocean*, Nov. 14, 1893, 8.

60 "Barry to Box Van Heest," *Daily Inter Ocean*, Dec. 4, 1893, 8.

61 "General Sporting Notes," *Chicago Tribune*, Dec. 14, 1893, 7; "Barry to Meet the Winner," *Daily Inter Ocean*, Dec. 14, 1893, 8.

62 "Pugilists Given Warning," *Salt Lake Tribune*, Dec. 27, 1894, 2.

63 "Connie Sullivan's 'Defy' Accepted," *Boston Daily Globe*, Jan. 2, 1894, 22; "Answers Connie Sullivan's Challenge," *New Haven Register*, Jan. 2, 1894, 1; "Sporting Miscellany," *Boston Journal*, Jan. 4, 1894, 3.

64 "Wrestling and Boxing Matches," *Chicago Tribune*, Jan. 9, 1894, 13.

65 "Barry Puts Out Cransden [sic]," *Brooklyn Eagle*, Jan. 23, 1894, 8; "Ended In A Clean Knock-Out," *Daily Inter Ocean*, Jan. 23, 1894, 8; "Lasted Just Three Rounds," *Worcester Daily Spy*," Jan. 24, 1894, 7.

66   "Glove Contests In Chicago. Plimmer's Partner Almost Knocked Out," *Brooklyn Eagle*, Feb. 7, 1894, 8; "The Police Interfered," *Daily Inter Ocean*, Feb. 7, 1894, 8; "Jimmy Barry Won," *The Evening Herald*, Feb. 7, 1894, 5; "Nothing Friendly About This," *Philadelphia Inquirer*, Feb. 8, 1894, 3.

67   "Sporting Notes," *Daily Inter Ocean*, Feb. 8, 1894, 8.

68   "Sporting Gossip," *Daily Inter Ocean*, Feb. 16, 1894, 8.

69   "In The Roped Arena," *Daily Inter Ocean*, Feb. 18, 1894, 9; <u>City Directory for Chicago Illinois – 1891</u> (R R Donnelley and Sons Company), 781- 82; <u>City Directory for Chicago Illinois–1892</u> (The Chicago Directory Company), 511–12; <u>City Directory for Chicago Illinois–1893</u> (The Chicago Directory Company), 561–62; <u>City Directory for Chicago Illinois–1894</u> (The Chicago Directory Company), 577-78; <u>City Directory for Chicago Illinois–1896</u> (The Chicago Directory Company), 662–63; <u>City Directory for Chicago Illinois–1898</u> (The Chicago Directory Company), 698–99; "Pat Fitzgerald Dead. Former Manager of Jimmy Barry Expires Suddenly in Denver, Supposedly of Heart Disease," *Chicago Tribune*, May 6, 1899, 7. Patrick and Frank Fitzgerald were children of Mary Fitzgerald who was the widow of Laurence Fitzgerald. Patrick was born in Peru, Illinois, in about 1892. It appears that their father had been a farmer who was living at Peru, Illinois, as early as 1870. See Year: 1870; Census Place: Peru, La Salle, Illinois; Roll: M593_244; Page: 670A; Image: 617; Family History Library Film: 545743. A Lawrence Fitzgerald was living at 38 Elm as early as 1876. He originally worked as a laborer and later as a confectioner. <u>1876 Lakeside Annual</u>

Directory 1877 (The Lakeside Press), 381 (Fitzgeralds living at 42 Elm); The Lakeside Annual Directory of the City of Chicago-1889 (Reuben H. Donnelly), 607 (Fitzgeralds living at 38 Elm).

70 "Abbott-Gilmore Match," *Daily Inter Ocean*, Feb. 24, 1894, Part 1, 6; "Abbott and Gilmore Tonight," *Chicago Tribune*, Feb. 28, 1894, 11; "Ready For The Mill," *Daily Inter Ocean*, Feb. 28, 1894, 8; "Knocks Gilmore Out," *Chicago Tribune*, Mar. 1, 1894, 11; "Gilmore Knocked Out," *Saint Louis Republic*, Mar. 1, 1894, 5; "Leon and Barry to Spar," *The Evening Herald*, Mar. 1, 1894, 5; "Stanton Abbott A Hard Fighter," *Philadelphia Inquirer*, Mar. 2, 1894, 4.

71 "Barry and Gorman," *Oshkosh Daily Northwestern*, May 1, 1894, 1; "Barrick [sic] and Gorman Matched," *Philadelphia Inquirer*, May 9, 1894, 3; "Barry-Gorman Matched," *Dallas Morning News*, May 14, 1894, 8; "It Is Settled," *Daily Telegram*, May 15, 1894, 1.

72 "General Sporting Notes," *Chicago Tribune*, May 24, 1894, 11; "Barry-Gorman Contest," *New Orleans Item*, May 25, 1894, 8; "Sporting Sprays–Everhardt The Victor," *New Orleans Item*, May 27, 1894, 5.

73 "The Contest Before the Olympic Club," *New Orleans Item*, May 31, 1894, 4.

74 "Gorman Defeated," *New Orleans Item*, Jun. 3, 1894, 4; "Jimmy Barry Beats Gorman," *Chicago Tribune*, Jun. 3, 1894, 4; "Jimmy Barry Proves the Boss Bantam," *Times Picayune*, Jun. 3, 1894, 8.

75 "Barry Looking for More to Conquer," *New Orleans Item*, Jun. 4, 1894, 8; "General Sporting Notes," *Chicago Tribune*, Jun. 6, 1894, 11; "Pugilistic. Barry and Trainer Depart,"

New Orleans Item, Jun. 6, 1894, 4; "Both Training Hard," *Boston Daily Globe*, Jun. 11, 1894, 7.

76 "Two Hot Matches," *Plain Dealer*, Jun. 16, 1894, 3; "Gilmore and Gallagher Matched," *Saint Louis Republic*, Jun. 16, 1894, 6; "Beaver Falls, Pa–Special," *Chicago Tribune*, Jul. 4, 1894, 11; "Barry to Retire," *The Saint Paul Globe*, Dec. 4, 1898, 10 (recapitulation of Barry's record list Harry Brooks).

77 "Sporting Notes," *Boston Journal*, Aug. 31, 1894, 8; No Headline, *New Orleans Item*, Sep. 5, 1894, 4; World War I Registration, Registration Location: New York County, New York; Roll: 1786971; Draft Board: 167 (provides date of birth); U.S. Census 1900; Census Place: Manhattan, New York, New York; Roll: T623_1121; Page: 14B; Enumeration District: 900 (reports birth in 1874 and immigration in 1884); U.S. Census 1910; Census Place: Manhattan Ward 12, New York, New York; Roll: T624_1013; Page: 8B; Enumeration District: 0304; Image: 1136; FHL Number: 1375026; U.S. Census 1910; Census Place: Manhattan Ward 12, New York, New York; Roll: T624_1014; Page: 24A; Enumeration District: 0321; Image: 631; FHL Number: 1375027; U.S. Census 1920; Census Place: Manhattan Assembly District 20, New York, New York; Roll: T625_1223; Page: 12A; Enumeration District: 1398; Image: 324.

78 "Leon And Barry to Battle," *Chicago Tribune*, Sep. 9, 1894, 4. Leon weighed 107 pounds when he arrived in Chicago. He predicted that he would weigh 108 pounds when he entered the ring. "Barry and Leon Still Training," *Chicago Tribune*, Sep. 14, 1894, 8.

79   "Leon And Barry To Meet," *Brooklyn Eagle*, Sep. 15, 1894, 2 ($1,000 purse with $1,500 side bets); "Barry and Leon," *New Orleans Item*, Sep. 15, 1894, 5 ($4,000 purse); "In My Day – A Champion Didn't Lose," *Chicago Times*, Mar. 21, 1937, 52.

80   "Jimmie vs. Casper," *Daily Inter Ocean*, Mar. 30, 1895, 5; Sugar, B.R., Boxing's Greatest Fighters (Globe Pequot, 2006), 291.

81   "Barry Defeats Leon. Chicago Bantam Wins The Fight In 28 Hard Rounds," *Chicago Tribune*, Sep. 16, 1894, 5; "Battle of Bantams. Barry of Chicago Whipped Leon of New York on Turf," *Oregonian*, Sep. 16, 1894, 6; "Barry Defeats Leon," *New Orleans Item*, Sep. 16, 1894, 5; "Barry's Face Hurt. He And Leon Show Broad Signs of Their Battle," *Chicago Tribune*, Sep. 17, 1894, 11.

82   "General Sporting Notes," *Chicago Tribune*, Sep. 25, 1894, 8.

83   "No Connors-Barry Match Made," *Chicago Tribune*, Sep. 18, 1894, 11; "Barry and Connors Cannot Agree," *Chicago Tribune*, Sep. 27, 1894, 8; "Connors and Barry Cannot Agree," *Chicago Tribune*, Oct. 9, 1894, 11; "Auditorium Events. Jimmy Barry Will Arrive In The City To-Night," *New Orleans Item*, Nov. 6, 1894, 2.

84   "Swings and Uppercuts," *Brooklyn Eagle*, Nov. 16, 1894, 4; "Fight Broken Up," *Fort Wayne Sentinel*, Nov. 17, 1894, 7; "Sporting Sprays, Pugilistic, Conners Is Here," *New Orleans Item*, Nov. 26, 1894, 2.

85   "Fistic Carnival," *New Orleans Item*, Dec. 2, 1894, 8.

86   "Bertrand-Church and Agnew-Sullivan Contests Come Off Tonight – Connors Is Ill," *Chicago Tribune*, Dec. 8, 1894,

4; "Fight Declared Off. Connors and Jimmy Barry Will Not Fight at New Orleans," *Morning Star*, Dec. 8, 1894, 1; "Tommy Ryan Arrives In New Orleans," *Chicago Tribune*, Dec. 9, 1894, 6; "Fistic Carnival. Jack Madden Will Meet Barry," *New Orleans Item*, Dec. 9, 1894, 8; "No Fight For Jimmy Barry," *Saint Louis Republic*, Dec. 13, 1894, 5; "Bowen Knocked Out," *Age Herald*, Dec. 15, 1894, 4; "New Orleans Is Aroused. The Killing of Bowen Causes a Wave of Social Reform to Sweep Over the City," *Daily Inter Ocean*, Dec. 17, 1894, 5.

87   "General Sporting Notes," *Chicago Tribune*, Dec. 25, 1894, 8; "No Match Made," *Daily Inter Ocean*, Dec. 27, 1894, 4; "'Parson' Davies Goes East," *Daily Inter Ocean*, Dec. 29, 1894, 4; "General Sporting Notes," *Philadelphia Inquirer*, Jan. 4, 1895, 4.

88   "Sporting Notes," *New York Herald*, Jan. 7, 1895, 11; "Any Bantam Will Do," *Morning Star*, Jan. 15, 1895, 1; "No Trust in Griffo," *Chicago Tribune*, Jan. 23, 1895, 5; Points for Pugilists," *Omaha World Herald*, Feb. 3, 1895, 12; "Sporting Miscellany," *World*, Feb. 14, 1895, 6; "Notes of the Boxers," *Brooklyn Eagle*, Feb. 17, 1895, 5.

89   "Live Sporting Notes," *New York Herald*, Jan. 28, 1895, 1; "Pugilism. Hercules Athletic Club Opens," *Plain Dealer*, Aug. 8, 1894, 3.

90   "The Australian Won," *Kansas City Star*, Jan. 4, 1895, 3; "Maciewski Saved a Knock Out," *Daily Inter Ocean*, Jan. 4, 1895, 3; "With a Leg and a Half," *Wheeling Register*, May 31, 1894, 1.

91   "Barry Can't Fight," *The {Decatur} Bulletin Sentinel*, Feb. 23, 1895, 3.

92 "Live Sporting Notes," *New York Herald*, Mar. 2, 1895, 11.
93 "For Billy Williams' Widow," *Daily Inter Ocean*, Mar. 7, 1895, 4.
94 "Matches for Ryan and Choynski," *Chicago Tribune*, Mar. 7, 1895, 11.
95 "McCall-Leon Fight Fails to Come Off," *Chicago Tribune*, Mar. 8, 1895, 11; "For Billy Williams Widow," *Daily Inter Ocean*, Mar. 8, 1894, 4.
96 "Dual Match Made," *Daily Inter Ocean*, Mar. 7, 1895, 4; "Fighters Leave for Kansas City," *Chicago Tribune*, Mar. 9, 1895, 7.
97 "Boxers In Clover," *Daily Inter Ocean*, Mar. 17, 1895, 11; "White and Siddons," *Philadelphia Inquirer*, Mar. 17, 1895, Part 2, 20.
98 "Bertrand Anxious to Fight," *Daily Inter Ocean*, Mar. 13, 1895, 4; "Notes of the Boxers," *Brooklyn Eagle*, Mar. 16, 1895, 4 (Barry and Madden will meet at 105 pounds); "Barry-Leon Match. Ireland and Italy Will Box Fifteen Rounds March 30," *Daily Inter Ocean*, Mar. 21, 1895, 4.
99 "The Sports," *Tacoma Daily News*, Oct. 13, 1894, 4; "With a Broken Hand," *Omaha World Herald*, Dec. 6, 1894, 3; "Ryan and Choynski Box," *Daily Inter Ocean*, Feb. 26, 1895, 4; "The Minor Attractions," *Daily Inter Ocean*, Mar. 22, 1895, 4; "A Draw in Choynski's Favor," *Plain Dealer*, Mar. 22, 1895, 3.
100 "Barry-Leon. Champion Rules Favorite Over Leon at 10 to 9," *Daily Inter Ocean*, Mar. 27, 1895, 4.
101 "The Barry-Leon Fights. Delegation of Sports to Visit Casper at His Training Quarters," *Daily Inter Ocean*, Mar. 24, 1895, 4; "Ziegler-Griffo Go Postponed," *Daily Inter*

Ocean, Mar. 25, 1895, 8; "Malachi Hogan The Referee. Barry and Leon's Managers Agree on the Popular North Sider," *Daily Inter Ocean*, Mar. 29, 1895, 4; "Barry and Leon to Meet Tonight," *Chicago Tribune*, Mar. 30, 1895, 7.

102 "Was a Police Finish. Barry-Leon Fight Stopped in the Fourteenth Round. Leon Hopelessly Beaten But A Draw Was the Verdict of the Referee," *Daily Inter Ocean*, Mar. 31, 1895, 10; "Casper Leon Knocked Out. Police Interfered or Jimmy Barry Would Have Been Given the Decision, Chicago Fight Declared a Draw After Fourteen Rounds of Unusually Lively Work. Italian Counted Out When the Officers Stepped Into the Ring – Honors for Several Rounds Were Nearly Even," *Chicago Tribune*, Mar. 31, 1895, 4; "Almost A Knock-Out For Barry," *Omaha World Herald*, Mar. 31, 1895, 6.

103 "Leon to Desert Ring for Track," *Plain Dealer*, Apr. 2, 1895, 3; "General Sporting Notes," *The Morning Times* (Washington, D.C.), Jan. 30, 1896, 3 ("Casper Leon ran second to Barry on two different occasions, once in a finish of twenty-eight rounds, and again in a police finish when the men were to go fifteen rounds.").

104 "General Sporting Notes," *Chicago Tribune*, Apr. 1, 1895, 11.

105 "Value of Height and Reach," *Saint Louis Republic*, Apr. 7, 1895, Part 2, 11.

106 "To Arrange for Three Fights," *Chicago Tribune*, May 3, 1895, 11.

107 "The Ring," *Jersey Journal*, Oct. 19, 1895, 4.

108 "Smith and Ryan Training," *Brooklyn Eagle*, May 24, 1895, 5.

109 "Barry Knocks Out Ross," *New York Herald*, Jul. 16, 1895, 10; "Only Two Rounds Needed Dave Ross of Somerset Proves Easy Plucking for the Boy From Chicago," *Omaha World Herald*, Jul. 16, 1895, 2.
110 "Boxing at Maspeth," *New York Times*, Oct. 22, 1891, 16.
111 "Varunas to Drop Boxing," *The World*, May 9, 1891, 7.
112 "No Money for the Peds," *The World*, Mar. 24, 1891, 3.
113 "Empire Athletic Club Incorporated," *New York Times*, Aug. 7, 1891, 6; "Handler and Lavigne to Box," *New York Times*, Aug. 20, 1891, 6; "They Were Evenly Matched," *New York Times*, Oct. 13, 1891, 3.
114 "Sporting Notes," *Daily Inter Ocean*, Sep. 4, 1895, 5; "Live Sporting Notes," *New York Herald*, Sep. 9, 1895, 9; "The Ring," *Jersey Journal*, Sep. 10, 1895, 4; "The Ring," *Jersey Journal*, Sep. 11, 1895, 3; "Jimmy Barry Will Have to Work to Win," *Chicago Tribune*, Sep. 13, 1895, 5; "Police Prevent a Fight," *Bridgetown Evening News*, Sep. 17, 1895, 2; "Barry-Madden Fight Is Stopped," *Chicago Tribune*, Sep. 17, 1895, 7; "Barry And Madden Do Not Meet," *Daily Inter Ocean*, Sep. 17, 1895, 3; "Barry-Madden Fight Postponed," *Saint Louis Republic*, Sep. 17, 1895, 4.
115 "Madden and Barry Meet Today," *Chicago Tribune*, Oct. 20, 1895, 7.
116 "Barry Wins In Four Hot Rounds. Madden Outclassed and No Match for Chicago's Little Champion," *Chicago Tribune*, Oct. 22, 1895, 7; "Jimmy Barry Bests Jack Madden. Chicagoan Thoroughly Outclasses the Game Brooklynite," *Daily Inter Ocean*, Oct. 22, 1895, 4; "Barry Defeats Madden," *New York Herald*, Oct. 22, 1895, 10; "Jimmy Barry's Trip," *Chicago Tribune*, Sep. 27, 1897, 4.

117 "Sporting Notes," *Daily Inter Ocean*, Nov. 5, 1895, 4.
118 "Two Great Bantams," *Philadelphia Inquirer*, Aug. 9, 1896, 9.
119 "Barry May Never Fight Again," *Brooklyn Eagle*, Dec. 2, 1895, 10; "Hand Is Still Good. Report of Jimmy Barry's Permanent Disability Untrue," *Daily Inter Ocean*, Dec. 3, 1895, 4.
120 "Chance For Champion Barry. May Get on a Match with Anthony of Australia," *Chicago Tribune*, Dec. 17, 1895, 8; "Sporting Chat," *Philadelphia Inquirer*, Dec. 27, 1895, 5.
121 "Barry And Leon Fight A Draw," *Chicago Tribune*, May 31, 1898, 4.
122 "Put Up, Connors," *Daily Inter Ocean*, Jan. 11, 1896, 4; "The Ring," *Jersey Journal*, Jan. 22, 1896, 7; "Fistic Program All Arranged," *Chicago Tribune*, Jan. 28, 1896, 8.
123 "Looks Like A Bantam Match," *Daily Inter Ocean*, Jan. 15, 1896, 7; "Will Outlast And Defeat Him. Murphy Has a Strong Opponent but Believes He Will Win," *Chicago Tribune*, Feb. 13, 1896, 7.
124 "Barry's Last Handball Game," *Chicago Tribune*, Jan. 26, 1896, 7.
125 "Off for El Paso," *Dallas Morning News*, Jan. 29, 1896, 2; "Is Off For The Fight," *Daily Inter Ocean*, Jan. 29, 1896, 4; "Pugs Arriving In Camp," *Chicago Tribune*, Feb. 2, 1896, 7; "Pugilism. Notes From the Carnival," *Plain Dealer*, Feb. 5, 1896, 8.
126 "Will Tender Him a Benefit. Jimmy Barry's Friends Preparing for a Big Demonstration," *Chicago Tribune*, Feb. 10, 1896, 8; "Handball at McGurn's," *Chicago Tribune*, Mar. 1, 1896, 7.

127 "Jimmy Barry's Hand Again 'Off'," *Chicago Tribune*, Mar. 20, 1896, 8; No Headline, *Plain Dealer*, Mar. 21, 1896, 8; No Headline, *Saint Louis Republic*, Mar. 23, 1896, 5.

128 "Much Talent Enlisted. Jimmy Barry's Benefit Should Be a Big Affair," *Daily Inter Ocean*, Apr. 5, 1896, 10.

129 "Foreign Talent Takes Part and a Good Entertainment Is Furnished," *Chicago Tribune*, Apr. 26, 1896, 5; "Handball Games Today," *Chicago Tribune*, Apr. 26, 1896, 6; "Saint Louis Boxers Victorious," *Saint Louis Republic*, Apr. 28, 1896, 5; "Jimmy Barry's Trip," *Chicago Tribune*, Sep. 27, 1897, 4.

130 "Points for Pugilists," *Omaha World Herald*, May 31, 1896, 10.

131 "General Sporting Notes," *Saint Louis Republic*, Jun. 3, 1896, 5.

132 "The Men In The Ring," *Philadelphia Inquirer*, Jun. 26, 1896, 5.

133 "General Sporting Notes," *Plain Dealer*, Jul. 25, 1896, 8.

134 "Champion Barry to Be Here," *Philadelphia Inquirer*, Aug. 2, 1896, 10; "General Sporting Notes," *New Haven Register*, Aug. 3, 1896, 7; "Two Great Bantams," *Philadelphia Inquirer*, Aug. 9, 1896, 9; "Fighting Gossip," *The Sun*, Aug. 17, 1896, 9.

135 "Barry Beats Flanagan. The Champion Proves That He Is an Artist in the Art of 'Hit and Get Away.' Local Boy Outclassed," *Philadelphia Inquirer*, Aug. 11, 1896, 5.

136 "Some Ring Talk," *Repository*, Aug. 30, 1896, 5; "A Challenge to the World," *Saint Louis Republic*, Sep. 2, 1896, 5.

137 "General Sporting Notes," *Plain Dealer*, Nov. 14, 1896, 3.

138 "Barry Has Rheumatism," *Daily Inter Ocean*, Oct. 2, 1896, 7; "Sporting Notes," *Daily Inter Ocean*, Oct. 26, 1896, 4.

139 "Sporting Briefs," *Philadelphia Inquirer*, Dec. 11, 1896, 7; No Headline, *Jersey Journal*, Dec. 14, 1896, 7; "Sporting Notes," *Boston Journal*, Dec. 26, 1896, 4; "The Barry-Kelly Match," *Brooklyn Eagle*, Dec. 27, 1896, 8; "Smashes On The Wind," *Philadelphia Inquirer*, Jan. 4, 1897, 5.

140 "Picks Fitz," *Daily True American*, Jan. 4, 1897, 2.

141 "Chat," *Reading Eagle*, Jan. 4, 1897, 3; "Fair Prospect," *Boston Daily Globe*, Jan. 4, 1897, 9; "A Lively Battle," *Plain Dealer*, Jan. 29, 1897, 3.

142 Barry, R., "Sammy Kelly – Premier Bantam," *Pearson's Magazine*, Vol. 30, Issue 1, 56-62.

143 "General Sporting Notes," *Plain Dealer*, Jan. 20, 1897, 3; "Dixon Defeats Murphy," *The Philadelphia Record*, Jan. 23, 1897, 11; "Live Sporting Notes," *New Haven Register*, Jan. 29, 1897, 9.

144 "Ed Smith's Comment," *Republic*, Jan. 19, 1918, 7A.

145 "Barry-Kelly Fight Results In A Draw," *Philadelphia Inquirer*, Jan. 31, 1897, 9; "Barry Meets His Match," *Boston Daily Globe*, Jan. 31, 1897, 84; "Bantams Fight A Draw," *Salt Lake Tribune*, Jan. 31, 1897, 3; "In My Day – A Champion Didn't Lose," *Chicago Times*, Mar. 21, 1937, 52.

146 "Gossip Of The Boxers," *Trenton Evening Times*, May 9, 1897, 3; "In My Day – A Champion Didn't Lose," *Chicago Times*, Mar. 21, 1937, 52.

147 "Kelly Knocked Out Plimmer," *Morning Times*, Mar. 10, 1897, 3; "Tad's Tid Bits," *New Castle*, Jan. 24, 1923, 16.

148 "Jimmy Barry And Ward Are Matched," *Chicago Tribune*, Feb. 21, 1897, 7.
149 "Jimmy Barry Gets The Decision," *Chicago Tribune*, Mar. 2, 1897, 3; "Jimmy Barry Gets Decision," *Boston Daily Globe*, Mar. 2, 1897, 22; "Barry Downs Ward," *Morning Star*, Mar. 2, 1897, 1; "Barry Gets The Decision," *Philadelphia Inquirer*, Mar. 2, 1897, 4; "Barry Was Given The Decision," *Saint Louis Republic*, Mar. 2, 1897, 5; "Awarded to Barry," *The Saint Paul Globe*, Mar. 2, 1897, 7; "Jimmy Barry. The Champion Bantamweight Bower and his Methods," *Fort Wayne News*, Mar. 10, 1897, 7.
150 "Was On His Way To Carson City," *Omaha Daily Bee*, Mar. 10, 1897, 5; "Sullivan And His Party," *San Francisco Chronicle*, Mar. 12, 1897, 9.
151 Advertisement, *Gazette Telegraph*, Mar. 7, 1897, 5.
152 "Sports In Denver," *Daily Journal*, Mar. 11, 1897, 1; "Davies On The Fight," *Omaha World Herald*, Mar. 12, 1897, 1.
153 "Parson Davies and His Pugilistic Stars," *Gazette Telegraph*, Mar. 11, 1897, 5; "'Parson' Davies' Special. As Now Scheduled, It Will Pass Through Salt Lake," *Salt Lake Herald*, Mar. 11, 1897, 2; "Parson Davies and His Pugilistic Stars," *{Colorado Springs} Gazette Tribune*, March 11, 1897, 5.
154 "Celebrated Pugilists Here," *Salt Lake Herald*, March 15, 1897, 7.
155 "Parson Davies' Colored Hercules. Robert Armstrong Is Ready to Fight Any Heavyweight. Jimmy Barry, the Champion Bantam, Is Also Looking for a Match," *San Francisco Call*, Mar. 17, 1897, 9.
156 "Chicago's Only Champion Fighter," *Chicago Tribune*, March 31, 1897, 8.

157 "Anthony To Barry. The Australian Bantam Is Willing to Fight for the Entire Purse," *San Francisco Call*, Mar. 17, 1897, 14; "Anthony And Barry. The Little Pugilists Will Fight in This City in April," *Morning Call*, Mar. 29, 1898, 9.
158 "Davies and Barry Reach Chicago," *Chicago Tribune*, May 7, 1897, 6.
159 "Pugilistic Briefs," *Chicago Tribune*, April 7, 1897, 8.
160 "General Sporting Notes," *Plain Dealer*, May 15, 1897, 3 (Ben Jordon wants to fight Palmer at 121 pounds); "General Sporting Notes," *Plain Dealer*, May 29, 1897, 3 (Palmer will fight in the future at 128 pounds).
161 "Barry Too Clever For Jimmy Anthony. He Landed As He Wished," *San Francisco Chronicle*, Apr. 27, 1897, 5; "Bantam Championship. Is Won by Jimmy Barry in a Fierce Twenty Round Fight," *Fort Wayne Daily Gazette*, Apr. 27, 1897, 1; "The World At Large," *Herald Weekly*, May 1, 1897, 2.
162 "Choynski-Fitzsimmons," *Aspen Daily Times*, May 1, 1896, 1.
163 "Omaha At A Glance," *Omaha World Herald*, May 3, 1897, 2.
164 "Amusements," *Omaha World Herald*, May 4, 1897, 4; "Amusements," *Omaha World Herald*, May 5, 1897, 6.
165 "Davies And Barry Reach Chicago," *Chicago Tribune*, May 7, 1897, 6.
166 "Parson Davies' String," *Grand Rapids*, Jun. 9, 1897, 1; Advertisement, *Kalamazoo Gazette*, Jun. 12, 1897, 4; "Had A Cork Leg, But Was A Boxer," *Chicago Tribune*, Jul. 2, 1897, 6; "Pugilists Arrive in Chicago," *Chicago Tribune*, Jul. 5, 1897, 5.
167 "Miscellaneous Sporting News," *Omaha World Herald*, Jul. 11, 1897, Part 3, 20; "Sullivan and Palmer May Meet,"

Philadelphia Inquirer, Jul. 12, 1897, 5; "Miscellaneous Sporting News," *Omaha World Herald*, Jul. 18, 1897, Part 2, 16 (asserting that Dave Sullivan claimed the 116 pound championship of America because of Barry's refusal to meet him); "General Sporting Notes," *Plain Dealer*, Jul. 20, 1897, 6 (discussions with Johnny Connors); "Around the Roped Arena, *Syracuse Daily Standard*, Jul. 30, 1897, 9; "Prospect In England Is Better. Charles E. Davies Discusses the Chances of the Ambitious Boxers on the Other Side," *Chicago Tribune*, Aug. 1, 1897, 38; "Jimmy Barry and Johnny Connors," *Chicago Tribune*, Aug. 5, 1897, 4.

168 "Only Short Bouts-Mayor Harrison Will Not Permit Twenty-Round Goes," *Chicago Tribune*, Oct. 13, 1897, 4.

169 "The Parson's Plans-Charles E. Davies In Saint Louis and Representing the Boxers-
Joins the Press Club Boys-And May Give a Royal Entertainment With Them in the Coliseum," *Saint Louis Post Dispatch*, Oct. 20, 1897, 5; "Col. Hopkins In Town-He Has Something to Say About the Creedon-McCoy Battle," *Saint Louis Post Dispatch*, Oct. 21, 1897, 7.

170 "General Sporting Notes," *Plain Dealer*, Jul. 30, 1897, 6; "Note of the Boxers," *Chicago Tribune*, Sep. 8, 1897, 4; "Sturch Knocks Out Richards," *Chicago Tribune*, Sep. 21, 1897, 4; "Jimmy Barry's Trip," *Chicago Tribune*, Sep. 27, 1897, "General Sporting Notes," *Plain Dealer*, Oct. 4, 1897, 3; "General Sporting Notes," *Plain Dealer*, Oct. 12, 1897, 12; "Gossip of the Ring," *Wilkes-Barre Times*, Jul 8, 1897, 3; "In the Sporting Boiler," *Philadelphia Inquirer*, Jul. 10, 1897, 4; "Sporting Notes," *Boston Journal*, Aug. 7, 1897, 3.

171 "Smith and Palmer Matched," *Dallas Morning News*, Aug. 11, 1897, 5 (Smith-Palmer at 122 pounds); "Dave Sullivan to Fight Palmer," *The San Francisco Call*, Aug. 21, 1897, 5; "Gossip of the Ring," *The Sun*, Aug. 25, 1897, 4; "Around the Roped Arena," *The Scranton Tribune (Morning Edition)*, Aug. 30, 1897, 2: "American Money," *Repository*, Oct. 18, 1897, 8 (Sullivan-Palmer at 116 pounds); "Sporting Notes," *Wilkes Barre Times*, Oct. 18, 1897, 3 (Palmer to retire); "Great Bantam Fight," *Des Moines Daily News*, Oct. 18, 1897, 1 (Sullivan to wear the stars and stripes); "Fighting," *The Sun*, Jan. 21, 1898, 4.

172 "'Pedlar' Palmer Injured," *New Haven Register*, Oct. 19, 1897, 2; "General Sporting Notes," *Plain Dealer*, Oct. 22, 1897, 6 (broke his wrist); "Palmer the Winner," *Daily Iowa Capital*, Oct. 19, 1897, 3 (After tire contest it was ascertained that Palmer had injured both hands during the eleventh round, the right being practically useless); "Sporting Notes," *Lloyds Weekly Newspaper*, Oct. 21, 1897, 23 (Palmer had to go to hospital for treatment of injured wing); "Poplar Hospital and the Pugilist," Charity Record, Nov. 4, 1897, 20 (Pedlar Palmer, the pugilist appears to be popular with the patients of the Poplar Hospital where he attended for an injured wrist caused by a fistic encounter with Dave Sullivan. As Palmer won 600£ on that occasion, and during the past two years he has won stakes amounting to 3,000£, it may seem scarcely right that he should be the recipient of free medical aid.)

173 "Palmer's Victory Over Sullivan Not Unexpected," *Saint Louis Republic*, Oct. 25, 1897, 6.

174 "Among the Pugilists," *Milwaukee Journal*, Oct. 2, 1897, 7.

175 "Among the Boxers," *The Evening Times*, Sep. 2, 1897, 6 (There is every intent to match Barry and Leon in New York); "Barry Willing to Meet Leon," *The Evening Times*, Sep. 8, 1897, 6 (Barry willing to meet Leon at between 108 and 112 pounds); "Among the Boxers," *The Times*, Sep. 17, 1897, 6 (Palmer intends to retire. He wants to come to America but not to fight); "Accepts an Offer to Fight," *The Times*, Sep. 26, 1897, 9 (Barry agreed that he was willing to meet Leon for $1,000); "A Bantam on His Travels," *The Evening Times*, Sep. 27, 1897, 6 (Barry willing to meet any English bantam at between 107 to 110 pounds); "General Sporting Notes," *Plain Dealer*, Oct. 4, 1897, 3 (Mike Small Barry's likely opponent in England).

Many writers have attempted to explain the weight classes that existed among lighter weight fighters at the time. Dan Cuoco took a shot at making sense of the situation in "The Paperweight Championship" posted to IBRO in April 2001. In part, he wrote:

At that time [the 1880s], the bantamweights were 105, the featherweights 115, and another, apparently nameless division, existed at 124-126.

Here's what happened: World bantamweight champion Tommy (Spider) Kelly agreed to 110 for his defense against Britain's Billy Plimmer in 1892, World featherweight king George Dixon increased that [featherweight] class from 115 to 118, and world

126-pound champion Young Griffo tried to take the weight of his class to 130. The next steps came when Billy Plimmer, having beaten Kelly, took the bantam limit to 112, and his successor Pedlar Palmer, lifted it to 116 with the National Sporting Club's blessings. Dixon then defended the featherweight title at 122, while the rapidly expanding Griffo just declared himself a lightweight.

So, the old 124-126 pound championship passed out of existence, the featherweight division came up to replace it, and the bantams came up to one pound above where the featherweight had been, The paperweights now moved up, too – to 100 and then to 105, exactly where the bantamweights had been five years before.

Jimmy Barry of Chicago was the first notable paperweight (or "flyweight"), though American record books have misguidedly listed him as "bantamweight" champion. Barry who turned pro in 1891 following an amateur career won the 100-pound title with a 17th round knockout over Jack Levy on December 5, 1893. This bout, fought with skin-tight gloves, was held in the small town of Roby, Indiana...

While this analysis might have applied some logic to the situation, there was no authority that consistently defined weight classes in the 1890s. There was no logical explanation of what was happening. See Goldman, H., "The Paperweight Championship," *Boxing Digest*, Oct. 1896. As explained in the text of this chapter the National Sporting Club called the Barry-Croot match as a fight at seven stones and ten pounds (108 pounds)—which does not fit any of the classes Cuoco identifies—and the international press consistently described the fight as for the bantamweight championship. No contemporary article has been located that refers to the match as a fight between paperweights.

In February 1904 Thomas S. Andrews, the author of annual boxing record books and a Milwaukee newspaper reporter, and Parson Davies successfully convened a meeting of club managers and newspaper writers in Detroit to form a National Boxing Association. The officers and directors were reported: President, William H. Considine of Detroit; Secretary-Treasurer, Thomas S. Andrews of Milwaukee; Directors, Charles E. Davies of the Southern Athletic Club of New Orleans, E. H. Bigham of Indianapolis, Dr. J. H. Message of Chicago's Battery D Athletic Club; James Manon of the Pittsburgh Athletic Club; and A. R. Bright, of the Milwaukee Athletic Club. As one of its first acts, the association established a uniform set of weight classifications that were to govern all fights in the United States. The eleven new classifications were: special (or "minimus") class, 105 pounds or lighter; light bantamweights, 110 pounds; bantamweights, 115; featherweights, 122; heavy featherweights 127; lightweights, 133; light welterweights, 140; welterweights, 148; middleweights, 158; light heavyweights, 175; and heavyweights, all men over 175. These classifications were to hold until the association's next meeting, when the officers and directors would review suggestions provided by prominent men interested in the boxing game in America.

See Dunn, M., Chicago's Greatest Sportsman, Charles E. "Parson" Davies at 481–483 (2011). If this classification system had existed in 1897 then the Barry/Croot fight would have been between light bantams.

The National Sporting Club of London finally established its own eight weight classes in 1909—twelve years after Jimmy Barry knocked out Walter Croot. Those weight classes were: flyweight 112 pounds; bantamweight 118 pounds; featherweight 126 pounds; lightweight 135 pounds; welterweight 147 pounds; middleweight 160 pounds; cruiserweight 175 pounds; and heavyweight over 175 pounds. If this system had existed in 1897 then the Barry-Croot match would have been between flyweights.

176 "May Fight Tonight," *Chicago Tribune*, Dec. 6, 1897, 4.
177 "At the Ringside," *Trenton Evening Times*, Oct. 4, 1897, 6; "Police," *The Times* [of London]," Dec. 8, 1897, 5.
178 See footnote 176 above; "Sporting Notes," *Lloyds Weekly Newspaper*, Oct. 24, 1897, 23.
179 "Gives Fight to Palmer," *Chicago Tribune*, Apr. 18, 1899, 4.
180 "Gossip of the Ring," *The Sun*, Nov. 7, 1897, 2 (Barry match to fight Croot on November 16, 1897); "Jimmie Barry Has A Match. Will Meet an English Bantam, Walter Croat [sic], on Nov. 15 [sic]," *Chicago Tribune*, Nov. 7, 1897, 7; "Miscellaneous Sports," *Omaha World Herald*, Nov. 14, 1897, 24; "John Fleming Dead," *The Philadelphia Record*, Nov 16, 1897, 11; "Death of Mr. John Fleming," *London Daily Mail*, Nov. 16, 1897, 6; "Sporting," *Otago Daily Times*, Dec. 20, 1897, 3.

181 "Gossip of the Ring," *Omaha Daily Bee*, Nov. 21, 1897, Part 3, 18; No Headline, *Jersey Journal*, Nov. 29, 1897, 6; "Among the Fighters," *The Evening Times*, Nov. 30, 1897, 2; "Jimmy Barry Pines For Pins of Old," *Chicago American*, Jan. 26, 1931. The date of this last article is uncertain as it is taken from a McGurn family scrapbook. The article is written by Jimmy Corcoran who was a long-time Chicago sportswriter for the *Chicago Herald-American*.

182 "Prize Fight Ends Fatally," *New Haven Register*, Dec. 7, 1897, 3; "Jimmy Barry Wins. Knocks Walter Croot Out in Twenty Rounds in London," *Trenton Evening Times*, Dec. 10, 1897, 6; "English Bantam Weight Dies," *Butte Weekly Miner*, Dec. 9, 1897, 8; "Barry Wins the Bantam Championship," *Daily Telegraph*, Dec. 7, 1897, 1; "The Fatal Glove Fight," *Lloyds Weekly Newspaper*, Dec. 19, 1897, 23.

183 "Barry Whips Walter Croot," *Kansas City Journal*, Dec. 7, 1897, 5; "Barry Knocks Out England's New Champion," *Chicago Tribune*, Apr. 9, 1943, 27. The number of corner men who have told a fighter before a final round that they could not win a match without knocking out their opponent probably cannot be numbered. How often a corner man believes what he is saying cannot be determined.

184 Some accounts say that the final blows were two left handers to the ribs and a right to the ear. See "Boxer Croot Dead," *Chicago Tribune*, Dec. 8, 1897, 6.

185 See note 183 above.

186 "Barry Popular In Chicago," *Chicago Tribune*, Dec. 8, 1897, 6; "Police," *The Times* [of London], Dec. 8, 1897, 5.

187 "English Bantam Weight Dies," *Butte Weekly Miner*, Dec. 9, 1897, 8 (states Croot died at 9:00 a.m.); "Jimmy Barry Wins. Knocks Walter Croot Out in Twenty Rounds in London," *Trenton Evening Times*, Dec. 10, 1897, 6 (states Croot died at 8:30 a.m.); "Lord Londale [sic] on Boxing," *Butte Weekly Miner*, Feb. 10, 1898, 11.

188 "Death In Ring Back 30 Years," *Reno Evening Gazette*, Feb. 7, 1923, 10.

189 "Police," *The Times* [of London], Dec. 8, 1897, 5; "Fatal Knock-Out Blow, Barry and Others Arrested. Charged With the Death of Croot," *Morning Star*, Dec. 8, 1897, 1; "English Bantam Weight Dies," *Butte Weekly Miner*, Dec. 9, 1897, 8 (states Croot died at 9:00 a.m.); "Victim Of The Ring. Young Croot Dead and Jimmy Barry Under Arrest," *New York Times*, Dec. 8, 1897, 7; "English Bantam Weight Dies. Walter Croot of Newcastle Succumbs to the Blows of Barry, the American – Participants Held to Answer, *New York Times*, Dec. 8, 1897, 7.

190 See footnote 186 above.

191 "Jimmy Barry Gets Off. Verdict of Accidental Death in the Case Against Him," *Daily Register Gazette*, Dec. 11, 1897, 2; "It Was An Accident. Jimmy Barry Was Not Responsible for the Death of Croot," *Grand Rapids Press*, Dec. 11, 1897, 3; "Jimmy Barry Cleared. Jury in Croot Case Says Death Was Accidental," *Philadelphia Inquirer*, Dec. 12, 1897, 6; "Police," *The Times* [of London], Dec. 15, 1897, 17.

192 "Croot Affair Not Settled," *Philadelphia Inquirer*, Dec. 15, 1897, 4; "In Bow Street Jail," *Boston Journal*, Dec. 15, 1897,

5; "Jimmy Barry and Others Released," *Bangor Daily Whig and Courier*," Dec. 22, 1897, 1.

193 "Barry Will Fight No More. Announces His Decision in a Letter to 'Parson' Davies-Lord Lonsdale on the Fight," *Chicago Tribune*, Dec. 25, 1897, 7; "Barry Says He Is Through," *Philadelphia Inquirer*, Dec. 26, 1897, 13; "Will Jimmy Barry Retire," *Philadelphia Inquirer*, Dec. 28, 1897, 14; "Jimmy Barry Home," *Trenton Evening Times*, Jan. 7, 1898, 6; "Jimmy Barry Desires A Match," *New York American*, Jan. 8, 1898, 7; "General Sporting Notes," *Plain Dealer*, Jan. 10, 1898.

194 "Jimmy Barry Home," *Trenton Evening Times*, Jan. 7, 1898, 6; "Sporting Gossip," *The Evening Times*, Jan. 7, 1898, 6; "Jimmy Barry Desires A Match," *New York American*, Jan. 8, 1898, 7.

195 "Jimmy Barry Arrives In Chicago. Willing to Fight Any One in His Class After He Rests Up," *Chicago Tribune*, Jan. 9, 1898, 6; "Barry Will Accept Skelly's Offer," *Chicago Tribune,* Jan. 10, 1898, 4.

196 "Anson in a Handball Match," *Chicago Tribune*, Jan. 23, 1898, 7.

197 "'Tod' Sloan [sic] in 'Frisco," *Kansas City Star*, Feb. 7, 1898, 3.

198 "Leon Will Meet Barry," *Chicago Tribune*, Jan. 27, 1898, 4; "'Parson' Davies Gets Offer," *Kansas City Star*, Jan. 29, 1898, 3.

199 "Purse for Barry and Sammy Kelly," *Chicago Tribune*, Jan. 29, 1898, 7; "The Ring. Bob Armstrong Knocked Out," *Time Picayune*, Jan. 30, 1898, 8.

200 "Notes of the Boxers," *Chicago Tribune*, Feb. 1, 1898, 4; "Big Purse for Leon and Barry," *Jersey Journal*, Feb. 2, 1898, 2; "General Sporting Notes," *Kansas City Star*, Feb. 7, 1898, 3.

201 "Fred Bogan – Is in Town, Looking For a Match," *Cincinnati Enquirer*, Jan. 15, 1898, 3; "Barry Coming," *Cincinnati Enquirer*, Jan. 27, 1898, 3; "A Match," *Portsmouth Daily Times*, Jan. 27, 1893, 8; "Tod Sloan Will Be In Cincinnati Tomorrow," *Cincinnati Enquirer*, Jan. 27, 1898, 3; "An Offer Made For Barry and Kelly," *Cincinnati Enquirer*, Jan. 29, 1898, 2; "Barry Here," *Cincinnati Enquirer*, Jan. 30, 1898, 2; "Jimmy Barry, The Champion Bantam Weight, Drew Well at People's," *Cincinnati Enquirer*, Jan. 31, 1898, 3; "Affairs Pugilistic," *Evening Herald* [Syracuse], Feb. 1, 1898, 2; "Local Men Will Have a Chance To Meet Jimmy Barry," *Cincinnati Enquirer*, Feb. 2, 1898, 3; "At Cincinnati. Danny Rewan Who Will Box Here Will Meet the Champion of the World Tonight," *Portsmouth Daily Times*, Feb. 5, 1898, 3; "Jimmie Barry – Made a Nice Set-To," *Cincinnati Enquirer*, Feb. 5, 1898, 3; "A Splendid Match," *Portsmouth Daily Times*, Feb. 7, 1893, 3; "Tod Sloan's Future," *Cincinnati Enquirer*, Feb. 8, 1898, 4; "Bets By Boxers Fatal," New York American, Feb. 9, 1898, 7; "Hooks and Jabs," *Trenton Evening Times*, Feb. 11, 1898, 6 (Bogan signed to fight Oscar Gardner at 122 pounds); "General Sporting Notes," *Kansas City Journal*, Feb. 23, 1898, 5.

202 "General Sporting Notes," *Plain Dealer*, Feb. 15, 1898, 6; "Barry Receives an Offer," *Chicago Tribune*, Feb. 17, 1898,

8; "General Sporting Notes," *Chicago Tribune*, Feb. 20, 1898, 7; "Local Sports," *Morning Herald*, Feb. 23, 1898, 5.

203 "Biggest Fight of Season. Casper Leon and George Munroe Meet in Fifteen-Round Bout Tonight," *New Haven Register*, Mar. 3, 1898, 9.

204 "Richie [sic] of Saint Louis Matched with Barry. The World's Bantam Champion Consents to Meet the Local Lad at Catch Weights," *Saint Louis Republic*, Mar. 7, 1898, 6; "Barry And Ritchie Matched. Champion Is to Meet the Saint Louis Boxer at the C.A.A. on Saturday Night," *Chicago Tribune*, Mar. 7, 1898, 9.

205 "Barry Receives an Offer," *Chicago Tribune*, Feb. 17, 1898, 8; "St. Patrick's Day Bouts. List of Fights To Be Held At Tattersall's," *Chicago Tribune*, Mar. 2, 1898, 4; "General Sporting Notes," *Kansas City Star*, Mar. 2, 1898, 2; "Grand Meeting of 'Pugs'," *Morning Star*, Mar. 2, 1; "Everhardt Is To Box Here," *Chicago Tribune*, Mar. 8, 1898, 5. Years later Connors said that on the night of this match the person who carried his bags was Jack Johnson the future world heavyweight champion who was down on his luck and thankful for anything he could earn. See "Johnson Was Poor Several Years Ago," *Chester Times*, Jan. 10, 1912, 6.

206 "To-Nights Chicago Fights, Everything Ready for the Western Fistic Carnival," *Philadelphia Inquirer*, Mar. 17, 1898, 4; "Jam At The Fights. Big Crowd Sees the Matches at Tattersall's," *Chicago Tribune*, Mar. 18, 1898, 4; "Fighting at Chicago. Jack Everhardt and Jimmy Barry Winners in Their Respective Bouts," *New York American*, Mar. 21, 1898, 9; "Fights On April 18," *Chicago Tribune*, Mar. 21, 1898, 9.

207 "Barry Defeats Ritchey. Little Fellows Have Good Fight of Six Rounds," *Duluth News-Tribune*, Mar. 27, 1898, Part 1, 2; "Pugilism. Barry Defeats Ritchie, *Plain Dealer*, Mar. 27, 1898, 9; "Jimmy Barry Defeated Ritchie," *Trenton Evening Times*, Mar. 28, 1898, 6; "Ritchie Praised by Siler," *Chicago Tribune*, Mar. 28, 1898, 9.

208 "Other News About the Fighters," *Chicago Tribune*, Apr. 17, 1898, 10; "Creedon and Stift," *Chicago Tribune*, Apr. 18, 1898, 9.

209 "All End In Draws. Six Fights at Tattersall's Without a Decision," *Chicago Tribune*, Apr. 18, 1898, 4; "Notes of the Boxers," *Chicago Tribune*, Apr. 22, 1898, 7.

210 "Killed In A Brawl," *Chicago Tribune*, Apr. 26, 1898, 4.

211 "Casper Leon Talks," *The Times* [Washington, D.C.], Jan. 30, 1898, 3; "Jimmy Barry Leaves for the East," *Chicago Tribune*, May 22, 1898, 5; "Barry Meets Leon Tonight," *Chicago Tribune*, May 30, 1898, 9.

212 "The Barry-Flanagan Bout," *Philadelphia Inquirer*, Jun. 2, 1898, 4; "Flanagan vs. Barry Tonight," *Philadelphia Inquirer*, Jun. 3, 1898, 4; "Flanagan And Jimmy Barry. Philadelphians Think Their Favorite Has the Better of the Chicago Champion," *Chicago Tribune*, Jun. 4, 1898, 7.

213 "Out of Doors," *Republic*, Aug. 1, 1898, 5; "The Bantams," *Repository*, Aug. 13, 1898, 2; "Barry-Ritchie Fight Tonight," *Chicago Tribune*, Aug. 13, 1898, 4; "Barry And Ritchie Box A Draw," *Chicago Tribune*, Aug. 14, 1898, 6; "Barry and Ritchie Draw," *Morning Star*, Aug. 14, 1898, 1.

214 "Pugilistic Notes," *Chicago Tribune*, Sep. 15, 1898, 4; "General Sporting Notes," *Detroit Free Press*, Sep. 21, 1898, 2.

215 "Rose and Jimmy Barry Matched," *Chicago Tribune*, Oct. 6, 1898, 4; "Roberson Wins Through A Foul," *Chicago Tribune*, Oct. 7, 1898, 7.

216 "Queenan Unable to Box," *Chicago Tribune*, Oct. 18, 1898, 4; "Notes of the Boxers," *Chicago Tribune*, Oct. 24, 1898, 4.

217 "New Incorporations," *Chicago Tribune*, Jan. 8, 1898, 14; "Notes of the Boxers," *Chicago Tribune*, Oct. 26, 1898, 4; "Waldorf Club Bouts," *Chicago Tribune*, Oct. 30, 1898, 6; "New Boxing Organization," *Chicago Tribune*, Dec. 3, 1898, 6.

218 "Carrig Gets The Decision," *Chicago Tribune*, Nov. 1, 1898, 6.

219 "Barry-McGovern Match Is Off," *Chicago Tribune*, Nov. 2, 1898, 4.

220 "Barry Draws With Leon. Outpoints, but Cannot Knock Out the Clever New-Yorker in Six Rounds," *Chicago Tribune*, Nov. 22, 1898, 4.

221 "Pugilistic Notes," *Chicago Tribune*, Nov. 30, 1898, 4.

222 "Pugilistic Notes," *Chicago Tribune*, Dec. 3, 1898, 6; No Headline, *Republic*, Dec. 29, 1898, 5

223 "Pugilistic Briefs," *Chicago Tribune*, Dec. 27, 1898, 4; "Pugilistic Briefs," *Chicago Tribune*, Dec. 29, 1898, 4; "Bantam Championship Fight," *Duluth News-Tribune*, Dec. 29, 1898, 1.

224 "Barry-Leon Fight Tonight. Old-Time Ring Foes to Meet Once More, This Time at Davenport-Other Good Contests," *Chicago Tribune*, Dec. 29, 1898, 4; "Bantams Fight To-Night. Barry and Leon Ready to Battle for the World's Championship," *Philadelphia Inquirer*, Dec. 29,

1898, 4; "Barry And Leon Draw," *Chicago Tribune*, Dec. 30, 1898, 4.

225 "Barry and Leon Draw. Old Foes Battle Twenty Hard Rounds at Davenport," *Chicago Tribune*, Dec. 30, 1898, 4; "Jimmy Barry and Casper Leon Stand Up Before Each Other at Davenport, Ia.," *Omaha World Herald*, Dec. 30, 1898, 7; "Draw For The Lightweights. Jimmy Barry and Casper Leon Fight 20 Rounds and Divide Money," *Republic*, Dec. 30, 1898, 2.

226 "Tattersall's Boxing Show," *Chicago Tribune*, Jan. 7, 1899, 4.

227 "General Sporting Notes," *Plain Dealer*, Jan. 8, 1899, 12.

228 "Things Unsettled," *Pawtucket Times*, Jan. 4, 1899, 2.

229 U.S. Census, Year: 1900; Census Place: Chicago Ward 23, Cook, Illinois; Roll: T623_272; Page: 7A; Enumeration District: 686.

230 Barry, Mary, dod 1899-02-09, Chicago, age 73, cert. #00001170, Cook County, Microfilm Roll 1033059, Item 2.

231 "Pat Fitzgerald Dead. Former Manager of Jimmy Barry Expires Suddenly in Denver, Supposedly of Heart Disease," *Chicago Tribune*, May 6, 1899, 7.

232 "Notes of the Boxers," *Chicago Tribune*, Mar. 14, 1899, 4.

233 "Some Sporting Talk," *Republic*, Jan. 19, 1899, 7; "'Kid' Lavigne in the City," *Chicago Tribune*, Mar. 30, 1899, 4.

234 "Fails To Put Out Stift," *Chicago Tribune*, Apr. 20, 1899, 7.

235 "George Ryan Loses On a Foul," *Chicago Tribune*, Jun. 8, 1899, 4.

236 "Knocks Out McCoy In First Round," *Chicago Tribune*, Aug. 19, 1899, 4; "Bouts at the Star Theater," *Chicago Tribune*, Aug. 3, 1899, 4.

237 "Barry And Harris Draw," *Chicago Tribune*, Sep. 2, 1899, 4; "Fast Bout At Chicago," *Omaha World Herald*, Sep. 2, 1889, 1; "In My Day – A Champion Didn't Lose," *Chicago Times*, Mar. 21, 1937, 52.

238 "Santry Easily Whips O'Malley. Interesting Bouts Furnished at the Frank Garrard Benefit," *Chicago Tribune*, Dec. 12, 1899, 4.

239 No Headline, *Decatur Herald*, May 15, 1900, 5; "Jimmy Barry to be a Jockey," *Fort Wayne News*, Jun. 19, 1900, 6; "Siler's Talk Of The Ring," *Chicago Tribune*, Sep. 1, 1901, 19: "To Revive Boxing Game," *Chicago Tribune*, Sep. 15, 1901, 18; "Handball Match At Barry's Court," *Chicago Tribune*, October 20, 1901, 20.

240 "Retired Fighter Aldermanic Candidate," *Chicago Tribune*, Jan. 13, 1902, 3; "Queer Timber for Alderman Unearthed in Chicago Primaries," *The Daily Review* [Decatur, Illinois], Mar. 10, 1902, 6.

241 "Robert E. Burke Dead," *New York Times*, Jul. 30, 1921.

242 "Robert E. Burke Is Indicted for Embezzlement," *Chicago Tribune*, Oct. 6, 1901, 1.

243 "New Club to Open Tonight," *Chicago Tribune*, Jan. 29, 1904, 11; No Headline, *Oshkosh Daily Northwestern*, Jun. 24, 1904, 6; "Benefit Nets $125. Boxing Meeting in Chicago to Help Out Jimmy Barry," *Boston Daily Globe*, Jun. 24, 1904, 8.

244 "Death Follows 'Prize' Fight," *Chicago Tribune*, Feb. 10, 1910, 1; "Chicago Boxer Dies from Hurts. 'Kid' Wilkowski

Expires Following Pugilistic Encounter," *The Daily Review* [Decatur, Illinois], Feb. 10, 1910, 5; "Boy Killed In Prize Fight," *Republic*, Feb. 20, 1910, 3.

245 "Jury Votes Blow Killed Boy Boxer," *Chicago Tribune*, Feb. 11, 1910, 6; "Cases of Boxers Continued," *Chicago Tribune*, Feb. 12, 1910, 11.

246 "Prize Fight Case Is Dismissed," *Chicago Tribune*, Mar. 12, 1910, 13.

247 "Prize Fighters Slugged Daft," *Piqua Daily Call*, Feb. 25, 1910, 5.

248 "Many Fighters Hold Good Jobs," *San Antonio Express*, Dec. 10, 1911, 6.

249 "Legislators See Boxing," *Morning Star*, May 7, 1913, 1.

250 "Barry Gives Up Army Ring Job," *Chicago Tribune*, Oct. 24, 1918, 11; "High Praise For New Fighters By Former Scrapper," *Republic*, Oct. 16, 1918, 3; "Group of Fistic Stars at Camp Gordon," *Republic*, Nov. 21, 1918, 3.

251 "Two Ex-Champions To Watch Wilde In His Yankee Debut," *Chicago Tribune*, Dec. 4, 1919, 17; "Rockford Fans At Fight Praise The English Champion," *Morning Star*, Dec. 7, 1919, 22.

252 "English Style Enables Wilde To Shade Barry," *Chicago Tribune*, Feb. 26, 1922, A1.

253 "Joe Williams Says," *El Paso Herald Post*, Apr. 21, 1934, 14.

254 U.S. Census, Year: 1920; Census Place: Chicago Ward 23, Cook (Chicago), Illinois; Roll: T625_334; Page: 4A; Enumeration District: 1297; Image: 590; "Former Boxing Champion Fighting For His Life," *Joplin Globe*, Jul. 21, 1936, 6; "The Payoff," *The Bee*, Jun. 28, 1937, 9.

255 "Save Two Women In Fire," *Chicago Tribune*, Feb. 21, 1912, 3; "Gilmore Recalls Old Bouts, *Chicago Tribune*, May 19, 1912, 8; "'Kid' Harry Gilmore Boxes Three Rounds," *Chicago Tribune*, Jan. 15, 1922, A3; "Fistic Fans Plan Testimonial to Harry Gilmore," *Chicago Tribune*, Mar. 9, 1924, A3; "Harry Gilmore, Famous Boxer Is Dead At 88,: *Chicago Tribune*, Sep. 11, 1942, 28.

256 "Jimmy Barry, Bantam King of '90s, Dies," *Chicago Tribune*, Apr. 5, 1943, 30; "Jimmy Barry Dead at 73," *Oregonian*, Apr. 6, 1943, 25; "Jimmy Barry, Retired Boxer, Dies at 73," *Suburbanite Economist*, Apr. 7, 1943, 49; "Hold Funeral Tomorrow For Jimmy Barry," *Chicago Tribune*, Apr. 6, 1943, 26; Cook County, Illinois Death Index, 1908-1988: James Barry, Apr. 4, 1943, File No. 10270, Cook County, Illinois.

257 Fights in 1891 include the following: "Athletic Shows To-Night," *Chicago Herald*, Jan. 24, 1891, 7; "Gilmore's Athletic Show," *Daily Inter Ocean*, Mar. 17, 1891, 6; "Ryan's Benefit," *Daily Inter Ocean*, Mar. 26, 1891, 6; "Ryan's Athletic Benefit," *Daily Inter Ocean*, Mar. 28, 1891, 6; "Tom Ryan's Benefit To-Night," *Daily Inter Ocean*, Mar. 31, 1891, 6; "Ryan Accepts M Millan's Defi," *Chicago Herald*, Jun. 7, 1891, 5; "Cleveland Meets Barry," *Chicago Herald*, Jun. 9, 1891, 6; "Want to Fight Tommy Ryan," *Chicago Herald*, Jun. 9, 1891, 6; "Some Clever Sparring Expected," *Chicago Tribune*, Jul. 12, 1891, 7; "Harry Gilmore's Exhibition," *Chicago Tribune*, Aug. 2, 1891, *Chicago Tribune*, 4; "Gleanings In Local Fields. Athletic Exhibitions at Evanston," *Chicago Tribune*, Aug. 7, 1891, 3; "Sporting Notes," *Chicago Herald*, Aug. 10, 1891, 5;

"Jack Mason Defeats Billy Cortor. A Match at McGurn's Handball Court – Other Events," *Chicago Tribune*, Aug. 25, 1891, 6; "Boxing at McGurn's Court," *Chicago Tribune*, Sep. 1, 1891, 6; "Sporting Notes and Queries," *Chicago Herald*, Sep. 21, 1891, 5; "Was No Match For Tommy White," *Chicago Tribune*, Sep. 27, 1891, 6 (Joe O'Leary is described as a pupil of Jem Mace from London).

258 Barry's reported fights can be found in the following: "Queenan And Baker," *Daily Inter Ocean*, Jan. 3, 1892, 6; "Made Good Guesses," *Daily Inter Ocean*, Jan. 14, 1892, 6; "Bowen And Murphy," *Daily Inter Ocean*, Feb. 10, 1892, 3; "The Ring," *Pittsburgh Dispatch*, Mar. 20, 1892, 6; "Boxing," *Daily Inter Ocean*, Apr. 2, 1892, 6; "Athletic Events," *Daily Inter Ocean*, May 21, 1892, 2; No Headline, *Fort Wayne Sentinel*, Aug. 10, 1892, 3; No Headline, *Fort Wayne Sentinel*, Aug. 18, 1892, 4; "Sporting Melange," *Daily Inter Ocean*, Oct. 14, 1892, 6; "Skill Of Athletes," *Daily Inter Ocean*, Oct. 30, 1892, 6; "Sporting Scraps," *Daily Inter Ocean*, Nov. 7, 1892, 6; "Fought A Draw," *Daily Inter Ocean*, Nov. 18, 1892, 6; "Romeo Where Art Thou?," *Daily Inter Ocean*, Nov. 15, 1892, 6; "Jackson And Lewis," *Daily Inter Ocean*, Dec. 2, 1892, 6; "Is Maher Sure To Lose," *Brooklyn Eagle*, Dec. 5, 1892, 7; "Gossip Of The Fighters," *New York Herald*, Dec. 5, 1892, 8; "Myer vs. McAuliffe," *Daily Inter Ocean*, Dec. 7, 1892, 6; "Won In Four Rounds," *Chicago Tribune*, Dec. 20, 1892, 7; "Fight to be Finished," *San Antonio Daily Light*, Dec. 29, 1892, 1.

259 The date of the fight with Billy Murphy is variously reported. For example, the Boxing Register reports the fight as taking place on February 12, 1893. Roberts, James

B. & Skutt, Alexander G., Boxing Register, Edition 4, (McBooks Press 2006), 65.

Presumably Barry's opponent was "Australian" Billy Murphy and not some other Billy Murphy. In January 1893 Billy Murphy was traveling to New York for a February 6, 1893 championship match with Johnny Griffin at the Coney Island Athletic Club. Murphy arrived at Boston on January 12, 1893 to train and would not have taken the long trip back to Chicago to fight a relative unknown bantamweight. Murphy lost his fight with Griffin and was badly beaten with rumors that he might die. He did not leave New York to return to California until February 21, 1893 and would not have been in Chicago on the prior day. Neither date seems likely.

260 "Athletics At Turner-Hall," *Chicago Tribune*, Jan. 16, 1893, 12; "All Sorts Of Sport," Kansas City Times, Jan. 18, 1893, 14; "Edward Kelly Knocked Out," *Daily Inter Ocean*, Mar. 9, 1893, 1; "Sporting Scraps," *Daily Inter Ocean*, Mar. 23, 1893, 9; "Reached No Result," *Chicago Tribune*, Apr. 9, 1893, 4; "In McGurn's Ring," *Daily Inter Ocean*, Apr. 11, 1893, 4; "Local Sporting Notes," *Chicago Tribune*, Apr. 14, 1893, 7; "Barry Will Box Smith," *Daily Inter Ocean*, Apr. 14, 1893, 4; "Sporting News," *Oshkosh Daily Northwestern*, May 5, 1893, 1; "General Sporting Notes," *Chicago Tribune*, Jun. 5, 1893, 12; "Sporting Notes," *Daily Inter Ocean*, Jun. 16, 1893, 4; "Will Fight At Roby," *Daily Inter Ocean*, Jul. 3, 1893, 4; "Smith vs. Griffin," *Daily Inter Ocean*, Part 1, 1; "Columbian Contests," *New Orleans Item*, Jul. 10, 1893,

5; "Smith Downs Griffin," *Bridgeton Evening News*, Jul. 11, 1893, 2; "Solly Smith Is Good," *Chicago Tribune*, Jul. 11, 1893, 6; "Corbett Matched To Fight Jackson," *Daily Inter Ocean*, Jul. 11, 1893, 3; "Settled Him In Four Rounds," *Elkhart Daily Review*, Jul. 11, 1893, 1; "Little Sol Smith Proves A Champion," *Times Picayune*, Jul. 11, 1893, 6; "Knocked Out By A Chance Blow," *New York Times*, Jul. 11, 1893, 2; "Smith Won In Four Rounds," *Plain Dealer*, Jul. 11, 1893, 5; "Dempsey and Dick Burge Matched," *Chicago Tribune*, Jul. 25, 1893, 7; "Pierce Is Particular," *Brooklyn Eagle*, Jul. 26, 1893, 2; "Both On Their Mettle," *Daily Inter Ocean*, Jul. 26, 1893, 4; "Pugilistic Gossip," *Daily Inter Ocean*, Jul. 29, 1893, Part 1, 4; "Sporting News," *Trenton Evening Times*, Aug. 3, 1893, 2; "The 'Kid's' Opponent," *Saginaw News*, Aug. 28, 1893, 7; "Prize Fight Declared Off," *Atlantic Daily Telegraph*, Sep. 5, 1893, 1; "Did Not Materialize," *Bay City Times*, Sep. 5, 1893, 1; "Live Sporting Notes," *New York Herald*, Oct. 28, 1893, 13; "Sporting Gossip," *New Orleans Item*, Oct. 30, 1893, 4; "To A Finish," *New Orleans Item*, Nov. 11, 1893, 4; "Fistic Stars Galore," *Daily Inter Ocean*, Nov. 12, 1893, Part 1, 8; "Are All Boxing Stars," *Daily Inter Ocean*, Nov. 13, 1893, 4; "Good Fistic Exhibit," *Daily Inter Ocean*, Nov. 14, 1893, 8; "Roby to be Opened Nov. 27," *Plain Dealer*, Nov. 18, 1893, 3; "Roby Club Officers Not Worried," *Chicago Tribune*, Nov. 21, 1893, 11; "Levy Asks For Another Trial," *Times Picayune*, Nov. 30, 1893, 1; "Barry to Box Van Heest," *Daily Inter Ocean*, Dec. 4, 1893, 8; "General Sporting Notes," *Chicago Tribune*, Dec. 14, 1893, 7; "Barry to Meet the Winner," *Daily Inter Ocean*, Dec. 14, 1893, 8.

261 This fighter was probably Harry Dalley who held himself out as the 105 pound champion of Australia and a protégé of Young Griffo. In February 1895 Dalley did attempt to arrange a fight with Barry. "Boxing Bouts At Paterson," *Brooklyn Eagle*, Feb. 5, 1895, 4.

262 The date of the fight with Billy Murphy is variously reported. For example, the Boxing Register reports the fight as taking place on February 12, 1893. Roberts, James B. & Skutt, Alexander G., <u>Boxing Register</u>, Edition 4, (McBooks Press 2006), 65.

Presumably Barry's opponent was "Australian" Billy Murphy – who was actually from New Zealand – and not some other Billy Murphy. In January 1893 Billy Murphy was traveling to New York for a February 6, 1893 championship match with Johnny Griffin at the Coney Island Athletic Club. Murphy arrived at Boston on January 12, 1893 to train and would not have taken the long trip back to Chicago to fight a relative unknown bantamweight. Murphy lost his fight with Griffin and was badly beaten with rumors that he might die. He did not leave New York to return to California until February 21, 1893 and would not have been in Chicago on the prior day. Neither date seems likely.

263 This fighter was probably Harry Dalley who held himself out as the 105-pound champion of Australia and a protégé of Young Griffo. In February 1895 Dalley did attempt to arrange a fight with Barry. "Boxing Bouts At Paterson," *Brooklyn Eagle*, Feb. 5, 1895, 4.

Chapter 2

264 The Cook County Illinois Death Index, 1908–1988 includes File 60 00488 for James H. Dalton who died on January 4, 1932. This is the death certificate for Captain James H. Dalton. The informant on the death certificate was Dalton's younger brother, Lawrence Vincent Dalton. He apparently reported that his father was born in Canada and that his mother was born in Ireland. This information appears to be reversed. Numerous other official records indicate that Captain Dalton's mother was born in Canada and that his father was born in Ireland. It may be that the person filling out the form entered the information incorrectly. See Ancestry.com. *Cook County, Illinois Death Index, 1908–1988* [database on-line]; Provo, UT, USA: Ancestry.com Operations Inc, 2008. Original data: Cook County Clerk. *Cook County Clerk Genealogy Records*. Cook County Clerk's Office, Chicago, IL: Cook County Clerk, 2008; U. S. Census, Year: 1860; Census Place: Cleveland Ward 11, Cuyahoga, Ohio; Roll: M653_953; Page: 1088; Image: 528; Family History Library Film: 803953; Year: 1870; U. S. Census Place: Cleveland Ward 11, Cuyahoga, Ohio; Roll: *M593_1192*; Page: *9B*; Image: *22*; Family History Library Film: *552691*; U.S. Census, Year: 1880; Census Place: Chicago, Cook, Illinois; Roll: 192; Family History Film: 1254192; Page: 502A; Enumeration District: 103; Image: 0727.

265 Nelson, J. Callahan & Hisckey, William F., Irish Americans and Their Communities of Cleveland (Cleveland State University, 1978), 70-85.

266 U.S. Census, Year: 1880; Census Place: Chicago, Cook, Illinois; Roll: 192; Family History Film: 1254192; Page: 502A; Enumeration District: 103; Image: 0727, and Illinois Death Certificate 60 00488 dated January 6, 1932 for Captain James H. Dalton. It is sometimes reported that he was born April 26 1854 or on April 26 1853. His birth date here is based on information provided by his brother Lawrence Vincent Dalton for Captain Dalton's death certificate.

267 U.S. Census, Year: 1860; Census Place: Cleveland Ward 11, Cuyahoga, Ohio; Roll: M653_953; Page: 1088; Image: 528; Family History Library Film: 803953.

268 *Chicago Tribune*, Nov. 2, 1884, 14. Gallagher was also from Cleveland, Ohio, and operated a saloon there. See "The Prize Ring-Fight between Jim Elliott and Charlie Gallagher, near Detroit-Brutal Exhibition-Elliott Declared the Victor-Alleged Unfair Ruling by the Referee," *New York Herald*, Nov.13, 1868, 8; "McCoole And Allen. The Boat Money Not Yet Given Up – Prospect of Another Match Gallagher," *Plain Dealer*, Jul. 7, 1869, 2.

On November 12, 1868 on Peach Island, near Detroit, Michigan, Charley Gallagher was defeated in twenty-three rounds by Jimmy Elliott. On February 23, 1869, Tom Allen fought Charley Gallagher on Carroll Island in the Mississippi River for the Heavyweight Championship of America and Gallagher won in two rounds. On August 17, 1869, in a rematch Allen knocked out Gallagher but the referee called the match a draw. "Sporting News. The Prize Fight Near Saint Louis. Allen Whips Gallagher in Eleven

Rounds, But is Cheated of his Victory by Saint Louis Scoundrels," *Cincinnati Daily Gazette*, Aug. 18, 1869, 3.

269 Before 1833, one-half mile north of where it entered Lake Michigan the Chicago River made a sharp bend south. There was a long sandbar between the river and its entry into the lake. A straight cut was made at the north end of the sandbar and a pier that was about 1,000 feet long was built on the north side of the redesigned river mouth. Another smaller pier was built on the south shore of the river. These piers were reconfigured many times between 1833 and the mid-1870s. During that period dredges were used to keep the river open removing three to four thousand cubic yards of sand each year. United States War Department, <u>Annual Reports of the War Department, Part 2</u>, (Govt. Print. Off., 1876), 433; See also "Chicago Lakefront and River Photographs, Midwest Manuscript Collection," The Newberry Library, Chicago.

270 Ancestry.com. Chicago Voter Registration, 1892 [database on-line]. Provo, UT, USA: Ancestry.com Operations Inc, 2001. Original data: Illinois State Archives microfilm (25 rolls).Chicago Voter Registration Schedule 1892, 32-33. James H. Dalton reported that he had lived in the county and the state for eighteen years. If accurate, this means that Dalton would have come to Chicago in about 1874. He applied to be registered on October 25, 1892, which was just before the elections that year.

271 The Chicago city directory for 1871 lists a steamfitter named James Dalton living at 420 S. Morgan Street. Later editions of the city directories report James and John

Dalton, both steamfitters, living at 420 S. Morgan. These are probably not James H. Dalton and John C. Dalton. This conclusion is based in part on the 1871 Chicago city directory which listed the place of nativity for residents. According to that directory, James Dalton reported that he was born in Newfoundland. There is nothing to suggest that the subject of this article was born in Newfoundland and therefore it seems unlikely that these are the children of William and Katherine Gallagher Dalton who were born in Ohio. See Chicago Census Report and Statistical Review etc., 1871 at 261.

272 "Marine Intelligence – General," *Daily Inter Ocean*, April 8, 1878, 6. There are claims asserted to the effect that Captain James H. Dalton was an expert clog dancer and won many prizes which may have helped him in boxing. This probably confuses the boxing tug boat captain with another James Dalton who worked in Chicago as a member of a minstrel company.

273 Stone, Fanny S., Racine, belle city of the lakes, and Racine County, Wisconsin: a record of settlement, organization, progress and achievement, Vol. 2, (S.J. Clarke, 1916), 171–172 (provides a biography of W. J. Higgie); Mansfield, John Brandt, History of the Great Lakes, Vol. 2, (J. H. Beers & Co., 1899), 772–773.

274 Vessel Owners Towing Co. is listed under "Tug Agents and Owners" in The Lakeside Annual Directory of the City of Chicago 1875-6, (Donnelley, Lloyd and Co.), 1323. The 1880 U.S. census lists James Higgie a Scotsman living at 625 Adams Street, Chicago, Illinois, as the president of

V.O.T. Co. Later Anthony G. Van Schaick was the company's treasurer. Van Schaick was a prominent member of the Chicago business community acting as a director of the Continental National Bank among other things.

275 Mansfield, John Brandt, History of the Great Lakes, Vol. 2, (J.H. Beers & Co., 1899), 773; Blue Book of American Shipping, Cleveland, Ohio: Marine Review, (1897), 405.

276 "Tug of War," *Daily Inter Ocean*, Oct. 28, 1876, 7; "A Tug War in Chicago," *Cincinnati Daily Gazette*, Jul. 31, 1878, 1; :Tug Men at Chicago Threaten to Strike," *Cincinnati Commercial Tribune*, Jul. 30, 1878, 2; "Miscellaneous Mentions," *Plain Dealer*, May 26, 1880, 4.

277 "The Vessel-Owners' Towing Company. An Exhibit of the Finances of the Line-the Election of Directors," *Daily Inter Ocean*, Jan. 10, 1877, 2; "The Vessel Owners' Towing Company," *Daily Inter Ocean*, Jan. 1, 1882, 3; "The Vessel-Owners' Towing Company," *Chicago Tribune*, Mar. 26, 1882, 16;

278 Advertisement, *Chicago Tribune*, Apr. 3, 1879, 7; "Prize-Fight," *Chicago Tribune*, May 8, 1879, 7; "Late Local Note," *Chicago Tribune*, May 8, 1879, 7; "Nose-Eating," *Chicago Tribune*, May 9, 1879, 5.

279 "The Prizering," *Chicago Tribune*, Mar. 23, 1879, 12.

280 "Athletics. Mike Donovan's Benefit," *Daily Inter Ocean*, Jun. 9, 1879, 2; "Sundry Sports," *Chicago Tribune*, Jun 7, 1879, 6 (Others who appeared at the benefit included fighters identified as Bennett, Ryan, Carey, Warren, and Ed Dorney).

281 "Brevities," *Daily Inter Ocean*, Aug. 29, 1879, 8; "Circuit Court," *Chicago Tribune*, Dec. 4, 1879, 7.

282 "Athletics," *Chicago Tribune*, Feb. 22, 1880, 7.
283 "Sporting," *Chicago Tribune*, Nov. 30, 1879, 3.
284 "Dock Notes," *Chicago Tribune*, Jul. 3, 1880, 11; "Rescued from Drowning," *Chicago Tribune*, Nov. 11, 1880, 7.
285 "Sparring," *Daily Inter Ocean*, Aug. 15, 1881, 6; "Steve Taylor Whipped," *New York Herald*, Apr. 1, 1881, 4.
286 "Prize Fight at New York," *Duluth News-Tribune*, May 17, 1881, 1; "Prize Fight," *Philadelphia Inquirer*, May 18, 1881, 1; "Prize Fight on a Barge," *Kalamazoo Gazette*, May 18, 1881, 1; "The Life of John L. Sullivan," *Winnipeg Free Press*, Apr. 2, 1927, 82.
287 "The Life of John L. Sullivan," *Winnipeg Free Press*, Apr. 2, 1927, 82; "The Life of John L. Sullivan," *Winnipeg Free Press*, Apr. 9, 1927, 66.
288 "Pugilistic," *Chicago Tribune*, Aug. 7, 1881, 16; "Sparring," *Chicago Tribune*, Aug. 13, 1881, 2.
289 See n. 19 above.
290 Hermann, Charles H., <u>Recollections Of Life & Doings in Chicago, From the Haymarket Riot to the End of World War I</u>, (Normandie House, 1945), 34-35.
291 "The Sparring Match," *Chicago Tribune*, Aug. 14, 1881, 6.
292 "Champion Pugilist," *Daily Inter Ocean*, Aug. 13, 1881, 4.
293 "The Sparring Match," *Chicago Tribune*, Aug, 14, 1881, 6.
294 See n. 15 above.
295 "Pugilism," *Chicago Tribune*, Aug. 28, 1881, 6; "The Ring. This Evening's Meeting," *Daily Inter Ocean*, Sep. 3, 1881, 2; "Athletic," *Chicago Tribune*, Sep. 4, 1881, 8.
296 "Pugilistic," *Chicago Tribune*, Sep. 6, 1881, 6.

297 "Pugilistic," *Chicago Tribune*, Sep. 25, 1881, 7; "A Prize-Fight Arranged," *Chicago Tribune*, Sep. 26, 1881, 8; "Pugilistic," *Chicago Tribune*, Oct. 1, 1881, 7.

298 "The Ring," *Daily Inter Ocean*, Oct. 3, 1881, 5; "Athletic," *Chicago Tribune*, Oct. 15, 1881, 6. There was an undercard that included two wonders (i.e., "I wonder where these two guys come from?") named Little Mack and Japanese Tommy. An eastern newspaper donated a gold medal valued at $100 for heavyweight fighters from Illinois.

299 Karamanski, Theodore J., <u>Schooner passage: sailing ships and the Lake Michigan frontier</u>, (Wayne State University Press, 2000), 127.

300 "Turbulent Tugmen. Adams Street Bridge Forced Open – Almost a Serious Accident," *Chicago Tribune*, Oct. 4, 1881, 5; "Bridgeless or Dangerous, The Great Thoroughfare to the North Side, Clark Street Referred To – When the Bridge Is Not 'Open' It Perhaps Had Better Be," *Daily Inter Ocean*, Oct. 4, 1881.

301 "A Protest. Vessel Owners and Tugmen Are in Wrath at the Treatment of the Shipping at the Bridges," *Daily Inter Ocean*, Jul. 14, 1875, 3. The text of the ordinance is found in this article.

302 "Mayor and Mariner a Difference Between Manager Higgie of the Vessel Owners' Towing Company and Carter H.," *Daily Inter Ocean*, Jun. 17, 1882, 6.

303 "A Just Judge," *Chicago Tribune*, Oct. 7, 1881, 11.

304 See, e.g., *In re Vessel Owners' Towing Co.*, 26 F. 172 (D. C. 1884); *In re Vessel Owners' Towing Co.*, 26 F. 169 (N. D. Ill. 1886).

Endnotes

305 "The Vessel-Owners' Towing Company," *Chicago Tribune*, Mar. 26, 1882, 16.

306 "The Ring," *Daily Inter Ocean*, Oct. 8, 1881, 7; "Pugilistic," *Chicago Tribune*, Oct. 11, 1881, 7.

307 "The Ring," *Daily Inter Ocean*, Oct. 10, 1881; 7; "Pugilistic," *Chicago Tribune*, Oct. 11, 1881, 7; "The Ring," *Daily Inter Ocean*, Oct. 15, 1881, 3.

308 "A Prize Fight," *Boston Journal*, Oct. 8, 1881, 6; "Sporting," *Detroit Free Press*, Oct. 8, 1881, 1; "The Ring," *Daily Inter Ocean*, Oct. 10, 1881; "Sporting Record," New Hampshire Patriot, Oct. 13, 1881, 4; "The Ring. Boxing Tonight," *Daily Inter Ocean*, Oct. 15, 1881, 3; "Athletic," *Chicago Tribune*, Oct. 15, 1881, 6. Comments long after this match suggest that Dalton performed poorly in this match. There is no clear evidence whether the planned match Morris-Dalton match actually took place.

309 "Athletics," *Daily Inter Ocean*, Oct. 22, 1881, 3.

310 "Other Notes," *Daily Inter Ocean*, Dec. 10, 1881, 7.

311 "Miscellaneous Notes," *Boston Daily Globe*, Dec. 18, 1881, 10.

312 "Men Who Are Looking For Capt. Dalton," *Chicago Tribune*, Jan. 22, 1882, 8.

313 "Sporting Notes – Captain Dalton's Reply," *Chicago Tribune*, Jan. 23, 1882, 5.

314 "The New Champion," *Daily Inter Ocean*, Feb. 13, 1882, 6; "The Hero of the Day," *Chicago Tribune*, Feb. 11, 1882, 5.

315 See n. 42 above.

316 "Paddy Ryan," *Chicago Tribune*, Feb. 26, 1882, 7

317 U.S. Census, Year: 1860; Census Place: Cleveland Ward 11, Cuyahoga, Ohio; Roll: M653_953; Page: 1028;

Image: 468; Family History Library Film: 803953. In the 1880 census of Cleveland John Donaldson reported that his profession was "professor." See U.S. Census, Year: 1880; Census Place: Cleveland, Cuyahoga, Ohio; Roll: 1007; Family History Film: 1255007; Page: 197D; Enumeration District: 34; Image: 0399.

318 "The Prize Ring," *Oshkosh Daily Northwestern*, Aug. 1, 1882, 2. In late June 1882, a man identified as John McCaffrey challenged Dalton to a London prize rule fight with or without gloves for any sum up to $250 with the fight to take place within five weeks. "Prize Fight at Chicago," *Chicago Tribune*, Jun. 29, 1882, 2.

319 "Elliott and Sullivan," *Chicago Tribune*, Dec. 22, 1882, 8.

320 No headline, *Rockford Daily Register*, May 9, 1883, 4.

321 "Dalton to Spar with Ryan," *Rockford Daily Register*, May 29, 1883, 4.

322 "How a Pugilist Trains," *Fort Wayne Sunday Gazetter*, Feb. 3, 1884, 6; "How a Pugilist Trains," *Piqua Morning Call*, Feb. 6, 1884, 3. These articles are republishing articles from the *Chicago Herald*.

323 "Lively Work With The Gloves," *Chicago Tribune*, Jan. 23, 1884, 6.

324 "In the Ring. 'Jim' Dalton defeats 'Mike' Driscoll according to the Marquis of Queensberry rules," *Chicago Tribune*, Jan. 24, 1884, 16.

325 Illinois Statewide Marriage Index, 1763–1900, Dalton, James and Kerwin, Mary Jane, 1883-01-13, Vol. OOE, Certificate 00068744 Cook County, Illinois.

326 "Pugilist Dalton Shot By His Wife," *New York Times*, Mar. 9, 1884.

327 "Shot By His Wife. Dalton, the Would-Be Pugilist Who Is Generally Knocked Out of Time on the First Round," *Chicago Tribune*, Mar. 8, 1884, 3; U.S. Census, Year 1880; Census Place: Chicago, Cook, Illinois; Roll: 184; Family History Film: 1254184; Page: 111A; Enumeration District: 5; Image: 0223.

328 "In General," *Chicago Tribune*, Mar. 12, 1884, 8.

329 "Knocked Out Of Time," *Chicago Tribune*, Mar. 11, 1884, 7.

330 Two Enemies With Gloves," *The New York Times*, Mar. 24, 1884; "A Glove Contest at Chicago," *The Patriot*, Mar. 24, 1884, 1; "Dalton's Buckles," *Chicago Tribune*, Mar. 13, 1884, 16.

331 "Sporting-With Small Gloves," *The Evening Gazette*, Apr. 29, 1884; "Athletics," *Salt Lake Tribune*, Apr. 30, 1884; No Headline, *Detroit Free Press*, Apr. 29, 1884, 1. In the first two cited sources Driscoll is incorrectly identified as "John" Driscoll. Parson Davies kept Dalton busy when he could. On April 21, 1884 the Captain acted as the referee for a collar-and-elbow wrestling match between John Rabshaw and Lew Moore.

332 "Done With Gloves," *Chicago Tribune*, May 11, 1884, 16. Stating that Goode would soon be matched with Captain Dalton.

333 "Mill at Chicago," *Salt Lake Herald*, May 21, 1884, 4.

334 "Dalton vs. Jem Goode," *Daily Inter Ocean*, May 20, 1884, 4; "The Manly Art," *Peoria Journal*, May 20, 1884, 1; "Bad For Jem Goode. He Loses His Match with Captain Dalton at Chicago," *Boston Daily Globe*, May 20, 1884, 1; "Pugilistic. Dalton Wins A Doubtful Victory Over Jem

Goode," *Chicago Tribune*, May 20, 1884, 6; "The Prize Ring," *National Police Gazette*, June 7, 1884, 10;

335 "The Ring. Local Bruisers Indulge In A Little 'Child's Play,'" *Chicago Tribune*, Dec. 6, 1884, 8.

336 "A Sweeping Challenge to Chicago Boxers," *Chicago Herald*, Jan. 11, 1885, 6; "Sharp Talk at McCaffrey," *Chicago Herald*, Jan. 11, 1885, 6; "Sporting Miscellany," *Boston Daily Globe*, Jan. 14, 1885, 13.

337 "After Captain Dalton's Scalp," *Chicago Herald,* Jan, 11, 1885, 6.

338 "Fighters, Wrestlers and Swordsmen," *Boston Daily Globe*, Jan. 20, 1885, 12.

339 "Dalton Knocked Out," *Chicago Tribune*, Feb. 3, 1885, 5.

340 "Burke Is A Good One," *Chicago Herald*, Feb. 3, 1885, 3.

341 "Cleary Knocks Out Dalton," *Cincinnati Enquirer*, Feb. 7, 1885, 7; "Dalton Knocked Senseless," *Chicago Herald*, Feb. 7, 1885, 1.

342 "New Albany and Chicago Railroad," *Chicago Times*, Jul. 14, 1885, 2.

343 "Dalton Matched Again," *Chicago Herald*, Feb. 14, 1885, 7.

344 "Wrecked At Midnight," *Chicago Tribune*, Feb. 26, 1885, 3; "How Dalton Rode," Feb. 27, 1885, 8; "Captain Dalton to the Front," *Chicago Herald*, May 10, 1885, 9; "How Dalton Rode," *Chicago Tribune*, Feb. 27, 1885, 8.

345 "The Glove Fight," *Chicago Tribune*, Mar 3, 1885, 6 (John Dalton sparred with Fred Sommers in a preliminary match.); "The Ring," *Chicago Tribune*, Mar. 8, 1885, 14 (John Dalton matched to fight Tom Hinch at the Park Theater on March 13, 1885 for a purse of $100.); "Burke

Greenfield at Battery D Tonight – The Program," *Chicago Tribune*, Mar. 23, 1885, 2 (Billy Dalton matched to fight Tom Hinch at Battery D for three or more rounds.)

346 "A Tame Set-To," *Chicago Tribune*, May 16, 1885, 6.

347 "One of the Bloodiest. A Sunday Prize Fight in the Great Northwest," *Boston Daily Globe*, Jun. 15, 1885, 4; "White vs. Black Pugilist," *New York Herald*, Jun. 15, 1885, 3; "Eight Rounds Hard Hitting," *Wheeling Register*, Jun. 15, 1885, 1. One newspaper claimed that Captain Dalton was managing Cardiff at this time. There is no evidence to support this claim. "Thompson Won't Fight Wilson," *Plain Dealer*, Jun. 17, 1885, 5.

348 "With Hard Gloves," *Chicago Tribune*, Jun. 15, 1885, 1.

349 "Capt. Dalton Badly Punishes a Saint Louis Man," *Chicago Tribune*, Apr. 4, 1886, 9.

350 "Sporting," *Daily Inter Ocean*, Jun. 6, 1886, 4.

351 "The King-Dalton Contest-King Fractures a Bone in His Wrist and Is Bested by the Chicago Man," *Chicago Tribune*, Jun. 13, 1885, 10; "The Twenty-Four Foot Ring," *Daily Inter Ocean*, Jun. 14, 1886, 2; "Jim Dalton, At 62, Proves He Has Lost None of Old Speed," *The Salt Lake Tribune*, Feb. 18, 1921, 12..

352 "Saloon-Keepers Surprised. Captain O'Donnell Calls upon Several Who Were Selling Liquors to Minors," *Daily Inter Ocean*, May 4, 1887, 1.

353 "The City In Brief," *Daily Inter Ocean*, May 7, 1887, 6.

354 "Miscellaneous," *Daily Inter Ocean*, Jun. 4, 1887, 7.

355 "Capt. Dalton Roughly Handled," *Chicago Tribune*, Feb. 2, 1888, 3; "Kinnard Punishes Dalton," *Daily Inter Ocean*, Feb. 2, 1888, 2.

356 "Died of Delirium Tremens," *Alton Daily Telegraph*, Feb. 29, 1892, 1.
357 "Captain Dalton's Benefit," *Daily Inter Ocean*, Jun. 30, 1888, 1; Miscellaneous Matters, *Chicago Tribune*, Jul. 1, 1888, 15.
358 No Headline, *Oshkosh Daily Northwestern*, Jan. 12, 1905, 6; "John L. Sullivan Will Lecture," *Sun*, Jan. 1, 1905, 9; "The Same John L. In Voice and Speech," *New Orleans Item*, Jan. 16, 1905, 6; "John L. Sullivan Made His Debut as a Raconteur," *Wilkes-Barre Times*, Jan. 17, 1905, 1.
359 Al Spink was only a year younger than Captain Dalton. In the early 1870s his older brother William was sporting editor of a Saint Louis newspaper called the *Globe Democrat*. William brought Al to work with that newspaper and Al's career took off. After the Saint Louis professional baseball team folded in 1875, Al helped acquire and build Sportsman Park and organize a new Saint Louis professional team. Al and his brother Charles started *The Sporting News* in March 1886. Al later gave up his interest in that paper and moved to Chicago where he wrote syndicated articles.
360 "Jim Dalton, At 62, Proves He Has Lost None of Old Speed," *The Salt Lake Tribune*, Feb. 18, 1921, 12.

Chapter 3

361 "When the White Elephant Was Young," *Plain Dealer*, Jun. 24, 1943, 6.
362 The M.C.L. was chartered by the state of Tennessee on January 28, 1852 and in Kentucky in 1854. It was intended

to provide a railroad line between Memphis and Louisville. Construction started in 1854. Railroad service reached Clarksville, Tennessee on October 1, 1859.

In 1859, the M.C.L.'s track was put into service from State Line, Kentucky (now called Guthrie) to Clarksville. Track to Memphis was finally finished with the help of Irish construction crews and opened April 12, 1861, two days after the attack on Fort Sumter, South Carolina.

After the Civil War began, the M.C.L. track and the bridge across the Cumberland River at Clarksville became a target of Union forces because cutting the track and destroying the bridge would disrupt the supply lines of Confederate forces. See "An Atrocious Outrage," *Richmond Dispatch*, Oct. 29, 1861 (reporting an attempt to burn the railroad bridge across the Cumberland River at Clarksville); "Capture of Fort Henry," *Richmond Daily Dispatch*, Feb. 8, 1862 (reporting the destruction of the railroad bridge which crossed the Tennessee River near Fort Henry); "Land Slide on the Memphis and Clarksville Railroad," *New Orleans Times Picayune*, Feb. 9, 1862 (reporting that a large force of laborers would be necessary to remove an obstruction caused by a land slide).

363 "News from the South," *New York Commercial Advertiser*, Jun. 10, 1861, 1; "The Election in Tennessee," *Philadelphia Inquirer*, Jun. 10, 1861, 1.

364 U.S. Census, Year: 1880; Census Place: Minneapolis, Hennepin, Minnesota; Roll: 622; Family History Film: 1254622; Page: 499A; Enumeration District: 254; Year: 1870; Census Place: Cleveland Ward 8, Cuyahoga, Ohio;

Roll: M593_1191; Page: 246A; Image: 17; Family History Library Film: 552690.

365 "Tennessee Legislature – Message of Gov. Brownlow," *New York Times*, Feb. 13, 1868; Andreas, Alfred T., History of Chicago, Vol. 3 (A.T. Andreas, 1886), 230; Herr, Kincaid A., The Louisville & Nashville Railroad, 1850-1963 (University Press of Kentucky, 1964); Acts of the State of Tennessee passed at the General Assembly (F.M. Paul, 1866), 33.

366 "Political," *Plain Dealer*, Apr. 2, 1868, 3; "The Constable Question," *Plain Dealer*, Apr. 28, 1869, 3; "Receiver's Sale," *Plain Dealer*, Oct. 6, 1875, 3; Cleveland Leader City Directory 1867, (Cleveland Leader Printing Company), 153; Cleveland Leader City Directory 1868, (Cleveland Leader Printing Company), 166 (In this edition John Gallagher is described as a grocer); W.S. Robinson & Co.'s Annual Cleveland Directory for the year ending April 1875, (W.S. Robinson & Co.), 230.

367 "Pugilism. Pat McKenney's Recipe," *Plain Dealer*, Jan. 7, 1888, 5.

368 "The Courts," *Plain Dealer*, Apr. 28, 1874, 3. There are several Julia Gallaghers in the 1870 census of Cleveland but there is only one Julia whose husband is John Gallagher. In 1867 a John Gallagher was charged with abusing his family but the charge was dismissed. It is not possible to determine whether this John Gallagher was Reddy's father. See "The Police Court," *Plain Dealer*, Sep. 26, 1867, 1.

369 "The Matrimonial Net," *Plain Dealer*, Feb. 19, 1885, 1 (charged with seduction); "Later City Items," *Plain Dealer*, Feb. 21, 1885, 1 (acquitted of charge of seduction because

of lack of corroboration); "Affie Moore Again," *Plain Dealer*, Nov. 11, 1890, 6 (arrested for burglary of safe); "A Cry of Dynamite," *Plain Dealer*, Nov. 12, 1890, 8; "Gallagher Won't Let 'er Go," *Plain Dealer*, Nov. 13, 1890, 6 (charged with complicity in a burglary); "Mrs. Gallagher's Troubles," *Plain Dealer*, Dec. 23, 1890, 3 (charged with battery of his wife); "Gallagher Didn't Go," *Plain Dealer*, Dec. 24, 1890, 6 (appears on charges of battery of his wife); "Gallagher Rearrested,: *Plain Dealer*, Feb. 26, 1891, 8 (released from the work house and arrested on indictment for burglary); "Very Smooth," *Plain Dealer*, Sep. 11, 1894, 5 (accused of providing a gun used in murder of police officer); "Arrested on Old Charge," *Plain Dealer*, Oct. 21, 1896, 10 (arrested on charge of grand larceny); "Doran Got His Prisoner," *Plain Dealer*, Dec. 28, 1896, 8 (arrested in Buffalo).

370 "A Cry of Dynamite," *Plain Dealer*, Nov. 12, 1890, 8.

371 See footnote 8 above; See e.g. City Directories for Cleveland, Ohio–1891 (Cleveland Directory Co.), 323; City Directories for Cleveland, Ohio–1892 (Cleveland Directory Publ. Co.) 321.

372 "Waylaid an Attorney," *Plain Dealer*, Dec. 18, 1889, 6 (stealing eggs and apples from grocery store); "Police Court," *Plain Dealer*, Jun. 1, 1892, 3 (taking and using a horse without permission); "Charged with Arson," *Plain Dealer*, Jan. 23, 1895, 4.

373 "Pugilism. Gallagher Coming," *Plain Dealer*, Feb. 2, 1893, 5; "Gallagher Challenges Patton," *Plain Dealer*, Mar. 19, 1893, 7; "A Two Round Fight," *Plain Dealer*, May 30, 1893, 8.

374 "Al Rumsey of Rumsey Park," *Plain Dealer*, Apr. 19, 1908, 53.

375 "The State Trades Assembly," *Plain Dealer*, Jan. 29, 1886, 2; "A.R. Rumsey charged with causing the death of John Curtis," *Plain Dealer*, Jun. 9, 1889, 6; "Judge Kelly's Court," *Plain Dealer*, Jun 11, 1889; "'Prof.' Rumsey's Hearing," *Plain Dealer*, Jun. 18, 1889, 6; "A Gift from Fitzsimmons," *Plain Dealer*, Apr. 17, 1896, 5; "Rumsey has the fever," *Plain Dealer*, Jul. 20, 1897, 10; "He Secures Big Buffalo Grain Handling Contract," *Plain Dealer*, Jan. 21, 1898, 8; "Mrs. Al Rumsey's Petition," *Plain Dealer*, Oct. 26, 1899, 8.

376 "Two New Sports In Town," *Chicago Herald*, Feb. 12, 1888, 3; Downs, Winfield Scott, Encyclopedia of American Biography," (American Historical Society, 1934), 168–169.

377 See footnote 3 above.

378 Hall, Henry, The Tribune book of open-air sports (The Tribune Assoc., 1887), 334; "The Cleveland Athletic Club," *Plain Dealer*, Dec. 12, 1938, 8.

379 "Amusements," *Plain Dealer*, Jun. 30, 1884, 4; When the White Elephant Was Young, *Plain Dealer*, Jun. 24, 1943, 6.

380 Advertisement, *Plain Dealer*, Feb. 18, 1885, 4; "Wrestling Matches," *Plain Dealer*, Feb. 18, 1885, 4.

381 "The Ring," *Chicago Tribune*, Jul 3, 1887, 8.

382 "Pugilism," *Plain Dealer*, Nov. 30, 1885, 3; "Knocked Out in the Third Round," *Repository*, Dec. 9, 1884, 5 (KO'd by Captain James H. Dalton at Louisville, Kentucky); "A Glove Fight," *Plain Dealer*, Jan. 21, 1885, 1 (lost in six rounds on a foul to a black fighter named Burgh); "Rev. J.H. Lewis; Youngstown; Mr. Arthur Collins; Cornell;

Little Willie Adkins, *Cleveland Gazette*, Jan. 24, 1885, 4 (defeated a Wilson in a fight at the Owl Club in Cleveland).
383 "Rabshaw to Gallagher," *Plain Dealer*, Dec. 1, 1885, 5.
384 "Wrestling. Faulkner and Burkhardt Draw," *Plain Dealer*, Jun. 1, 1886, 6.
385 "Pugilism," *Plain Dealer*, Jul. 29, 1886, 5; "Jimmy Connolly's Strong Points," *Plain Dealer*, Aug. 12, 1886, 5; "The Sporting World. Gallagher Defeats Connolly in a Six Round Glove Contest," *Plain Dealer*, Aug. 20, 1886, 5.
386 "The Pugilists," *Plain Dealer*, Aug. 24, 1886, 8.
387 "S.C. Bittle vs. 'Reddy' Gallagher," *Plain Dealer*, Aug. 25, 1886, 5; "Bittle and Gallagher," *Plain Dealer*, Aug. 29, 1886, 3.
388 "Sparring at the Academy," *Plain Dealer*, Sep. 11, 1886, 5; "The Sporting World. Le Blanche and Reddy Gallagher Spar with Soft Gloves," *Plain Dealer*, Sep. 12, 1886, 7.
389 "A Ball Player's Sad Death," *Plain Dealer*, Aug. 11, 1886, 8; "Sporting Notes," *Plain Dealer*, Sep. 17, 1886, 5.
390 "Fighting to a Finish. Jimmy Carroll and Dick Collier Fight Twenty-Two Rounds," *The New York Times*, Sep. 17, 1886.
391 "Sluggers Slapped. Judge Jones Expounds the Law to the Grand Jury," *Plain Dealer*, Oct. 9, 1886, 6.
392 "Did Gallagher 'Stop' Rumsey?" *Plain Dealer*, Nov. 5, 1886, 5.
393 No Headline, *National Police Gazette*, Apr. 5, 1884, 10; No Headline, *National Police Gazette*, Apr. 12, 1884, 10.
394 "Sporting Notes," *Plain Dealer*, Nov. 17, 1886, 2.
395 "Wrestling. Marc and Gallagher," *Plain Dealer*, Nov. 19, 1886, 6.

396 "Gallagher and Evans," *Plain Dealer*, Dec. 31, 1886, 5; "Gallagher Will Get Business," *Plain Dealer*, Dec. 31, 1886, 5; "General Sporting Notes," *Plain Dealer*, Jan. 13, 1887, 2.

397 "The Ring. The Proposed Mitchell-Gallagher Fight," *Chicago Tribune*, Jul. 3, 1887, 8.

398 "A Battle for Blood. Desperate Fight Between Reddy Gallagher and the Veteran Pete McCoy at Cleveland," *Plain Dealer*, Jan. 26, 1887, 2; "McCoy-Gallagher Mill," *Dallas Morning News*, Jan. 26, 1887, 1; "'Escaping' Fan at Boxing Bout, but Judge Next Day," *Plain Dealer*, Dec. 4, 1932, 21.

399 "Judge Kelly," *Plain Dealer*, Jan. 28, 1887, 8; "'Escaping' Fan at Boxing Bout, but Judge Next Day," *Plain Dealer*, Dec. 4, 1932, 21.

400 "In the World of Sports," *Chicago Tribune*, Jan. 27, 1887, 5; "A Just Sentence. Professional Pugilists are Given a Chance to do Honest Work," *Daily Gazette*, Jan. 27, 1887, 3; "Shocked Their Feelings. Pete McCoy and His Trainer sentenced to Fines and Imprisonment at Cleveland," *Daily Inter Ocean*, Jan. 27, 1887, 3; "Pugilist McCoy Skips," *New York Herald*, Jan. 28, 1887, 9.

401 "McCoy And Files. Their Bail Forfeited and a Capias Issued," *Plain Dealer*, Jan. 28, 1887, 8.

402 "'Reddy' Galingher [sic] Acquitted," *Chicago Tribune*, Feb. 3, 1887, 6; "'Reddy' Gallagher On Trial," *Plain Dealer*, Feb 3, 1887, 8.

403 "Gallagher and Fogarty," *Plain Dealer*, Jan. 31, 1887, 5; "Fogarty Wants To Fight Gallagher," *Plain Dealer*, Feb. 6, 1887, 6.

404 "Ross Wins Three Falls," *New York Herald*, Feb. 27, 1887, 14.

405 "Will Gallagher And Collier Fight?" *Plain Dealer*, Oct. 27, 1886, 4. Collier did put on an exhibition with George La Blanche at Curry's hall on October 2, 1886. "The La Blanche Benefit," *Plain Dealer*, Oct. 3, 1886, 6.

406 "The Next Cleveland Fight," *New York Herald*, Mar. 10, 1887, 8; "Stray Bits," *Daily Inter Ocean*, Mar. 10, 1887, 2 (Collier is incorrectly identified as Dick Pooler in this article.).

407 "A Quick Knock Out. Reddy Gallagher Whips Dick Collier In One Minute and Seven Seconds," *New York Herald*, Mar. 19, 1887, 9; "Knocked Out In A Round," *Chicago Tribune*, Mar. 19, 1887, 3; "Sporting. The Ring," *Daily Inter Ocean*, Mar. 19, 1887, 1; "Fights and Fighters," *The Morning Herald {Baltimore}*, Mar. 27, 1887, 4.

408 "Dempsey's Plucky Fight. He Breaks His Arm In His Fight With Gallagher," *Chicago Tribune*, May 3, 1887, 3; "Dempsey Breaks His Arm," *Kansas City Star*, May 3, 1887, 1; "Dempsey's Right Arm Broken. Served As Sullivan Was In His Encounter With 'Reddy' Gallagher," *New York Herald*, May 3, 1887, 2; "Dempsey Disabled," *Plain Dealer*, May 3, 1887, 2; "Miscellaneous," *Toronto Daily Mail*, May 4, 1887, 3.

409 "Sullivan Will Be Here Next Week," *Plain Dealer*, May 5, 1887, 2; "General Sporting Notes," *Plain Dealer*, May 8, 1887, 3; "Sullivan Party Here," *Plain Dealer*, May 11, 1887, 6; "Sporting World. John L. Sullivan Spars and Talks of His Future," *Plain Dealer*, May 12, 1887, 2.

410 "General Sporting News," *Plain Dealer*, May 12, 1887, 2; "General Sporting Notes," *Plain Dealer*, May 15, 1887, 6.

411 "Gallagher May Go On A Tour," *Plain Dealer*, May 21, 1887, 2; "General Sporting Notes," *Plain Dealer*, May 29, 1887, 7.

412 "Gallagher May Go On A Tour," *Plain Dealer*, May 21, 1887, 2; "General Sporting Notes," *Plain Dealer*, May 26, 1887, 6; "Paragraphic Penciling of Passing Events Pertinently Put, *Plain Dealer*, Jun. 3, 1887, 3.

413 "Sporting Notes," *The Daily Argus News*, Jun. 1, 1887, 1; "The Belt Given to Kilrain," *Bridgeport Morning News*, Jun. 6, 1887, 1; "Kilrain Has the Diamond Belt," *Indianian Republican*, Jun. 9, 1887, 4;

414 "General Sporting Notes," *Plain Dealer*, Jun. 10, 1887, 6; "Gallagher Will Join the New Company," *Plain Dealer*, Jun. 13, 1887, 5.

415 "Fighter Who Just Missed Being A World's Champion. Reddy Gallagher, Giving Away Big Weight, Once Fought a Draw With Charley Mitchell When the Englishman Was in His Prime – Story of His Brief Career in the Ring and His Most Important Contests," *Saint Louis Republic*, Feb. 7, 1904, Part III, 26.

416 "Charles Mitchell and 'Reddy' Gallagher to Fight," *Chicago Tribune*, Jun. 28, 1887, 3; "The Ring," *Daily Inter Ocean*, Jun. 28, 1887, 2; "The Sporting World. Pugilism. Gallagher To Fight Mitchell," *Plain Dealer*, Jun. 28, 1887, 5; "Telegraphic Summary," *The Sun* [Baltimore], Jun. 28, 1887, 1.

417 See footnote 19 above.

418 See footnote 16 above; "P.R. Gallagher, Sports Expert, Is Dead At 73. Pneumonia Fatal to Former Boxer and Post Columnist," *Denver Post*, Nov. 13, 1937, 5.
419 "The Prize Ring. Charlie Mitchell Defeats Reddy Gallagher for Points in Cleveland," *Chicago Tribune*, Jul. 29, 1887, 3 (The article claims Gallagher was knocked down in the third round but was on his feet in an instant. Given other accounts of the fight this was probably a slip rather than a knockdown.).
420 "Nobody Killed," *Lake Superior Review and Weekly Tribune*, Jul. 29, 1887, 1; "Mitchell On His Muscle. The Scientific Pugilist Declared to Have Defeated 'Reddy' Gallagher at Cleveland. A Sharp Battle Fought, Both Men Using Their 'Dukes' With Decided Vigor. Gallagher Makes a Good Impression, Both on His Antagonist and the Spectators," *Plain Dealer*, Jul. 29, 1887, 2.
421 "Think Well of Gallagher," *Plain Dealer*, Aug. 7, 1887, 5.
422 "Reddy Gallagher. The Well-Known Middle Weight In the City," *Detroit Free Press*, Mar. 30, 1890, 13.
423 "General Sporting Notes," *Plain Dealer*, Aug. 3, 1887, 5; "General Sporting Notes," *Plain Dealer*, Aug. 28, 1887, 2.
424 "General Sporting News," *Plain Dealer*, Aug. 9, 1887, 5; No Headline, *Repository*, Aug. 13, 1887, 3.
425 "Reddy Gallagher Looking For Davis," *Plain Dealer*, Sep. 4, 1887, 7; "General Sporting Notes," *Plain Dealer*, Sep. 6, 1887, 4.
426 Advertisement, *Newark {Ohio} Daily Advocate*, Sep. 8, 1887, 1; "An Athletic Combination," *Newark {Ohio} Daily Advocate*, Sep. 9, 1887, 2 (quoting the Kansas City *Times*); Advertisement, *Newark {Ohio} Daily Advocate*, Sep. 10,

1887, 1; Advertisement, *Newark {Ohio} Daily Advocate*, Sep. 13, 1887, 1.

427 "Gallagher and Collier," *Plain Dealer*, Nov. 3, 1887, 4.

428 Early articles referred to Costello as "a Cleveland newspaper man." "Miscellaneous Items of Interest," *Chicago Tribune*, Oct. 26, 1887, 6; "Sporting Gossip," *Saint Louis Post Dispatch*, Oct. 27, 1887, 8. Later articles mention Costello by name. "Bittle Coming to Fight Gallagher," *Plain Dealer*, Nov. 3, 1887, 4; "Business for Gallagher And Thompson," *Plain Dealer*, Nov. 10, 1887, 4; "Pugilism. Gallagher Challenges McCaffery," *Plain Dealer*, Nov. 12, 1885, 5.

429 "The Jap Falls On Gallagher," *Plain Dealer*, Nov. 13, 1887, 3.

430 "The Johnson Gallagher Match," *Plain Dealer*, Nov. 12, 1887, 5; "The Johnson-Gallagher Match," *Plain Dealer*, Nov. 3, 1887, 3; "Wrestling. Johnson defeats Gallagher," *Plain Dealer*, Nov. 18, 1887, 5.

431 "Reddy Gallagher's Winter Programme," *Chicago Herald*, Dec. 8, 1887, 3.

432 "The Gallagher-Riley Match," *Plain Dealer*, Dec. 15, 1887, 4; "Local Happenings," *Hamilton Daily Democrat*, Dec. 17, 1887, 3; "Fighter And Manager At War," *Plain Dealer*, Dec. 21, 1887, 6; "Reddy Gallagher's Fights Off," *Chicago Tribune*, Dec. 22, 1887, 6.

433 "General Sporting Notes," *Plain Dealer*, Jan. 17, 1888, 5; "Sporting And Athletic," *Trenton Evening Times*, Jan. 19, 1888, 2.

434 "Reddy Gallagher Wins," *Cincinnati Commercial Times*, Feb. 8, 1888, 3; "Bittle Loses the Battle," *Daily Inter Ocean*, Feb.

8, 1888, 2; "With Three Ounce Gloves," *New York Herald*, Feb. 8, 1888, 8; "Won By Gallagher," *St. Paul Daily lobe*, Feb. 8, 1888, 5; "The Ring. The Bittle-Gallagher Fight," *Toronto Daily Mail*, Feb. 9, 1885, 2.

435 "General Sporting Notes," *Plain Dealer*, Feb. 4, 1888, 5; "Parson Davies' Big Scheme," *Chicago Herald*, Feb. 5, 1888, 3; "Evans and Muldoon. To Start out under Parson Davies Auspices with Special Offers to All Comers," *Cincinnati Commercial Tribune*, Feb. 6, 1888, 2; "Muldoon on Wrestlers," *Chicago Tribune*, Feb. 5, 1888, 14; "Miscellaneous Notes," *Chicago Herald*, Feb. 5, 1888, 14.

436 "Sporting Notes," *Daily Inter Ocean*, Feb. 11, 1888, 2; "Sporting Notes," *Detroit Free Press*, Feb. 13, 1888, 5; "Cleveland's Champion Boxer," *Daily Inter Ocean*, Feb. 12, 1888, Part 1, 3; "Sporting News," *Daily Inter Ocean*, Feb. 14, 1888, Part 1, 6; "Lewis Downed McMahon," *Chicago Tribune*, Feb. 15, 1888, 6; "Jack Fogarty Says That Gallagher Fears to Fight Him," *Plain Dealer*, Feb. 24, 1888, 6.

437 "Sporting Matters. The Big Combination. An Excellent Exhibition at the Casino," *Detroit Free Press*, Feb. 28, 1888, 2.

438 "General Sporting Notes," *Plain Dealer*, Mar. 8, 1888, 5 (quoting from the Detroit Free Press); "Gallagher And Lewis Matched," *Plain Dealer*, Mar. 20, 1888, 5; "A Lewis-Gallagher Draw," *Daily Inter Ocean*, Mar. 22, 1888, 2; "News of the Week," *Morning Sun Herald*, Mar. 29, 1888, 6; "News Summary," *Atlantic Daily Telegraph*, Mar. 31, 1888, 3.

439 "Gallagher In Town, *Plain Dealer*, Mar. 13, 1888, 6.

440 "Sporting," *Daily Inter Ocean*, Mar. 28, 1888, 3. In 1999 a book was published claiming that there never was an Otto Floto and that the name was simply invented by the publishers of the *Denver Post*. This is a stunningly ill-informed assertion because Floto's activities in Chicago with Parson Davies in the 1880s are well documented and his activities in Denver were extensive. See William E. Studwell, W.E., Conrad, C., Schueneman, B.R., Circus Songs: An Annotated Anthology (Psychology Press, 1999), 13.

441 "Gallagher And Mannen To Spar," *Plain Dealer*, May 11, 1888, 6; "Gallagher And Mannen Matched," *Plain Dealer*, May 16, 1888, 5.

442 "Deaths," *Plain Dealer*, May 23, 1888, 5; "Pugilism. The Mannen-Gallagher Match," *Plain Dealer*, May 29, 1888, 5.

443 "Swimming. Pank and Gallagher To Race," *Plain Dealer*, Jun. 24, 1888, 6; "General Sporting Notes," *Plain Dealer*, Jul. 13, 1888, 5; "Gallagher And Mannen To Fight," *Plain Dealer*, Jul. 13, 1888, 5.

444 "Reddy Gallagher May Go West," *Plain Dealer*, Aug. 8, 1888, 5; "General Sporting Notes. Reddy Gallagher and Ed Smith Will Fight in Colorado," *Chicago Tribune*, Aug. 14, 1888, 3.

445 "Pugilism. The Gallagher-Smith Match Off," *Plain Dealer*, Aug. 25, 1888, 5.

446 "Gallagher Wants to Try Wall," *Chicago Tribune*, Aug. 10, 1888, 6.

447 "General Sporting Notes," *Plain Dealer*, Jul. 13, 1888, 5.

448 "Daly vs. Gallagher," *Saint Louis Post Dispatch*, Sep. 27, 1888, 8.

449 "A 'Scrap' On Stage," *Saint Louis Republic*, Sep. 29, 1888, 6; "The Sporting World," *Plain Dealer*, Oct. 1, 1888, 5.
450 "A Boxing Match," *Saint Louis Republic*, Oct. 2, 1888, 6.
451 "Gallagher-McManus," *Saint Louis Republic*, Oct. 5, 1888, Part 1, 3.
452 "Daly's Benefit," *Saint Louis Republic*, Dec. 14, 1888, Part 1, 6.
453 "General Sporting Notes," *Plain Dealer*, Dec. 21, 1888, 5; "About The Pugilists," Saint Louis Republic, Dec. 21, 1888, Part 1, 6; "Reddy Gallagher Coming," *Saint Louis Post Dispatch*, Dec. 21, 1888, 12; "Dan Daly's Benefit," *Saint Louis Post Dispatch*, Dec. 22, 1888, 8.
454 "The Sporting World. Gallagher and McAuliffe," *Plain Dealer*, Jan. 17, 1889, 5.
455 "Daly's Benefit," *Saint Louis Republic*, Dec. 13, 1888, Part 2, 15.
456 "The Old Kennard House," *Plain Dealer*, Sep. 11, 1944, 8; "The Old Kennard House," *Plain Dealer*, Sep. 13, 1944, 4; "The Old Kennard House," *Plain Dealer*, Sep. 16, 1944, 4.
457. "Mitchell Driven to Bay," *Chicago Tribune*, Dec. 28, 1888, 6; "Charley Mitchell In A Row," *Chicago Herald*, Dec. 28, 1888, 5; "Kilrain And Mitchell Unpopular," *Plain Dealer*, Dec. 18, 1888, 2; "Bloody Barroom Work," *Galveston Daily News*, Dec. 29, 1888, 1; "Charley Mitchell Assaulted by Roughs In Cleveland," *Toronto Daily Mail*, Dec. 31, 1888, 2; "Fight Without Stakes," *Boston Daily Globe*, Dec. 28, 1888, 10; "The Old Kennard House," *Plain Dealer*, Sep. 18, 1944, 8.
458. "Athletic. Graham Defeats McGuire," *Plain Dealer*, Dec. 20, 1888, 5; "Athletic. 'Greek George' and Graham," Plain

Dealer, Dec. 26, 1888, 5; "Athletics. Gallagher Throws Graham," *Plain Dealer*, Jan. 3, 1889, 5.
459. "General Sporting Notes," *Plain Dealer*, Feb. 19, 1889, 5; "General Sporting Notes," *Plain Dealer*, Feb. 22, 1889, 6
460. "Pugilism. California Work For Gallagher," *Plain Dealer*, Mar. 22, 1889, 5.
461. "Sporting Smalltalk," *Critic Record*, Apr. 15, 1889, 3; "Carroll to Fight La Blanche," *Plain Dealer*, Apr. 24, 1889, 1.
462. "Sporting Notes," *New York Herald*, May 17, 1889, 8.
463. "Another Unfortunate," *Plain Dealer*, May 30, 1889, 8.
464. "Gallagher To Fight McCarty," *New York Herald*, Jul. 17, 1889, 8; "Pugilism. The Gallagher-McCarty Match," *Plain Dealer*, Sep. 26, 1889, 5; No Headline, *Saginaw News*, Dec. 23, 1889, 3; "Pugilism. Is Reagan A Weakener," *Plain Dealer*, Feb. 26, 1890, 5; "Heal Wants A Fight," *Plain Dealer*, Feb. 27, 1890, 5.
465. "Pugilism," *Plain Dealer*, Mar. 13, 1890, 5; "Sporting Notes," *Pittsburgh Dispatch*, Mar. 14, 1890, 6; "Pugilism. Gallagher And McCarthy Matched," *Plain Dealer*, Mar. 26, 1890, 5; "Gallagher and McCarthy Matched," *Pittsburgh Dispatch*, Mar. 27, 1890, 6; "Reddy Gallagher and McCarty Matched," *Salt Lake Herald*, Mar. 27, 1890, 3; "Brief Telegrams," *The Deseret News*, Mar 27, 1890, 1.
466. "General Sporting Notes," *Plain Dealer*, Mar. 29, 1890, 5; "Reddy Gallagher," *Detroit Free Press*, Mar. 30, 1890, 19.
467. "On Hoosier Soil. A Fifty-three Round Prize Fight Occurs at Shelby, Ind.," *Fort Wayne Sentinel*, Apr. 9, 1890, 1.
468. "'Reddy' Gallagher At San Francisco," *Chicago Tribune*, Apr. 15, 1890, 2; "He Was Not In It. Professor Corbett Plays

With Dominick McCaffrey. Programme for Ladies' Night at the Olympic Club – Arrival of 'Reddy' Gallagher. Jack Kitchen Going East," *The Morning Call*, Apr. 15, 1890, 2.
469. "Proud of Corbett," *Pittsburgh Dispatch*, Apr. 18, 1890, 1; "Prospective Prize Fighter," *Jackson Citizen Patriot*, May 15, 1890, 3; "Athletic Sport," *The Morning Call*, May 15, 1890, 8.
470. "Fitz Was Awkward When He First Landed," *The Pittsburgh Press*, Oct 16, 1902, 14.
471. "General Sporting Notes," *Chicago Tribune*, May 29, 1890, 6.
472. "'Bleeding' the Gamblers," *The New York Times*, Oct. 19, 1892.
473. "The Sporting World," *Leadville Daily Herald*, Nov. 25, 1883, 3; "The Sporting World," *Leadville Daily Herald*, Nov. 28, 1883, 4; "The Sporting World," *Leadville Daily Herald*, Dec. 6, 1883, 4; "The City in Brief," *Leadville Daily Herald*, Dec. 28, 1883, 4.
474. "P.R. Gallagher, Sports Expert, Is Dead At 73. Pneumonia Fatal to Former Boxer and Post Columnist," *Denver Post*, Nov. 13, 1937, 5.
475. See footnote 16 above.
476. "Glover and Ashton to Meet," *Chicago Herald*, Jun. 22, 1890, 13; "The Ashton-Glover Match," *Chicago Tribune*, Jul. 2, 1890, 7; "Ashton Ready for Clover Hard Thumping Contests Promised for the Battery D Show Tomorrow," *Inter Ocean*, Jul. 2, 1890, 6.
477. "Knocked Senseless," *Chillicothe Constitution*, Jul. 3, 1890, 5; "It Cost Brennan Dear," *Chicago Herald*, Jul. 4, 1890, 1; "His Final Battle-Billy Brennan Fatally Injured in a Set-To

at Battery D," *Chicago Tribune*, Jul. 4, 1890, 7; "Pugilist Brennan Dead," *Saint Louis Post Dispatch*, Jul, 4, 1890, 4; "Brennan's Last Fight," *St. Paul Daily Globe*, Jul. 5, 1890, 5.

478. "Desperate and Brutal," *Chicago Tribune*, May 22, 1890, 6; "The Loser Won," *Saint Louis Post Dispatch*, May 22, 1890, 12; "General Sporting Notes," *Chicago Tribune*, May 24, 1890, 6; "The Prize-Fighter's Death," *Newark Sunday Call*, Jul. 6, 1890, 1.

479. "The Fatal Fall," *Chicago Tribune*, Jul. 4, 1890, 1; "His Death Accidental," *Daily Inter Ocean*, Jul. 6, 1890, 1.

480. "Fatal Sparring Match," *Chicago Tribune*, Jul. 5, 1890, 3; "The Brennan Killing," *Saint Louis Post Dispatch*, Jul. 5, 1890, 5; "The Ring. Girarard and Gallagher released by Coroner's Jury," *The Toronto Daily Mail*, Jul 7, 1890, 8.

481. "Pugilism. Dempsey's Clever Exhibition," *Plain Dealer*, Jul. 20, 1890, 7; "The Sullivans," *Kalamazoo Gazette*, Sep. 7, 1890, 1.

482. "Midnight Maundering," *Leadville Daily and Evening Chronicle*, Oct. 10, 1890, 4; "Gallagher Defeats the Jap," *Aspen Weekly Times*, Oct. 18, 1890, 1; "Gallagher Defeats the Jap," *Aspen Daily Chronicle*, Oct. 18, 1890, 1; "Gallagher Defeats the Jap," *Aspen Daily Times*, Oct. 18, 1890, 1; "Wrestling. Gallagher Defeats the Jap," *Plain Dealer*, Oct. 22, 1890, 5.

483. "Another Wrestling Match," *Aspen Daily Chronicle*, Oct. 22, 1890, 3; "Another Wrestling Match," *Aspen Daily Times*, Oct. 22, 1890, 1.

484. "Possible Matches," *The Morning Call*, Dec. 12, 1890, 3.

485. "Men Who Handle the Gloves," *The {Baltimore} Morning Herald*, Mar 22, 1891, 6.
486. "Sporting Miscellany," *Boston Daily Globe*, Jun. 1, 1891, 3; "Among the Big Pugilist," *Spokane Daily Chronicle*, Jun 1, 1891, 1.
487. "On the Diamond," *Los Angeles Times,* Jun 24, 1891, 4; "General Sporting Notes," *Chicago Tribune*, Jun. 28, 1891, 4.
488. "With the Gloves," *The Morning Herald*, Jul 26, 1891, 6; "General Sporting Notes," *Chicago Tribune*, Aug. 24, 1891, 5.
489. "General Sporting Notes," *Chicago Tribune*, Aug. 8, 1891, 7.
490. "Injudicious Training," *The Star*, May 20, 1904, 1.
491. "Mitchell The Victor," *Chicago Tribune*, Sep. 24, 1891, 6; "Reddy Gallagher Knocked Out," *Chicago Herald*, Sep. 24, 1891, 1; "'Young Mitchell' Wins. The Great Middleweight Contest In San Francisco. Gallagher Had the Best at First," *The Salt Lake Tribune*, Sep. 24, 1891, 2; "The Denver Man Beaten. 'Young Mitchell' Whips 'Reddy' Gallagher In Thirteen Rounds. California Pugilist Slower Than Masterson's Pet But a Firmer Man and Harder Hitter etc.," *Kansas City Star*, Sep. 24, 3; "Prize Fight. 'Young Mitchell' Knocks 'Reddy' Gallagher Out in Thirteen Rounds," *Albuquerque Morning Democrat*, Sep. 25, 1891, 1; "Mitchell The Winner. Reddy Gallagher Defeated in a Thirteen Round Contest at San Francisco," *Aberdeen Daily News*, Sep. 25, 1891, 1; "Arenic," *San Francisco Chronicle*, Sep. 28, 1891, 8.
492. "Sporting News," *Los Angeles Times*, Sep. 29, 1891, 4.
493. Year: 1888; Arrival: New York , United States; Microfilm Serial: M237; Microfilm Roll: M237_525; Line: 43; List

Number: 1251; "Romance of An Actress," *The Salt Lake Tribune*, Mar. 30, 1892, 5.
494. "Divorced In Four Minutes," *New York Herald*, Oct 21, 1892, 10.
495. Advertisement, *San Francisco Chronicle*, Jan. 18, 1891, 3.
496. "Gossip of the Stage," *Chicago Herald*, Jun. 6, 1891, 10.
497. See footnote 126 above.
498. "At the Hotels," *The Salt Lake Tribune*, Jul. 28, 1891, 8.
499. "A Cow Puncher's Bride," *The Salt Lake Herald*, Jan. 22, 1892, 1; "Millie Price Dow's Sister," *Aspen Daily Chronicle*, Jan. 28, 1892, 1; "Wouldn't Be Outdone by a Cowboy," *The Arizona Republic*, Jan. 29, 1892, 1.
500. See footnote 131 above.
501. "The Prize Fighters," *Morning Olympian*, Oct. 3, 1891, 1; "The Ring," *The Toronto Daily Mail*, Oct. 9, 1891, 2.
502. "Notes of the Fighters," *Chicago Tribune*, Jul. 4, 1892, 12; "Notes," *Boston Daily Globe*, Oct. 10, 1892, 2; "Sporting Miscellany," *Repository*, Nov. 15, 1892, 4; "General Sporting Notes," *Chicago Tribune*, Nov. 28, 1891, 7; "Blows," The *Toronto Daily Mail*, Dec 1, 1891, 2.
503. "The Great Game. Some Bitter Reflections Concerning Boulder's Defeat," *Boulder Daily Camera*, Nov. 11, 1895, 1; Colorado School of Mines-Alumni Association, *The Mines Magazine* (Colorado School of Mines Alumni Association, 1915), Vol. 5, 228 and 251 (describing a game between the school and the D.A.C. during the "dark ages" of football and contending that members of the team needed brass knuckles to participate in a game with the D.A.C.); *The Sigma Chi Quarterly: the official organ of the Sigma Chi Fraternity* (The Fraternity 1902-03), Vol. 22, 405-06

(describing plans of Denver Sigma Chi members to form an all-university team including players from Michigan, Pennsylvania, Stanford, DePauw, Princeton, Wisconsin, Columbia, Lehigh, Cornel, Chicago, Minnesota and Illinois) to play a Thanksgiving day football game with a D.A.C. team led by Reddy Gallagher).

504. "Around The World On Wheels For the Inter Ocean," *Daily Inter Ocean*, Jun. 2, 1895, 24.
505. "Gossip Of The Fighters," *New York Herald*, Nov. 28, 1892, 8.
506. "Pugilistic," *San Francisco Chronicle*, Apr. 11, 1892, 8; "Pugilistic," *San Francisco Chronicle*, Apr. 18, 1892, 8.
507. "Gallagher Wants More Money," *The Evening Herald*, Dec. 3, 1892, 4; "Reddy Gallagher and Jack Dempsey," *Dallas Morning News*, Dec. 18, 1892, 8; "Will Fight Dempsey," *Aspen Daily Leader*, Dec. 18, 1892, 1; No Headline, *Freeman*, Jan. 7, 1893, 5; "Sporting Notes Of Interest," *New York Herald*, Jan. 10, 1893, 8.
508. "Entirely Too Coarse. Pugilist Smith's Work Does Not Please the Referee," *Aspen Daily Chronicle*, Jan. 31, 1893, 1; "Gallagher Wins," *Boulder Daily Camera*, Jan. 31, 1893, 1; "Ended In A Row," *Omaha World Herald*, Jan. 31, 1893, 5; "Masterson in the Ring," *The Daily Record*, Jan. 31, 1893, 5; "Exciting Fight At Denver," *Macon Telegraph*, Feb. 5, 1893, 8.
509. "Pugilism, Gallagher Coming," *Plain Dealer*, Feb. 2, 1893, 5; "A Two Round Fight," *Plain Dealer*, May 30, 1893, 8.
510. See footnote 16 above.
511. "Silver's Friends," *Clinton Daily Age*, Jul 13, 1893, 1 (State Silver League meets at Coliseum Hall); "Western

News Items," *The Desert News*, Jun. 2, 1894, 16 (The Denver Manufacturers Exchange holds exposition at Coliseum Hall); No Headline, *The New York Times*, Aug. 31, 1894 (the Colorado prohibition party convention held at Coliseum Hall); "Denver to Have Cycle Show," *The New York Times*, Oct. 29, 1895 (the first cycle show west of Chicago); "Bryan's Platform Breaks," *The New York Times*, Jan. 19, 1899 (William Jennings Bryant appears at Coliseum Hall). These are but a few examples of the events held at the Coliseum.

512. "Corbett An Invalid. The Champion a Very Sick Man and May Never Fight Again," *Sioux Valley News*, Apr. 27, 1893, 5.
513. "What's Become of Denver Ed Smith," *Rochester Evening Journal and Post*, Apr. 12, 1926, 26.
514. "Couldn't Knock Gallagher Out," *Rockford Daily Spectator*, Jul. 5, 1893, 2; "Gallagher Wins from Smith," *Chicago Tribune*, Jul. 5, 1893, 6.
515. "Sporting Notes," *Daily Inter Ocean*, Mar. 3, 1895, 4; "Reddy Stops Fighting," *Plain Dealer*, Mar. 4, 1895, 3.
516. "To Fight Oct. 3," *The World*, Sep. 27, 1894, 1; "Denver Fight," *Reno Evening Gazette*, Oct. 3, 1894, 3; "Smith and Farrell," *Plain Dealer*, Oct. 4, 1894, 3; "Farrell Fouled Smith," *St. Paul Daily Globe*, Oct. 4, 1894, 5; "Foul Fight. Lawrence Farrell No Match For Denver Ed Smith," *The Evening Bulletin*, Oct. 4, 1894, 1; "Won the Fight on a Foul," *Wheeling Register*, Oct. 4, 1894, 1; "Won On A Foul," *The {Baltimore} Morning Herald*, Oct. 4, 1894, 2.
517. "At The Columbia," *Idaho Statesman*, Oct. 14, 1894, 3.
518. In public records prior to her marriage Mary's name is given as "Sheehy." These records include the passenger

manifest at the time of her immigration, the 1880 U.S. Census, and her Colorado marriage license. See footnote 154 above. However, when she provided information to the Encyclopedia of American Biography she reported her maiden name as "McSheehy." See footnote 16 above. Such changes are common among Irish immigrants.

519. Mary Gallagher provided her account of her family's genealogy after Reddy had died. See footnote 16 above. New York incoming passenger records show that Honorah Allman arrived at New York with her daughter Mary Sheehy on October 13, 1873. See Year: 1873; Arrival: New York, United States; Microfilm Serial: M237; Microfilm Roll: M237_383; Line: 12; List Number: 1105; Timothy Allman arrived in New York on September 29, 1873, two weeks before Honorah and Mary. See Year: 1873; Arrival: New York, United States; Microfilm Serial: M237; Microfilm Roll: M237_382; Line: 53; List Number: 1049. Subsequent records indicate that Timothy and Honorah were husband and wife and that Honorah had three children who became Timothy's step children: Mary, John, and Roger. Honorah and Timothy also had a daughter Margaret who was born about 1877 and who would have been a half-sister of Mary Gallagher. See U.S. Census, Year: 1880; Census Place: San Francisco, San Francisco, California; Roll: 77; Family History Film: 1254077; Page: 61A; Enumeration District: 150; Image: 0123. An obituary for Mary Gallagher indicates that at her death she was visiting a sister, Margaret Dale, in Pasadena, California. See "Mary Gallagher Widow of Post Columnist, Dies," *Denver Post*, Feb. 16, 1994. The 1930 census indicates that

Mary A[llman] Dale born about 1878 lived in Pasadena in 1930 with her husband Frank and three children. See U.S. Census, Year: 1930; Census Place: Pasadena, Los Angeles, California; Roll: 169; Page: 1B; Enumeration District: 1245; Image: 173.0. Mary's obituary also indicates that she had sisters Nora Tyree and Ellie Beckett who lived in Los Angeles. The 1930 census indicates that Nora Tyree was born in California in 1874 and lived in Los Angeles. See U.S. Census, Year: 1930; Census Place: Los Angeles, Los Angeles, California; Roll: 141; Page: 14B; Enumeration District: 226; Image: 918.0. For an undetermined reason Nora is not enumerated with the rest of the family in the 1880 census. Nora would have been another half-sister of Mary Gallagher. California voter registration records indicate that an Elnora Beckett was registered to vote in San Jose, California between 1916 and 1936. See California Voter Registrations, 1900-1968 [database on-line]. Provo, UT, USA: Ancestry.com Operations Inc, 2008. Original data: State of California, United States. Great Register of Voters. Sacramento, California: California State Library. She was then registered in Los Angeles beginning in 1946. California Voter Registrations, 1900–1968 [database on-line]. Provo, UT, USA: Ancestry.com Operations Inc, 2008. Original data: State of California, United States. Great Register of Voters. Sacramento, California: California State Library.

520. "Wrestling at Denver," *Morning Olympian*, Apr. 6, 1895, 2; "In a Wrestling Contest," *The Morning Call*, Apr. 6, 1895, 2; "Dunn Draws With Gallagher," *Philadelphia Inquirer*, Apr. 4, 1895, Part II, 20. Reddy wrestled Harry Dunn of

Australia to a draw. Gallagher obtained a fall in Greco-Roman style but after more than two hours of collar-and-elbow wrestling the match was called a draw. "Telegraphic Notes of Sports," *San Francisco Chronicle*, Apr. 7, 1895, 5.
521. "The Ring. Welterweights Fight at Denver," *Salt Lake Herald*, Dec. 8, 1894, 2; Shirked Their Duty," *Denver Post*, Nov. 26, 1895, 1 (Gallagher fined $25 for acting as referee); "The McCoy-Martin Fight," *Daily Journal*, Jul. 3, 1900, 1 (referred the fight at Telluride).
522. "The Ring," The Salt Lake Herald, May 11, 1895, 5; Miletich, Lou, Dan Stuart's Fistic Carnival (Texas A & M University Press, 1994), 11–16.
523. "Corbett In Denver," *The Salt Lake Herald*, Aug. 5, 1896, 7; "Corbett Spars in Denver," *San Francisco Chronicle*, Aug. 6, 1896, 5; "The Latest News," *Tombstone Prospector*, Aug. 6, 1896, 1; "Choynski After Fitzsimmons," *The Morning Times*, Aug. 31, 1896, 3; "A Chance for Fitz," *The State*, Aug. 31, 1896, 5; "Boxing," *The San Francisco Call*, Sep. 5, 1896, 10; "Corbett's Queer Announcement," *San Francisco Chronicle*, Sep. 30, 1896, 5; "Five Thousand Dollars Put Up," *The Morning Call*, Oct. 4, 1896, 9.
524. "Parker-Carrig Prize Fight," *Telluride Journal*, Mar. 25, 1899, 8. Pat Fitzgerald of Chicago was Carrig's trainer and came to Denver with him for the Parker match. Fitzgerald was the long-time trainer and close friend of the bantamweight champion of the world, Jimmy Barry. In early May Fitzgerald died of a heart attack in his Denver hotel room fully dressed.
525. Laws passed at the session of the General Assembly of the State of Colorado (Bradford Printing Co., 1899), Ch. 123, Prize

Fighting, 309; "By Sandy Griswold," *Omaha World Herald*, Part III, 23 (explaining the impact of the Cannon Law).

526. DeArment, Robert K., <u>Bat Masterson: The Man and the Legend</u> (University of Oklahoma Press, 1989), 353-369; "A Good Thing. Push it Along," *Daily Journal*, Apr. 8, 1899, 1; "Result of the Prize Fight Law," *Durango Democrat*, Apr. 20, 1899, 1.

527. "Denver Club Flying High," *Aspen Tribune*, Apr. 23, 1899, 1; "Big Fight Goes to Denver," *Chicago Tribune*, May 5, 1899, 5.

528. "Dixon Again. Greatest Fistic Battle Seen in Denver, Colored Boy Had All the Better of It. White Stood Up to His Punishment. Fought Coolly and With Much Pluck. After the 13th Round He Was Never Dangerous. Made Desperate Rally in the Last Round. But He has Too Far Gone to Do Very Much Execution.," *Boston Daily Globe*, Jul. 12, 1899, "Dixon Still the Featherweight. Gets Decision in Twenty-Round Fight With Tommy White," *Daily True American*, Jul. 13, 1899, 2.

529. DeArment, Robert K., <u>Bat Masterson: The Man and the Legend</u> (University of Oklahoma Press, 1989), 353–369; No Headline, *Svensk Amerikanska Western {Denver, Denver County}*; Aug. 2, 1900; 8; "About the Boxers," *Boston Globe*, Aug. 3, 1900, 4.

530. "Few Fighters Ever Get Rich," *Duluth News Tribune*, Apr. 15, 1906, Section S, 2.

531. "What Prizefighter Has the Most Wealth," *Freeman*, Feb. 23, 1907, 7. "Richest Prize-Fighter," *Boston Journal*, Feb. 5, 1907, 8.

532. "Coliseum Hall Is Destroyed by Fire," *Fort Collins Weekly Courier*, Sep. 30, 1908, 1.
533. "News – Gossip About Fights – Fighters," *Trenton Evening Times*, Oct. 15, 1907, 11 (purchase price reported to be $135,000); No Headline, *Palestine Daily Herald*, Oct. 19, 1907, 4; "Retired Fighter Buys Hotel," *Washington Herald*, Oct. 24, 1907, 8.
534. "Fights Of Old West," *Oregonian*, Nov. 20, 1932, 45.
535. "Title Battle Makes Pitts Big Promoter," *Chicago Tribune*, Sep. 10, 1916, 4.
536. "P.R. Gallagher, Sports Expert, Is Dead At 73. Pneumonia Fatal to Former Boxer and Post Columnist," *Denver Post*, Nov. 13, 1937, 1; Reddy Gallagher, Sports Writer, Who Fought Draw With First Dempsey, Dies," *Dallas Morning News*, Nov. 14, 1937, Sec. IV, 6.
537. "Schrembs Is Now Bishop 22 Years," *Plain Dealer*, Feb. 18, 1933, 7. This article states that Francis Fergus was one of twenty-nine men to be ordained by Bishop Schrembers on March 11, 1933 at St. John's Cathedral in Cleveland.
538. "Scribe Left Fortune," *Montana Butte Standard*, Nov. 19, 1937, 1
539. See footnote 16 above.

Chapter 4

540. U.S. Census, Year: 1880; Toledo, Lucas County, Ohio; Roll: 1043; Family History Film: 1255043; Page: 365A; Enumeration District: 43; Image: 0624; "The News In Toledo. Interesting Sketch of Majesty's Career – A Graduate of the Toledo High School," *Toledo Daily Commercial*, Feb.

26, 1891, 2; "The Majesty Tragedy. Further Account of the Affair," *Toledo Daily Blade*, Feb. 26, 1891, 2.

541. <u>1885 Bloomington [Illinois] Directory including Normal and Stevensonville</u>, (Chas. O. Ebel & Co.), 271, Majesty, H.A., bds., 206 E. Chestnut.

542. See n.2 at 43; "The Majesty Obsequies," *Toledo Daily Blade*, Feb. 27, 1891, 2; "A Sad Ending. Arthur Majesty, Formerly of Bloomington, Killed By A Brute in a Prize Fight," *Bloomington Bulletin*, Feb. 26, 1891, 4; "Majesty Murdered. The Skilled Lightweight Boxer and Pugilist, Formerly of This City, Killed In a Prize Fight in Ohio," *Daily Pantagraph*, Feb. 26, 1891, 4.

543. <u>R.L. Polk & Co.'s Toledo Directory, 1882-83</u> (R.L. Polk & Co. 1883), 186; "The Peoria Athletic Combination," *Daily Pantagraph*, May 5, 1884, 4; "Peoria Athletes," *Peoria Journal*, May 5, 1884, 4.

544. There was a strong connection between the cities of Peoria, Illinois, and Toledo, Ohio. In the 1880s Illinois farmers east and west of the Illinois River brought their grain to river terminals where it was shipped by boat to Peoria. At Peoria the grain was loaded on rail cars for shipment on the Toledo, Peoria and Warsaw R.R. (the "T. P. & W.") to Toledo, Ohio. At Toledo the grain was delivered to dealers and elevators along the shore of the Maumee River. Toledo, at the west end of Lake Erie, was the home of many grain dealers who had the grain loaded on Great Lakes ships for transport to the East Coast. In bypassing delivery to Chicago at the south end of Lake Michigan these businesses avoided the higher freight rates charged there and shortened the distance that the grain would be transported

on the Great Lakes. Majesty's employer in Toledo had been one of many grain dealers in Toledo. "Suing An Elevator Company," *Plain Dealer*, May 14, 1885, 2.
545. "A Failure and a Fraud," *Daily Pantagraph*, Dec. 23, 1884, 6; "A Pugilistic Fraud," *Peoria Journal*, Dec. 24, 1884, 4.
546. "Alf Greenfield and Party to Spar at Danville Tonight," *Chicago Tribune*, Apr. 7, 1885, 2.
547. "Other Events, Sudden Termination of a Sparring Entertainment on the North Side" *Chicago Tribune*, Apr. 12, 1885, 11; "The Police Stopped the Fight," *The Boston Globe*, Apr. 13, 1885, 8; "Not Allowed To Fight," *New York Times*, Apr. 13, 1885.
548. "Sparring at the Park," *Chicago Tribune*, May 23, 1885, 2; "A Four-round Fight in Chicago," *Sacramento Daily Record*, May 25, 1885, 1.
549. "Tomorrow's Athletic Event," *Chicago Tribune*, Jun. 12, 1885, 2.
550. "Athletic. Burke Stays Five Rounds With Sullivan," *Chicago Tribune*, Jun. 14, 1885, 10; "In Ugly Temper," *Chicago Herald*, Jun. 14, 1885, 6; "Won By A Scratch," *St. Paul Daily Globe*, Jun. 14, 1885, 1.
551. "The Midgets. Tommie Warren, the Pacific Slope Marvel, and Prof. Majesty, Bloomington's Clever Sparrer," *Daily Pantagraph*, Jul. 20, 1885, 4.
552. "Sparring For Points. The Four-Round Discussion With Soft Gloves Between Majesty and Warren," *Daily Pantagraph*, Jul. 21, 1885, 4; No Headline, *Bloomington Bulletin*, Jul. 21, 1885, 4.
553. "With Soft Gloves," *Chicago Tribune*, Jul. 21, 1885, 2.

554. "Majesty Will Challenge Warren," *Bloomington Bulletin*, Jul. 22, 1885, 4; "Will Try It Again," *Daily Pantagraph*, Jul. 22, 1885, 3.

555. "Tommy Warren's Record. Sketch of the Pugilist Who Vanquished Havlin – Story of His Different Battles," *Boston Globe*, Nov. 30, 1888, 6 ("It is stated on good authority that a great many of the pugilists he is credited with knocking out in Grand Rapids, Indianapolis and other cities, were one and the same person that travelled around with him, and each city assumed a different name."); "No Settlement is Near," *Chicago Tribune*, Oct. 26, 1890, 3 ("Warren belongs to a class of fighters who infinitely prefer to put up fake fights than the genuine article."); "Wave the Olive Branch," *Chicago Tribune*, Nov. 9, 1890, 4 ("Warren has made a boast that he never goes into a ring unless he knows what the result of the battle will be and he no doubt continues to make good his boast."); "In a Suicide's Grave," *Chicago Tribune*, Mar. 1, 1891 ("A few years since he [Majesty] practically made Tommy Warren's reputation for him, the scene of operation being the small towns of this State. Warren was making a tour of the State, offering to stop any man of his weight in four rounds. Majesty would go from town to town in advance, and, assuming different names, would meet Warren and be put to sleep with the greatest regularity. All the time he was under salary to Warren.").

556. "Local Sparring Events. The Park was comfortably filled last evening," *Chicago Tribune*, 6.

557. "A Coming Fight In Kentucky," *Chicago Tribune*, Jan. 15, 1886, 6.

558. "A Sharp Fight At Louisville," *Chicago Tribune*, Jan. 19, 1886, 5; "Majesty Mangled In A 'Mill,'" *Chicago Herald*, Jan. 19, 1886, 1; "The Sporting World," *Cincinnati Enquirer*, Jan. 19, 1886, 2; "Pith of the News," *Daily Inter Ocean*, Jan. 19, 1886, 1; "Had No Respect for Majesty," *Daily Freeport Journal*, Jan. 19, 1886, 1; "Had No Respect for Majesty," *Elkhart Weekly Review*, Jan. 21, 1886, 4; "Feather-Weight Sparring," *St. Paul Globe*, Jan. 21, 1886, 1.
559. "Will Tackle Warren Again," *Cincinnati Enquirer*, Jan. 20, 1886, 2.
560. "Warren Whips Murphy," *Chicago Tribune*, Feb. 6, 1886, 6; "The Fight Of The Feather Weights. Tommy Warren Whips Johnny Murphy in Good Shape in Eight Rounds," *The Sun*, Feb. 8, 1886, 3.
561. "Amusements," *Bloomington Bulletin*, Mar. 10, 1886, 4.
562. "Bloomington's Feather-weight Again Done," *Peoria Journal*, Mar. 11, 1886, 1; "The Sparring Exhibition," *Bloomington Bulletin*, Mar. 11, 1886, 4.
563. "Forty-Five Rounds. Warren Knocks Out Barnes, Formerly Champion Feather-Weight," *Washington Critic*, Mar. 23, 1886, 1; "A Long and Bloody Battle," *Chicago Tribune*, Mar. 24, 1886, 1; "The Feather-Weight," *Chicago Tribune*, Mar. 25, 1886, 5 (Barnes wants a rematch with Warren).
564. "Stopped by the Police," *Chicago Tribune*, Apr. 3, 1886, 1. There was a Pat Cahill who fought on the East Coast in this same general era. See e.g., "It Was A Draw, *Brooklyn Eagle*, Dec. 17, 1891, 1.
565. "In the Field of Sports," *Chicago Tribune*, Apr. 24, 1886, 3; "An Unjust Decision," *Chicago Tribune*, May 11, 1886, 1; "Manifestly Unfair," *Chicago Tribune*, May 12, 1886,

3 (Warren thinks that Mitchell should have been given the decision). One article identifies Warren's opponent as William Smith but this appears to be incorrect. See "Tommy Warren's Record," *Boston Globe*, Nov. 30, 1888, 6.
566. "Tom Warren Still Champion," *Dallas Morning News*, Jun. 1, 1886, 6 (opponent called Jim Johnson); "Warren Defeats Johnson," *Daily Inter Ocean*, Jun. 1, 1886, 5 (opponent called Pike Johnson); "Sporting Notes," *Omaha World Herald*, Jun. 1, 1886, 2 (opponent called "unknown from Cadillac, Michigan"); "Tommy Warren Wins Again," *Times Picayune*, Jun. 6, 1886, 16 (opponent called John C. Johnson of Cadillac); "Warren's Record," *Boston Globe*, Nov. 30, 1888, 6 (opponent called John alias "Pug" Johnson).
567. "A Match Arranged," *Daily Inter Ocean*, Jun. 13, 1886, 1.
568. See n. 16 above.
569. No Headline, *Streator Daily Free Press*, Jun. 10, 1886, 3.
570. "A Quick Knockout. Paddy Welch of Chicago, Does Up Arthur Majesty in Two Rounds," *Saint Louis Post Dispatch*, Jun. 19, 1886, 12; No Headline, *Streator Daily Free Press*, Jun. 21, 1886, 3 (quoting an article from the *Bloomington Bulletin*).
571. No Headline, *Streator Daily Free Press*, Jun. 23, 1886, 3.
572. "Fragments," *Daily Pantagraph*, Jul. 6, 1886, 4.
573. "The Ring. Paddy Welch Knocked Out," *Chicago Tribune*, Jul. 7, 1886, 2; "A Knockout. The Result of the Myers-Welsh Hard Glove Contest. Five Coaches and a Brass Band," *Daily Pantagraph*, Jul. 7, 1886, 5; "Myers-Welsh. The Fistic Encounter Won by the Former at Braidwood Last Evening," *Streator Daily Free Press*, Jul. 7, 1886, 3;

"The Ring. Paddy Welch Knocked Out," *Chicago Tribune*, Jul. 7, 1886, 2.
574. "Look Out for Indictments," *Daily Pantagraph*, Feb. 7, 1887, 3.
575. "Arthur Majesty Killed. The Plucky Little Peorian Has His Neck Broken in a Boxing Contest – Great Regret Expressed Among His Friends Here," *Peoria Transcript*, Feb. 26, 1891, 1: "Arthur Majesty," *Peoria Journal*, Feb. 26, 1891, 1.
576. "Fragments," *Daily Pantagraph*, May 27, 1887, 4.
577. "They Will Meet Again," *Daily Pantagraph*, Jun. 10, 1887, 4.
578. "In the Arena of Sports," *Chicago Tribune*, Jul. 18, 1887, 3.
579. "Warren Plays With Majesty," *Daily Inter Ocean*, Jan. 22, 1888, 5; "A Fizzle of a Fight," *Chicago Tribune*, Jan. 22, 1888, 11; No Headline, *Grand Forks Herald*, Jan. 26, 1888, 2.
580. "The Majesty Tragedy," *Toledo Daily Blade*, Feb. 26, 1891, 2
581. "Personals," *Elkhart Daily Review*, Dec. 30, 1890, 2.
582. "A Tragedy In The Prize Ring. Arthur Majesty The Victim," *Toledo Daily Commercial*, Feb. 26, 1891, 2; <u>R.L. Polk and Company, 1891 Toledo City Directory</u> (R.L. Polk & Co.), 551; U. S. Census 1920; Census Place: Toledo Ward 6, Lucas, Ohio; Roll: T625_1408; Page: 4B; Enumeration District: 80; Image: 1115.
583. "Arthur Majesty Killed," *Toledo Daily Blade*, Feb. 25, 1891, 2.
584. "Lively Prize Fight at Peoria," *Chicago Tribune*, Jan. 3, 1891, 7; "Battling Fight in Peoria," *Saint Louis Republic*, Jan. 3, 1891, 6.
585. "Siddon and Lewis to Fight," *Chicago Tribune*, Jan. 2, 1891, 6; "To Fight To A Finish," *Daily Inter Ocean*, Jan. 2, 1891, 3; "Light-Weights Matched," *Saint Louis Republic*, Jan. 3, 1891, 6; "Will Fight To-Night," *Fort Wayne Sentinel*, Jan.

9, 1891, 1; "A Light-Weight Battle," *Daily Inter Ocean*, Jan. 9, 1891, 2.
586. "The Siddons-Lewis Fight Postponed," *Chicago Tribune*, Jan. 10, 1891, 6.
587. "Arthur Majesty," *Peoria Journal*, Feb. 26, 1891, 1.
588. "Seville Not a Ringer," *Toledo Daily Commercial*, Feb. 26, 1891, 2.
589. *Seville* v. *State of Ohio*, 15 Lawyers' Reports Anno. 516 (1892); "A Tragedy In The Prize Ring," *Toledo Daily Commercial*, Feb. 26, 1891, 2.
590. "The News In Toledo. Interesting Sketch of Majesty's Career – A Graduate of the Toledo High School," *Toledo Daily Commercial*, Feb. 26, 1891, 2.
591. "Details Of The Fight. The Eighteenth Round Ends Majesty's Life," *Toledo Daily Blade*, Feb. 25, 1891, 2 (Seville knocked Majesty out with a swinging right hand uppercut); "The Associated Press Account," *Toledo Daily Blade*, Feb. 26, 1881, 2 (Majesty fell backward against and through the ropes onto his face); "Killed In The Prize Ring. Arthur Majesty of Toledo, O., Fatally Injured by Dave Seville," Saint Louis Republic, Feb. 25, 1891, 5 (Majesty fell backward against and through the ropes onto his face); "Killed In A Glove Contest," Daily Inter Ocean, Feb. 26, 1891, 2 (Majesty fell backward against and through the ropes onto his face); "Killed in the Ring. The Brutal Murder of a Prizefighter by His Opponent," *Evening News*, Feb. 26, 1891, 2 (Majesty said: "I can't see, him me, if you want to."); "Arthur Majesty," *Peoria Journal*, Feb. 26, 1891, 1 (Majesty said: "I can't see, him me, if you want to."); "A Sad Evening. Arthur Majesty, Formerly of Bloomington,

Killed By A Brute In a Prize Fight," *Bloomington Bulletin*, Feb. 26, 1891, 4 (Majesty said: "I can't see, him me, if you want to."); "Majesty Murdered," *Daily Pantagraph*, Feb. 26, 1891, 4 (Majesty said: "I can't see, him me, if you want to."); "Knocked Out Of Life. Arthur Majesty, the Hero of Many Battles, Receives His Death Blow in the Ring," *Chicago Herald*, Feb. 26, 1891, 5.

592. "The Associated Press Account," *Toledo Daily Blade*, Feb. 26, 1891, 2. "Killed In The Prize Ring. Arthur Majesty of Toledo, O., Fatally Injured by Dave Seville," *Saint Louis Republic*, Feb. 25, 1891, 5; "Killed In a Glove Contest," *Daily Inter Ocean*, Feb. 26, 1891, 2.

593. *Seville* v. *State of Ohio*, 15 Lawyers' Reports Anno. 516 (1892); "The Majesty Obsequies," *Toledo Daily Blade*, Feb. 27, 1891, 2.

594. "Arthur Majesty Killed," *Toledo Daily Blade*, Feb. 25, 1891, 2.

595. "All Participants Arrested," *Toledo Daily Blade*, Feb. 26, 1891, 2; "Frank McHugh's Arrest," *Toledo Daily Blade*, Feb. 26, 1891, 2; "A Tragedy In The Prize Ring," *Toledo Daily Commercial*, Feb. 26, 1891, 2.

596. "A Tragedy In The Prize Ring," *Toledo Daily Commercial*, Feb. 26, 1891, 2.

597. *Seville* v. *State of Ohio*, 15 Lawyers' Reports Anno. 516 (1892); "Charged With Murder," *Toledo Daily Commercial*, Feb. 27, 1891, 2; "Bound Over for Manslaughter," *Newark Daily Advocate*, Mar. 3, 1891, 1; "That Fatal Prize Fight," *Newark Daily Advocate*, Mar. 3, 1891, 3; "Bound Over to the Grand Jury," *Newark Daily Advocate*, Mar. 5, 1891, 1.

598. "Trial Begun," *Repository*, Apr. 3, 1891, 2.

599. "The Courts," *Plain Dealer*, Jun. 24, 1891, 3.
600. Ohio, County Marriages, 1790–1950, Franklin, Franklin County, Ohio, digital folder number: 4016221.
601. "Even His Wife Deserts Man," *The Richwood Gazette*, Aug. 20, 1891, 1.
602. "Telegraphic Brevities," *New York Times*, Mar. 2, 1892.
603. "Couldn't Receive Him," *Wheeling Register*, Mar. 4, 1892, 1.
604. "Both Must be Hanged," *Plain Dealer*, Sep. 4, 1892, 2; "Asks For A Pardon," *Plain Dealer*, Oct. 14, 1892, 2.
605. "The Verdict Reduced," *Plain Dealer*, Jun. 6, 1894, 2.
606. "Pugilist Arrested," *Wheeling Register*, Apr. 21, 1896, 8.
607. "Pugilism. Taking Long Chances," *Plain Dealer*, Nov. 20, 1896, 6; "After Lavaek," *Plain Dealer*, Jan. 20, 1897, 3.
608. "Dave Seville Whipped," *Newark Daily Advocate*, Aug. 6, 1897, 4.
609. "The Contest A Draw," *Marietta Daily Leader*, Mar. 18, 1898, 1; "The Contest A Draw," *Saginaw News*, Mar. 18, 1898, 3.
610. "Club Will Be Ousted," *Jackson Citizen Patriot*, Sep. 26, 1901, 4.
611. "Held For Murder," *Repository*, Sep. 21, 1910, 16; "Unknown Man Is Murdered," *Piqua Leader Dispatch*, Sep. 22, 1910, 1; "Al Kaufman Comes Today," *The Sun*, Sep. 22, 1910, 10.

INDEX

Abbot, Stanton 34
Adelphi Athletic Club 103
Aiken, Charles 24
Allen, Tom 125-126, 140, 157-158
American Protective Association 157
Amateur Athletic Union 50
Anderson, John 133
Anderson, Tom 148-150
Angle, Bernard John 81
Anthony, Jimmy 53-54, 59, 64-69, 74-75
Anson, Cap 15, 80-83
Armstrong, Bob 49, 61-70, 84
Arthur, Billy 17
Ashton, Jack 202, 226
Auditorium Club (New Orleans) 41

Baker, Henry 32
Barnes, Tommy 235
Barrett, Tommy 17
Barry, Garrett 3
Barry, Margaret 3, 7-8
Barry, Michael 3, 7-8

Barry, Thomas J. 3, 8, 102, 112
Barry & O'Neil 108
Bartley, Frank 34-35, 97, 103
Battery "D" 23
Bertrand, Joe 43-44, 70
Bittle, Sam, 169-170, 187-189
Boden, Mike 24
Bogan, Fred 28, 85, 94
Bowen, Andy 24-25, 41, 69
Bowen, Jack 139
Bradburn, William 133, 151, 160, 169
Brady, James 171
Brennan, Billy 66, 202-205
Broadway Athletic Club 59-60
Brown, Billy "Kid" 68
Brown, Clara ("Carrie") Tripp 199
Brown, Harry 199
Brown, Sailor 203
Brucks, John 132
Brunell, F. H. 177-78
Burke, Jack 35, 140, 152-54, 157, 158, 161,

183, 186-87, 202, 229-31, 236-38
Burke, Robert Emmett 107-08
Butler, Joe 64-65
Butt, Dr. Edward 249
Byrnes [Burns], Jack 130-31

Caledonia Club (Philadelphia) 56
Cardiff, Patsey 155, 158-59, 183, 227-28
Carrig, Jack 220
Carroll, Jimmy 171-73, 179, 183, 198, 200, 205, 208, 307
Carroll, Paddy 160, 204, 236-37
Casino Theater 11, 20, 190, 239
Chandler, Tom 128, 132, 139-40, 149-151, 189
Cheney, Lee 227, 239
Chester, Florence 209-211
Chicago Athletic Club 10, 86, 239
Chicago Carriage Lamp 8
Childs, Frank 43, 69, 84, 95

Choynski, Joe 43, 45, 49, 52, 59, 61-66, 68, 88-89, 95, 219
Christol, Lucien Marc 174-75
Cleary, Mike 140, 145, 152-55, 161, 215
Cleveland, Al 23, 36
Cleveland Athletic Club 168, 172, 180, 185, 189
Clifford, Harry 133
Clow, John 155, 201, 215
Cohn, Louis M. 38, 44
Cole, John 50
Coliseum 66, 206, 214-15, 222
Collier, Dick 172, 179-80, 187
Collins, John 190
Connolly, James "One Eyed" 145, 169, 229
Connors, Johnny 30-31, 37, 39, 41-42, 70, 86-87, 112
Cook, Hiram 67
Corrothers, James David ix, 2, 18
Costello, Bob 34-36
Costello, Thomas, 175, 178, 183, 187-88, 192, 196-97, 221

Index

Cougle, Abe 200
Coulon, Johnny 110-112
Coyle, Pat 232
Cranston, Young 32
Creedon, Dan 43
Cribb Club 192
Crook, Ed 238
Croot, Walter 2, 60, 73, 75-82
Cross, Dr. Jesse George 226
Cyberboxingzone 21, 25, 39, 58

Dalley, Harry 55-56
Dalton, James H. "Captain" 123-162
Dalton, John C. 155
Dalton, Kate 124
Dalton, Lawrence 124
Daly, Charley 193
Daly, Dan 192-95
Daly, Jack 94
Davies, Charles E. "Parson" 11, 19, 24, 29, 39, 43-44, 48-49, 51, 53-75, 80, 82-89, 111, 130-135, 140, 144-149, 151, 183, 189-191, 202-05, 219, 227-234, 237, 241

Davies, Vere 146
Dempsey, Jack 36, 41, 156, 164, 170, 180, 182-88, 193, 195, 198, 201-08, 213, 218, 222
Dixon, George 54, 60-61, 72, 221, 288
Doherty, Tom 133
Dohony, James 200
Donaldson, John 131, 143
Doner, Joe 24
Donovan, Mike 127, 140-41
Donnelly, Ben 17, 210
Dorney, Ed 131, 133, 139
Dow, C. H. 210
Dow, Merrill C. 210
Doyle, Austin 144
Doyle, Con 34, 36
Driscoll, Mike 146, 148
Dunn, Richard T. 228
Dunne, Jerry 145
Duplessia, Ed 139

Eaufeldt, Max 27
Eck, Thomas 139
Elliott, Jimmy 125-26, 144-45, 151
Elms, Joe 42
Empire Theater 32, 33

Erne, Frank 50
Essig, Charles 17, 95
Euker, John 102
Evans, "Punk" 244
Evans, William 145

Falvallo, Michael 50
Farley, Barney 200
Farrell, Lawrence 158, 217
Faulker, James 179
Fell, Jim 188
Fergus, Rev. Francis T. 223
Fergus, Michael 223
Ferguson, Joe 24
Files, John 176
Fitzgerald, Frank 31, 34, 55, 69, 103
Fitzgerald, Jack 31
Fitzgerald, Patrick 17, 29, 34-35, 97, 103
Fitzsimmons, Bob 36, 40, 51, 54-55, 63, 66, 172, 200, 207, 213, 218-21
Fitzwilliams 157
Flanagan, Steve 32, 54, 56-58, 60-61, 92-93, 101, 105
Flood, John 130
Floto, Otto 43, 65, 164, 191-92, 219-223

Flynn, Charley 226-228
Flynn, James F. 7-8
Fogarty, Jack 179-80, 188
Forbes, Harry 95-96
Forbes, George 175, 177
Fort Dearborn Athletic Association 95
Fox, Richard K. 134, 184-85
Franks, Harry 229
Fulda, L. R. 198

Gallagher, Andrew 124
Gallagher, Charley 125
Gallagher, Ellen 166
Gallagher, Frank 166
Gallagher, Jimmy 37
Gallagher, John 166-67, 214
Gallagher, Julia 166
Gallagher, Mike 125
Gallagher, Patrick J. "Reddy" 11, 65-66, 163-224
Gallagher, Robert 166
Gallagher, Terry 167
Garden City Athletic Club 11
Gardner, Oscar 88, 253
Garrard, Frank 17, 19-20, 33, 43, 107, 202-205
Gibbons, Austin 20
Gibbons, Pete 133

Index

Gilmore, Harry 9, 11-19, 23, 27, 29, 33-38, 40, 43, 61, 95, 107-112, 189-90, 203-04, 241
Glickauf, Harry 43
Glover, Frank 169, 202, 238
Goddard, Joe 215-16
Golden, Paddy 139
Goode, Jem 148-152, 159, 161, 227-28
Gorman, Jimmy 30, 35-38, 72
Graham, J. W. "Captain" 197
Greater New York Athletic Club 95
Greenfield, Alf 151, 229, 238
Greeninger, Louis 42
Griffin, Johnny 28, 72, 86

Hall, Jim 24, 207, 213-14
Hall, John H., 242, 246-47, 250
Harding, William 134
Handler, Jimmy 50
Harris, Harry 103-106
Harris, Joe 207
Harris, Sammy 95-96
Harrison, Carter 70, 144-147
Harrison, Carter, Jr. 70, 110
Hart, Sig 44, 70, 105

Haugh, Maxey 88
Herget, John 164, 198
Hill, Harry 129-30
Hogan, "Kid" 37
Hogan, Malachi 39, 45, 96-97, 100-01, 106
Houseman, Lou 84, 86
Hoven, Eddy 37
Hudson Athletic Club 50
Hudson, "Cammy" 94
Huguelet, Joe 105
Hutchin, George L. 227
Hutchins, Judge J. C. 176

Illinois Wesleyan University 226, 240
Immaculate Conception Church 3-4, 112
Ingram, J. C. 123, 129, 136-37

Jackson, Peter 24, 29, 80, 208-211, 215
Johnson, Jim 237
Johnson, John C. 237
Johnson, Pike, 237
Johnson, William B. 188

Kelly, Dan 17
Kelly, Ed 193-94

Kelly, Sammy 60-62
Kelly, Tommy 16
Kennard House 196
Kennedy, James C. 50
Kerrigan, Patsy 183
Kerwin, George 86
Kerwin, Mary Jane 146
Ketchum, Valentine H. 242-43, 250
Kilrain, Jake 159, 183-85, 195-197
Kinnard, Tom 159-60
King, Jack 157, 234

La Blanche, George 156, 170-73, 183, 187, 198, 208, 214
Lomasney, Charles 238
Lannon, Joe 183, 199
Latham, George 30 Lavigne, "Kid" 109
Lenox Athletic Club 90
Leon, Casper 35-48, 56-57, 60-71, 70, 72, 75, 82-86, 90-92, 95-103, 105, 111
Leonard, Bennie 110
Leonard, Jack 96
Levy, Jack 28, 30, 37

Lewis, Evan "the Strangler" 156, 189-90, 219, 241
Lewis, Jack 103
Lewis, "Sparrow" 243
Liederkranz Hall 153
London's National Sporting Club 67, 71-72, 75, 78-81
Lyons, Young 53

Maciewski, Frank 42
Macy, Tom 244
Macziewski, Herman Arthur, Magesky, Magesty, Majesty 225-256
McCall, Barney 21, 70
McCarthy, Billy 199
McCarthy, Cal 54
McCarthy, Dan 130
McCarthy, Eugene 139
McCarthy, Joseph 108-09
McLaughlin, James 139
Madden, Billy 130-32, 142
Madden, Jack 41-43, 48-51, 54-55, 72
Madison Square Garden 34
Maher, Peter 54-55, 65
Mannen, Pete 192

Index

Masterson, Bat 65-66, 164, 192-93, 201, 207-08, 214-16, 219-21
McAlpin, "Soap" 140
McAuliffe, Jack 8-11, 194
McAuliffe, William 138
McCormick Hall 133, 139-40, 142
McCormick, Jack 103-04, 217
McCormick Place 131
McCoy, "Kid" 97, 103
McCoy, Pete 175-80, 187, 202
McDonald, Mike 39, 123, 128, 131-35, 142-44, 149-50
McDonongh, John 160
McFarland, Packey 110
McGlenn, "Kid" 86
McGovern, Terry 95, 102
McGrath, Joe 32-36
McGuire, Jim 54
McGuire, John 197
McGurn, Ellen 9-13, 108
McGurn, Michael 3, 9-13
McGurn, William 14, 44, 78, 97
McHugh, Frank 247, 249
McHugh, Mike 236
McInerney, Jack 20, 204
McKenny, Patrick 166
McManus, Hugh 193-95
McNamara, Dr. Francis 52-53
McSheehy, Honorah O'Connor 216-18
McSheehy, Mary 164, 216-18
Mellington, Young 23
Memphis, Clarksville and Louisville Railroad ("M.C.L.") 165-66
Mitchell, Charley 140, 145, 151, 157-58, 164, 183-186, 195-97
Mitchell, Young 198, 207-10
Morris, Con 139-40
Morris, Joe 231
Mullen, James 166
Munroe, George 86
Murphy, "Torpedo" Billy 20, 42, 54, 60, 105
Murphy, Frank 19, 36
Murphy, George "Dutch" 210-11
Murphy, Jimmy 24-25
Murphy, Johnny 235

Murphy, Johnny W. 54, 58, 202-207
Murphy, Pierce 237
Murphy "Toothless" 236
Myer, Billy 11, 39, 189-90, 237-41
Myer, Eddie 39, 237-41

Needham, Danny 42, 241, 253
Nelson, David 244
Nelsonville Athletic Club 245, 251
Nolan, Harry 237
Nolan, Peter 193, 197
Nolan, Walter 96

O'Leary, Dan 43
O'Leary, Jim 96
O'Leary, Joe 21, 23-24, 36
O'Rourke, Tom 49, 54, 63, 90, 95, 207, 221
Olympic Club (New Orleans) 30, 35, 37, 212
Olympic Club (Cincinnati) 42
Owens, Williams 133

Palace Sporting Club 83
Palmer, Pedlar 53, 67, 72-78, 88-89

Pank, Harry 180-83, 192
Parker, Kid 220
Parson Davies' Specialty Company 66, 189
Plimmer, Billy 33, 42, 53, 58-59, 63, 88
Polo Athletic Club 88
Pooler, Dick 168
Pope, Link 86, 191, 238
Popp, Willie 90
Preston, William L. 136-37
Price, Millie 209-11

Quade, Bobby 27-28

Rabshaw, Lewis 168
Raymond, Robert 243
Reeves, Jack 176
Ritchie, Johnny 86-87, 93-94, 111
Rhoden, Charley 105
Rooke, George 140-41
Ross, Duncan C. 133, 168, 174
Rosser, Emil 244-248
Rotchford, Billy 86-89, 111
Rough On Rats 199
Rumsey, Albert H. 167, 169, 173-74, 178
Ryan, Mike 183

Index

Ryan, Paddy 53-54, 134, 141-45, 149, 152, 161
Ryan, Tommy 41-43, 49, 51-53, 103

Santry, Eddie 43
Schaefer, Willie 110
Schooll, Joeseph 139
Schroder, Rudy 232
Schuthelm's Old Garden 194
Scully, John 139
Second Regimental Armory 24, 34, 44
Seville, David 245-54
Sharkey, Jack 111
Sharkey, Tom 105, 219
Sharp, Rufus 43
Shea, Pete 28-32, 36
Sheridan, Mickey 110
Sheriff, William "the Prussian" 145-46
Sherman, Charles E. 38
Sherwood, Dr. Francis R. 203
Shields, Anne 3
Shields, John 4
Shields, Mary 2
Shrosbee, Al 17, 20-21, 59, 86, 89
Siddons, George 20, 243, 253
Sielf, Dick 105

Siler, George 34, 39, 87-88, 92, 95
Skelly, Jack 50, 82-83
Sloane, Jack 36
Sloane, Tod 80-81, 83, 85
Small, Mike 72, 75
Smith, Connie 32
Smith, Denver Ed 192, 214-16
Smith, Jem 185
Smith, Jess 213
Smith, John 159
Smith, O. H. 183
Smith, Richard 81
Smith, Soapy 201
Smith, Solly 28, 33, 72, 86, 253
Smith, William 171
Snee, Martin 11, 190, 219
Sorakicki, Matsada 187
Spaulding & Co. 80
Spink, Alfred "Al" 158, 160-61
St. Bernard Athletic Club 83
Stanton, Ernie 76
Star Theater 103, 107, 209
Stenger's Hall 34
Stephens, Alfred 246-47, 251
Stift, Billy 19-20, 86, 103
Sturch, Joe 71, 93-94

Saunders, Charles 133, 227
Sullivan, Dave 70, 72-74, 78
Sullivan, John L. 49, 51, 53-54, 124, 129-134, 139, 141-145, 148-151, 157, 159-61, 182-84, 186, 195-96, 218, 227, 229-31, 234
Sullivan, Spike 82, 88
Sullivan, William 109

Taylor, James 127
Taylor, Steve 129
The Eye 227
Toronto Athletic Club 90
Tattersall's 43, 86, 88-89
The Wicklow Postman 53-55
Thompson, Mervine 168, 187
Tighe, James G. 50
Tighe, William C. 50
Tivoli Theater 32, 201
Tracy, A. B. 245-47
Tri-City Athletic Club 96-97
Trinity Athletic Club 96-97
Turner Hall 19
Tuthill, Gus 221

Union Garden Hall 49

Van Heest, Johnny 25, 31, 253
Van Praag, Sol 39
Varuna Boat Club 50

Walters, Big "Sandy" 39
Walters, Emma 216
Ward, Dick 22, 36
Ward, Jack 61-63, 74
Warren, Tommy 189, 227-237, 239-243, 253
Washburne, Hempstead 24
Waverly Rink 160
Waverly Theater 43
Welsh, Paddy 238-39
White, Charley 90, 112
White Elephant 168
White, Frankie 110
White, Johnny 92
White, Tommy 14, 17, 19-20, 25, 29, 33-34, 39, 43, 56, 61, 71, 78-82, 86, 94, 97, 99-100, 112, 160, 203, 221, 253
Wilde, Jimmy 111
Wilkowski, Albert 108-09
Wilkowski, Ignatz 109
Williams, Abe 133, 139, 227, 236

Williams, Billy 43
Wilson, Billy 155
Wilson, Gus 188

Yingling's Hall 169

Zachritz, Will 193-94

CPSIA information can be obtained at www.ICGtesting.com
Printed in the USA
BVOW011035060313

314861BV00010B/141/P